Seesaw

Yorick Blumenfeld

SEESAW

Cultural Life in Eastern Europe

HARCOURT, BRACE & WORLD, INC., NEW YORK

To those in Eastern Europe
who—despite the lack of any outlet—continue to create
in the hope of a freer tomorrow

Contents

List of Illustrations

(Between pages 150 and 151)

All the photographs in this book were taken by the author.

Painting by Eva Brydlova

Milos Forman with his wife

Guyla Illyes

Gabor Garai

Jiri Trnka

Belgrade Museum of Modern Art, exterior

Belgrade Museum of Modern Art, interior

Alina Szapocznikowa

Tadeusz Brzozowski

Krzysztof Penderecki

Andrei Gulyashki

Seesaw

CHAPTER I

Introduction: A Cultural Awakening

A gradual cultural awakening is the most meaningful development occurring in the communist regimes of Eastern Europe in the mid-sixties. Culture, in all its forms, has acquired exceptional significance because it is involved in a perpetual tug of war with the dictatorship of the proletariat. In the shifting seesaw movement that results, the great majority of the population is rooting for the underdog artists and intellectuals, while the communist apparatus is reluctant to drag the cultural opposition down to an unpopular defeat, as in Czechoslovakia. The tensions, however, continue to mount until either reforms are granted or repression is enforced. The lack of equilibrium is perpetuated by the awareness among communist bureaucrats that, while internal changes are essential, successful reform could result in their fall from power. Because the arts are the most effective media for expressing protest and exposing those abuses the party tries to cover up, the communist leadership correctly recognizes the arts as one of the most dynamic oppositional factors to the dictatorship of the proletariat. Culture consequently becomes both the indicator of the state of political freedom and the champion of political progress.

The dramatic events in Poland and Czechoslovakia in 1968 clearly revealed culture's impact. In Warsaw the closure of a drama by the nineteenth-century poet Adam Mickiewicz provided the spark that set off student riots all over Poland and provoked the most serious political crisis in that country since the October revolution of 1956. In Prague, the Communist Party's inability to find a modicum of coexistence with the writers ultimately proved a crucial factor in the overthrow of Party Secretary Antonin Novotny and in the subsequent invasion of Soviet and Warsaw Pact troops. The Czechoslovak intelligentsia had played a leading role in defying the communist bureaucracy and temporarily succeeded in abolishing both censorship and rigid control of the mass media. For a few, hopeful summer months the Czechs lost their fears and found their voices. This phenomenon was so clearly distasteful to the neighboring communist regimes that they used tanks to suppress it. Unlike the Hungarians in 1956, the Czechs had tried to combine Western democratic forms with a communist economic base. The suppression of their effort to humanize communism represented a tragedy not only for the Czech people, but also for those of the neighboring communist states. This mid-summer rape set the clock back a number of years. Now the Czechoslovak intelligentsia will be forced back into the repugnant state of "internal exile" which characterizes so many artists and writers in Eastern Europe. The immediate future looks dark, but it seems unthinkable that the infamous guns of August 1968 will crush the creative hopes of the East Europeans.

Most communist regimes still regard art as a medium of indoctrination and propaganda. This explains why Marxism-Leninism has been unable and unwilling to encourage innovation in any of the arts; why, after fifty years, its influence on world culture has been so largely negative. Although a majority of the communist leaders do not want to return to the era of Stalinism and the "cult of personality," their efforts to bring the arts down to the level of the workers and peasants have not been exactly stimulating to the intellectual community. At best, the communist party secretaries, such as Gomulka, Kadar, and Ceausescu, are cultural eunuchs who suspect any artistic level higher than their own, and whose instinct it is to emasculate rather than to patronize the arts. Nobody will remember the sayings of the Polish Party Secretary or the Bulgarian Premier a generation from now. But those arts—which they barely managed to tolerate—will have assumed their place in the world's cultural heritage.

It is complex to trace the impetus for the present cultural awakening. It seems to have numerous sources: rebelliousness against the narrow outlook of those in power, revival of national consciousness, growth of polymorphism in Marxism, which has given greater latitude to the intellectuals, long pent-up strivings of individual creators, greater economic flexibility of the socialist regimes, conflict of generations, and, finally, the inherent strength of truthful expression in these mendacious societies. The events in Poland and Czechoslovakia in the late sixties have shown that the cultural situation is marked by great fluidity. Each country is proceeding at its own pace. Nor do the many cultural forms flourish side by side at the same time. East Germany lags behind all the other countries, except Albania, in every respect. In Russia—which, theoretically, is supposed to set the pace and tone for cultural forms in the communist world—painting, music, architecture, cinematography, sociology, philosophy, to mention but a few, are all conventional, if not musty. Consequently, rather than cover the states as a bloc, I have selected the cultural highlights of each country. I have attempted, not to present a survey, but to sketch an impressionist tableau of diversity and movement. This book will examine, in detail, music and painting in Poland, theater and cinema in Czechoslovakia, poetry and satire in Hungary, architecture and the philosophical periodical in Yugoslavia, literature in Bulgaria, television in Rumania, opera in East Germany, and the cultural minirevolution in Albania.

It is exceptionally hazardous to attempt historically valid generalizations as to the direction, pace, or even duration of the general cultural amelioration. What is valuable in the study of cultural developments in Eastern Europe is to get an idea of their tenuousness. For example, freedom of musical composition in Poland was absolute, while in East Germany it was tightly restricted; abstract painting was tolerated in Czechoslovakia and forbidden in Bulgaria; novels condemning the cult of personality were published in Hungary, were promoted in Czechoslovakia, and remain suppressed in Poland. There are no hard and fast rules. Economic conditions greatly affect the state of the arts, if only because relative prosperity permits the Party to divert some appropriations from industry, yet East Germany, which enjoys the highest standard of living, has the lowest quotient of political and cultural flexibility.

5

The question could be asked: Does a *Zeitgeist* exist in the area? On the surface there doesn't appear to be anything in the mid-sixties to compare with the gloom prevailing under Stalinism. But the euphoria characterizing the intellectuals and the students in Prague after the overthrow of Novotny was restricted to Czechoslovakia.* Perhaps alienation comes closest to describing the current mood in Eastern Europe. Alienation is seen not so much as a general estrangement that occurs when the political machinery contradicts the hopes of men, but, specifically, as a total disillusionment with all aspects of applied Marxism-Leninism. The average East European intellectual of the mid-sixties is not motivated by fear, great hopes, or selfless idealism. He does not see a Statue of Liberty under a rainbow on the horizon. Rather, he is marked by a deliberately cautious spirit. He always reveals that trace of anxiety which marks the recidivist. He understands the frailty of the cultural flower. He knows a few degrees of Party frost could put an end to the creative spirit of the Czech film industry. He is a man who looks over his shoulder before taking a step forward.

Like Metternich, who waged a lifetime struggle against "modern ideas," Brezhnev, Gomulka, and even Zhivkov try to restrain experimentation or innovation in the arts. They respond to appeals for greater intellectual freedom by demands for unity and threats of disciplinary action. However, no government is entirely insensitive to international public opinion. Polish ideologists, for instance, as narrow-minded and fanatic as they may be, feel a swelling national pride and derive a certain propaganda value from being able to tell the world: "This is the type of music that can be composed under communism! This is how free we Poles are!" While it is possible to say things in Polish films that would not be allowed in print, there is also a limit beyond which the arts are not permitted to advance. The leading socialist theoretician on culture, the Hungarian phi-

* Although all such generalizations always raise innumerable questions, by "intellectual" I mean that category of professionals whose lives are committed to serious study, reflection, speculation; by "intelligentsia" I mean that recognizable class of well-educated and articulate individuals who constitute a self-conscious, and usually avant-garde, elite within that society.

† During the 1956 Hungarian revolution, when Lukacs was already seventy-one, he was named a minister in Imre Nagy's Cabinet. When the revolution was

6

losopher and literary critic Georgy Lukacs† (b. 1885), wrote in his latest book, *On the Exceptional* (1966), that "One of the reasons for the mistrust toward art, as is often found in extreme idealists and ideological representatives of religions, is the spontaneous tendency of true art toward worldly immanence." And the mistrust of the leading party cadres is undoubtedly due to the distorted and often warped idealism of its leaders. They believe not only that Marxism established the scientific foundation for political action, but also that it is the only theoretical system for defining or explaining all problems of knowledge—from abstract painting to serial music, or from economics to genetics. When a film, a book, or even a poem, through symbolism or abstraction, manages to bring Marxist assumptions into question, the dogmatist sees no alternative but to ban it. Dialogue, he believes, would only spread a heretical message and confuse the people.

The dialectical weakness of the party cadres and their leaders, their unwillingness and inability to enter into a rational or meaningful exchange, naturally enhances the stature of the East European intellectual. To be a writer still carries much of its prewar glamour and prestige, despite the fact that many second-rate writers became, and in a few instances remain, reliable political instruments of the dictatorship of the proletariat. Creative artists, as leaders of the intelligentsia, are still thought to transmit the highest aspirations of their people. The aesthetic avant-garde serves as a cultural nervous system to the political avant-garde. Intellectuals have retained their identity as a social class, as innovators in the society. The very act of writing or painting, it is felt, makes them responsible for the spiritual and political health of the country. However, intellectuals are on their guard. They do not say everything they think, nor do they believe every word they utter. Creation continues all the time, but a large percentage of what is being produced remains unseen by the public; it is hidden

---

suppressed, Lukacs was arrested and initially deported to Rumania. However, he was permitted to resume his philosophical writings after four months and became the only leader who was never tried by the Kadar government or forced to recant his deeds publicly. This was not only a sign of magnanimity on the part of Kadar but also a recognition of Lukacs's prestige as a Marxist. Lukacs was readmitted to the Hungarian Communist Party at his own request in 1968.

in the artist's studio or in the writer's drawer. Some intellectuals, protesting against the party's attempts to absorb them into the socialist propaganda machine, tend toward introversion, obfuscation, and escapism. The fact is that the penalties for incurring party disfavor are great, the material or physical reward for being a martyr nil. Although East European artists and literary figures are, by and large, a privileged minority, the risks they must take in presenting new ideas are formidable.

Communist leaders, such as Janos Kadar, have become adept at exploiting the vanity, the need for reward, and even the greed of individual artists. Travel abroad, either individually or as a member of a delegation, is held out as a carrot for good behavior. And the ideological bosses are expert at encouraging a Kafkaesque atmosphere of uncertainty. Self-censorship, it has been noted, is more effective than outright suppression. It is also more insidious because it exploits the creator's instinct of self-preservation. The ultimate result is that artists frequently are unable to withstand the pressures and compromise their integrity. Often their fate depends on the blindness or ignorance of the local censor or the cultural administrator. Lest one think things have changed so radically under communism, however, it must be remembered that in the mid-nineteenth century the postal authorities of the Austro-Hungarian Empire read as many letters as they could and threw the remainder away, in case they might contain subversive information. Censorship at Vienna's Burgtheater was so rigorous under the Hapsburgs that plays in which nobles married commoners were forbidden. In Poland, Czarist censorship stifled nearly all indigenous cultural forms. Moreover—a pace-setter for recent socialist campaigns against long-haired beatniks—only officials of the Dual Monarchy were permitted to wear a mustache or moderate-length whiskers. A full-fledged beard was regarded as suspicious even then and could draw imprisonment.

In the twenty years of socialism that followed the ravages of World War II, the artists and intellectuals of Eastern Europe were surrounded by men with ashen, worn-out, and sometimes tortured faces; bureaucratic mediocrity was raised to an almost religious level, with a gradual erosion of human values. After the Hungarian revolution, to fight directly against the dictatorship of the proletariat appeared increasingly futile. It requires an incredible effort of will to produce even an echo in this heavy, smog-laden atmosphere. While retaining their fighting spirit, many of the older writers, painters, and poets have developed fatigued souls. They have been metaphorically bureaucratized, Sanforized, and tarred and feathered Red. Their *Weltschmerz* is a combination of nostalgia for the prewar past, a fatalistic attitude toward the present, and an ostrichlike posture toward the fate of the prewar generation. In addition to experiencing this feeling of debilitation, the writers and artists of the small nations of Central Europe are further burdened by their geographic and linguistic isolation. A suffocating futility results from being, let us say, an untranslatable Hungarian poet. Who, for example, has heard of the mystic lyricist Sandor Weores? He is totally unknown in the West. And yet, if he had written in English or French, he would most certainly be as recognized as T. S. Eliot or St. John Perse. The realization that one cannot be understood or appreciated except by a few compatriots produces an agonizing loneliness.

For twenty years now, the East European has been quasi-isolated from the Occident. While some of the naïveté and the painful search for identity of the cineasts, painters, and poets is much appreciated by the West, to the creators themselves the cultural segregation is terrifying. Links with their counterparts beyond the Iron Curtain are extremely important to the cultural communities of Prague, Warsaw, Bucharest, and Budapest. It is more than just coming back and saying to one's colleagues, "I walked down the Champs-Elysées last week," or, "Look at this tie I bought at Burberrys." Contacts signify the end of spiritual isolation. Nearly all the members of the East European intelligentsia display a strong wish to return to the mainstream of modern European culture. But the dangers of renewed contact are also great: Communists are disturbed by "Americanization" of their cultural life and are doing their utmost to combat it. I have frequently heard intellectuals suggest that it has been beneficial to be removed from much of the vulgarization that has occurred in the Occident during the last two decades—ranging from television commercials to Playboy Clubs.

They want no part of the waist-high culture. They are contemptu-
ous of America's "culture industry," which treats the arts as if they
were a kind of Borden's Camembert. Socialism has succeeded in
decommercializing much of culture. Behind the Curtain, supply
and demand have been subordinated to ideological requirements.

Despite the exceptional allure of the West, three of the most
influential phenomena of postwar intellectual life in America—
homosexual irony (camp, if you will), the popularization of psychology, and Jewish consciousness (as furthered by such writers as
Bellow, Mailer, and Malamud) —have not yet filtered through the
Curtain. Homosexual aesthetes do not swarm the fine arts as they
do in the West. In Budapest one still senses the influence of Jewish
intellectuals on the skepticism and humor once so prominent in
that capital's intense cultural life. In Prague there remain some
Jews who gained prominence during the period of Novotny's overthrow, but elsewhere culture has been impoverished by the Nazi
extermination. However, nothing is so remarkable as the degree to
which the intelligentsia under socialism has been isolated from the
influence of psychology and sociology, ranging from Freud to Mar-
shall McLuhan. Western thinkers are generally oriented to an
analytic, Freudian style of thought, but in the Soviet Union today
even words like "libido," "projection," and "sublimation" are not
recognized. Instead, poets, historians, essayists, critics, novelists,
sociologists, editors—in fact, the whole gamut of intellectuals dealing with the written word—tend to think symbolically. They are
accustomed to reading and interpreting well-hidden, Aesopian allusions. They find significant political metaphors in even the simplest
statements. The simpler the thought, the bigger fool one is regarded
for not perceiving its controversial potentialities.

The extent to which the Soviet Union has ceased to be a true
cultural influence everywhere, from Prague to Bucharest, is astounding. Moscow is today seen as the center of the great cultural
void. The tendency is to negate that which is Russian and to
admire everything Western—from Edward Albee to patent leather
boots, from Dr. Kildare to Carnaby Street stockings, from Andy
Warhol to the miniskirt. Simultaneously, a curious phenomenon
has developed, in which the state is being replaced as patron

of the arts by those in the Occident who can bestow gold. The one certain sign of international acceptance has become convertible currency whether earned by Polish composer Penderecki in commissions from the West German radio, by Czech cinematist Forman through financial offers from Carlo Ponti, or by Czech author Ladislav Mnacko, who published his novels in Austria. The ruble, on the other hand, is regarded as a symbol of economic exploitation. No one is interested in going to Moscow for pleasure. Soviet culture is viewed as being burdened by the sullenness of a predominantly peasant population. Some Warsaw sociologists I talked to felt that John Maynard Keynes was right when he wrote in 1925 in his *Short View of Russia* that the Soviets were making a gross miscalculation in exalting "the boorish proletariat above the bourgeoisie and the intelligentsia, who, with whatever faults, are the quality of life and surely carry all the seeds of human advancement."

When orthodox Soviet writers came to Prague in the summer of 1968 the get-togethers were decidedly awkward. They came close to resembling a dance of sixteen-year-olds with forty-year-olds. The continued efforts of the Russians to impose ideological conformity a full fifty years after the October revolution is looked upon with unfeigned contempt.* All Polish painters are fully aware, for instance, that nonrepresentational art shows are still being closed in Moscow; that an exhibit of Marc Chagall's works was quickly declared a nonevent (despite the fact that he had been Commissar of Art in his native city of Vitebsk); and that Soviet expressionist Oskar Rabin's paintings are denounced by the Soviet press as "crude jokes," while Rabin himself is described as being "unpleasantly sick." The Moscow Union of Painters declared that "Rabin casts a shadow on Soviet ideology, distorts the true image of our reality in the eyes

* Ekaterina Furtseva, the Soviet Culture Minister, maintained in 1968 that the emphasis in ballet should be placed on "realism" and not on abstract movement. "We do not share the opinion of some ballet lovers who approve of the sexual direction ballet has taken," she said. Furtseva claimed that it was unpleasant for her to see "sexual figures on the stage." The unhappy director of the Bolshoi Ballet, Igor Moiseyev, countered that "Sex is not abstract." But such an argument would hardly prevail upon the dowdy Furtseva.

of the foreign observer and gives grounds for undeniable propaganda against our country." Far less ridden by rigidity and dogma than its Russian counterpart, the intelligentsia of Eastern Europe has not lost its stereoscopic vision of life.

The specter of modernism continues to haunt the arts in the communist states. The Bolsheviks initially gave the avant-garde comprehensive and officially sanctioned power. But once Stalin assumed control, modernism was banned. Stalin could not understand why Chagall painted cows green—much less what his romanticism had in common with Marxism-Leninism. The Stalinist concept of socialist realism in the arts, as originally formulated by Lunacharsky and elaborated by Zhdanov, progressively strangled the growth of new cultural forms. Socialist realism is still seen by the various party demagogues as the "most purposeful art" of all time. To men like Walter Ulbricht, its objective is to speed up the "onrushing inevitability" of communism. For this type of pithecanthropus, history must always be viewed in terms of the first monkey that stood up on its hind legs and began the triumphant march toward communism. However, the concept of a "socialist realism" is as absurd as that of a "Jewish realism" or a "capitalist realism." Because the party teleologists have been burdened by an authoritarian compulsion for consistency, the debate on the meaning of socialist realism has now raged for twenty years. The polemicists are faced with insoluble dilemmas, such as whether to include Kafka and Picasso within the definition of realism by enlarging it to infinity, or to exclude them and consequently proscribe reality. As communists permanently in search of a system, they viciously reject anyone who might depict reality as an inscrutable tangle or who could see a world of absurd illusions, unconnected by any logic. The unfulfilled dreams, the shattered hopes and illusions, the atmosphere of dejection of other literatures do not exist for socialist realists. Their approach is similar to that of the theoreticians, critics, and pseudo philosophers who spent countless hours expounding the absurd artistic credo of national socialism: Equal energies are being squandered interpreting the dialectical character and material existence of socialist realism. And as socialist realism undergoes continuing redefinition, its meaning is persistently di-luted. Now even the communist intellectuals in Eastern Europe recognize that the metamorphosis of socialist realism has caused great confusion not only among the artists, but also in the minis-tries of culture. With sharp irony, one Hungarian poet pointed out to me that socialist realism was always much more effective in analyzing the negative aspects of contemporary civilization than in portraying the future utopian communism, or even in describing communism's present positive features. (Nobody gives an owl's hoot about the electrification of collective farms, the increases in the national output of steel, or the opening of three new filling stations in Budapest.) It is remarkable that even the vision of the utopian communism of the future is viewed in terms of denial: *i.e.*, the day when there will be no more drunks, no poor, no beatniks with long hair, no jazz, no junkies, and—yes—even no money. For a convinced communist, an earthly paradise becomes a string of negatives.

Although the concept of socialist realism is suffering decimation from all sides, this does not mean that a strenuous rear-guard action is not being mounted from Moscow. The perennial problem is how to make literature politically militant without stifling it and, con-versely, how to encourage art that is also politically useful. The editor of the journal *Moskva* was writing in the summer of 1966 that "workers in literature and art must demonstrate all the beauty and heroism of the Soviet working class." And in the Soviet youth organ, *Komsomolskaya Pravda,* writers were publicly appealing for living prototypes of the "young and positive hero." To the great annoyance of the editors, no candidates stepped forward in this search for the "New Soviet Man." However, the idealogues are not discouraged. The Hungarian theoretician Bela Kopeczi, in a lengthy article on socialist realism published in 1966, wrote that "the period is now closed in which even Marxist critics preferred to avoid the term 'socialist realism' because, apparently, they thought it had been discredited by dogmatism." Kopeczi, who sees socialist realism as a "historical category," wrote that there now appears to be agreement that it should be defined as "the aesthetic expression of socialist society at the present stage of development." Kopeczi maintains that "socialist realist literature and art are distinguished from bourgeois literature and art primarily by active humanism." (No matter that the socialist realist usually measures culture in quantitative rather than qualitative terms: so many millions of books, so many hours of concerts, so many miles of celluloid.) This Hungarian spokesman claims socialism offers the intellectuals something that the capitalist system could never offer: "It calls upon them to promote human progress, with their own specific means, by relying upon the forces of society instead of engaging in Don Quixote-like battles." When comparing Kafka's *Trial*, Hemingway's *The Old Man and the Sea*, and Sholokhov's *Human Destiny*, communists esteem their views of reality as readily identifiable: "Bourgeois" (or "decadent") literature portrays the isolated man conscious of his miserable lot—and only occasionally still capable of heroic exertion; progressive "socialist" literature always suggests the possibility of harmony and sense in life. Kopeczi sees the writer not as an isolated individual but as a worker, the scope of whose existence and activity within society exerts a freeing influence. He concludes that "The socialist realist writer and artist know well that their art is part of a general struggle on a social scale against alienation; they know that alienation must be eliminated not only in 'thinking,' in 'consciousness,' but in 'mass existence' as well."

As I have said, the word "alienation" continues to haunt party theologians. It is becoming the termite that threatens to undermine the entire theoretical foundation of socialism. Alienation was to have disappeared with the end of the class structure. Now the party leadership has to admit that, while theoretically the growth of alienation among the socialist working class is inadmissible, in fact it exists. The proletarian described by Marx now finds himself dominated by the profoundly impersonal institutions of his party's creation. Instead of feeling envy or resentment against the big capitalist boss with the cigar, the socialist worker now feels a total lack of human contact with the technocrat who is running the factory and who appears in a chauffeur-driven limousine. East European literature is, consequently, much more intensely concerned with the problems posed by alienation than, let us say, John Osborne is with the problem of the oppressiveness of the "Establishment." A gradual separation of art from social obligations, from realism, is a direct result. For example, the new Czech writers seem haunted by a kind of anarchical and romantic aestheticism and appear engrossed by such subjects as the hero in an amoral environment.

What to do? Speaking at the Hungarian Communist Party Congress in the fall of 1966, Hungarian ideologist Istvan Szirmai said, "Historical experience teaches us that the suppression of non-Marxist trends cannot replace the fight for essentials carried out within the Party, that their administrative suppression can only lead to ideological isolation, to our isolation." And the villain of 1956, Party leader Janos Kadar, emphasizing that a more broad-minded position is essential, added with moderation, "We don't ask for conformism from anyone, not even from communists. They are not conformists, either. We say that individuality, too, should develop and offer society what it can."

Among the communists themselves, no such conformity as was demanded by Stalin now exists. This is clearly illustrated by the divergent attitudes of the various parties to a writer such as Franz Kafka. In Russia, Kafka is still considered a second-rate literary figure whose work plays a priori into the hands of the bourgeoisie. His short stories appeared in Russia for the first time in 1965 and were cited as examples of regressive artistic development. The Poles published limited editions of Kafka's works from 1957 to 1961 and almost nothing of his since then. One Bulgarian critic claimed Kafka's writing is "distinguished by a flight from the social-political problems of the age in which he lived, as well as by complete confusion when faced with the negative in human nature and the despair and pessimism connected with it." Another Bulgarian, who could not decide whether or not Kafka was a decadent author, concluded that "Kafka is individual evidence of the end of capitalism." The Rumanians and the Hungarians have translated some of his works, including *The Trial* and *The Castle,* but the East Germans maintain that his concept of alienation is irrelevant to modern socialist conditions. The negative attitude of Comrade Ulbricht's companions has infuriated the Czechs, who have now fully rehabilitated Kafka. When I visited Prague in 1965, I was

15

taken to the house where Kafka lived, adjoining a church in the medieval town. There was no plaque, nothing to indicate Kafka had grown up there. Now this situation has been corrected, and Czechs will freely admit that the world of Kafka is most relevant to their experience. They still have to deal with an endless procession of faceless bureaucrats. Kafka, in effect, became the hero of the 1968 revolution.

All the regimes of the bloc attempt to "buy off" their intellectuals by giving them enviable sinecures at various libraries, universities, and publishing houses, by granting high royalties, by providing large apartments and weekend houses, and even by permitting trips abroad. The East Germans provide a special "intelligence pension" for their faithful intellectuals. The Poles, on the other hand, are specialists at dispatching large cultural delegations to France and England. (However, about four out of five of those sent are in the lowest category of their creative field and in the top category of political reliability.) Except in music and painting, the Polish regime has increasingly restricted free expression in the entire cultural sphere. The result is that honest Polish intellectuals must remain silent. The writers who sit in the drab, smoke-impregnated atmosphere of the "Grand" or *"Europejskie"* cafés in Warsaw have deep lines of irony that mar their smiling masks. They still pride themselves on being in the avant-garde, on being the developers of Western culture in Eastern Europe; it is the only way they can maintain their self-respect. But even their pride is beginning to wear thin. Sipping espresso, they boldly charge every shadow on the political horizon like medieval knights. In their writings they are timid, opportunistic, and unwilling to come to grips with difficult contemporary issues.

"Over ten years have passed since the last wave of literary debuts expressed some new, original ideas," said one Polish critic. As a consequence, Polish readers are becoming indifferent to the authors. And the authors, rather than develop new formulas, which the censors might reject, tend to refine and distill what passed in earlier works.

The masked despair and stagnation of the Polish intellectuals does not embarrass the regime. Quite the contrary, Gomulka forces

16

the writers to absent themselves from the increasingly bitter ideological struggle. He has deprived dozens of outspoken professors of their jobs. Whenever and wherever a solitary intellectual does raise his voice, he is quickly stifled by the statutes of the "decree on particularly dangerous offenses during the period of reconstruction of the state." For condemning this decree as a "code of lawlessness," one of the foremost thinkers of the October 1956 revolution, Professor Leszek Kolakowski (b. 1927), was expelled from the Polish United Workers' Party in 1966. Speaking at a student rally at the University of Warsaw, Kolakowski said there was no reason to celebrate the tenth anniversary of the Polish October because there was still no democratic freedom in the country. Kolakowski's position was that pious dialectics would never make up for unfulfilled expectations.

Professor Kolakowski then lay low until March 1968, when he participated at a meeting of the Warsaw branch of the Union of Writers, which was protesting the ban of Mickiewicz's play at the National Theater.* So heavy-handed was the regime's treatment of the arts, so oppressive had Polish censorship become, that Kolakowski told his colleagues that "the national culture is being dwarfed under innumerable blows." He publicly argued that the student riots and mass demonstrations were "caused by the hopelessness of the situation and proved the incompetence and lack of ability of the cultural leadership." Where Latin-American students would first attack the Ministry of Justice or the police headquarters, hundreds of Warsaw students, armed with bats and bricks, stormed

---

* Mickiewicz's *Dziady* (*Forefathers' Eve*) was long on the reading list of every Polish high school. The audiences in 1968, however, laughed too loudly at such lines as, "the only things that Moscow sends us are jackasses, idiots, and spies," and applauded too vigorously such inflammatory verse as: ". . . full well I know / The kind of grace the Muscovite will show / Ripping the fetters from my feet and hands / To rivet on my spirit yet heavier bands!" So the authorities imposed a ban on further performances of the play. Gomulka said, by way of excuse, "We could not allow it to become a springboard for anti-Russian attacks." However, the anti-Russian content of nineteenth-century Polish literature is so great that to ban classics on the ground that they might now arouse anti-Soviet sentiment would place the regime in the embarrassing position of repudiating a large part of Poland's national heritage.

17

the Ministry of Culture—illustrating to what degree culture has become a focal point of contention.

The Polish communist leadership reacted in a desperate fashion to the mass demonstrations: Kolakowski and a host of other professors, writers, and journalists were summarily dismissed from their jobs. Entire departments of Warsaw and Cracow universities were shut. And an old-fashioned campaign was initiated against "Zionists," who were held responsible by Gomulka for the "spiritual instigation" of the student riots. In a country where hardly any Jews survived (the prewar population of about three and a half million was reduced to a mere thirty thousand by the Nazis), traditional anti-Semitic sentiment was once again exploited for reasons of political expediency. The official party paper, *Trybuna Ludu,* published a simple man's guide to Zionism, whose logic made it clear that Karl Marx himself would have been invited to leave People's Poland. The state-controlled Polish press went so far as to accuse Jews of having worked hand in glove with the Gestapo and suggested that only very few Jews actually did any fighting in the final uprising of the Warsaw ghetto. But even a full-scale pogrom would not solve Poland's troubles.

Back in the mid-fifties Kolakowski had already made a list entitled "What Socialism Is Not." Among the items mentioned were: "A state in which racist agitators enjoy full freedom; a state that does not mind being hated, so long as it is feared; a society in which it is a crime to be brother, sister, son, or wife of a criminal." Now the Polish United Workers' Party seemed in a rush to implement Kolakowski's sarcasm. Relations between the intellectuals and Gomulka went as low as they could go without degenerating into bloody insurrection. Polish critic, composer, and former parliamentarian Stefan Kisielewski, who had called the Gomulka regime "the dictatorship of neoignoramuses," was clubbed into unconsciousness by secret policemen disguised as workers. When I think of the witty, urbane conversations I had with this disarming, impish anarchist, the scene becomes particularly painful. Kisielewski had long been campaigning for greater intellectual freedom, and at a 1967 Congress of the Union of Writers he had declared he could "no longer be dependent on the good will of people whose names are shrouded in official mystery and whose low intellectual level in numerous instances prevents them from even understanding the meaning of the articles or books they are censoring." If there had to be censorship, suggested Kisielewski, at least let it be publicly acknowledged.

The Polish intellectuals could no longer excuse the regime's actions. They were convinced that normal methods of protest and limited demands could produce no results and were examining more radical measures of dissent. Even men of differing political and religious convictions became united in their demand for change. The chances were that Gomulka would eventually be replaced by someone even more autocratic. In this struggle, the intellectuals, the students, and the liberal communists did not appear to have sufficient support for their cause to prevail. Instead, the outlook was that a nationalist would come to power on a platform that would suppress the dissidents, "Zionists," and intellectuals.

A few authors, such as the satirist Slawomir Mrozek, who lives in Italy, and the poet Zbigniew Herbert, who lives in Paris and Vienna, have been able to escape the noxious atmosphere in which writers execute literary stunts with the same lack of feeling as circus acrobats performing somersaults. Opposed to the strong current of obscurantism that dominates much of Polish writing, Herbert (b. 1924) specializes in miniatures of refined irony that have earned him a European reputation. Herbert rejects all poetical devices. His poetry is clear, compact, austere, almost classic in form. His free-verse poem, "The Emperor's Dream," is a typical example of his writing.

He dreams he is a wood louse who scurries across the floor looking for food. Suddenly, overhead, he sees an immense foot about to crush him. The emperor hunts for a crevice in which to squeeze. The floor is smooth and slippery. Yes, nothing is more ordinary than the dreams of emperors.

In another poem, "The Emperor," written in 1957, he maintains the delicate equilibrium between fantasy and condemnation.

Once upon a time, there was an emperor.
He had yellowish eyes and bestial jaws.

And he lived in his palace, a palace crammed with marble and police.
In the night he awoke and screamed fearfully.
Nobody loved him.
As for him, what he loved was to roam the country and inspire fear.
And even to have himself photographed with children who laughed in
  between the flowers.
When he died, no one dared remove his portraits from the walls.
You, yes, you! Look in your house: Maybe, just maybe, somewhere at home
  remains his likeness.

One prominent Polish critic has written that Herbert fathoms the depths of common experience after having conquered, through his discerning intelligence, "the paralysis of the will caused by the temptation of the absurd." More complex and sophisticated than "The Emperor" is Herbert's poem on "The Study of the Object," in which he tries to extract meaning from the shadow of an object that does not exist. To Herbert, the world is inscrutable, opaque, and infinitely mendacious. The truth cannot be detected, but only created from the bottom up, by adding the simplest elements.

Most beautiful is the object that does not exist.
Neither blindness nor death can take away the object that does not exist.
Mark the place where stood the object that does not exist by a black square.
It will be a simple dirge for the beautiful absent.
Empty space more beautiful than the object,
More beautiful than the place it leaves.
It is a preworld,
A white paradise for all possibilities.

Herbert is one of those exceptional phenomena—a satirist who is allowed to live abroad and to publish at home—which mark Polish culture. But even Herbert admits, "In our time it is very difficult to be a joyful gardener of words." Those poets who must live in Poland soon withdraw from an active role. They become austere, aloof, and obscurantist. Their works often read like anacrostics; they are full of mysticism. No wonder that the Polish public has turned to Elizabethan poetry, especially the works of Donne, Drayton, Spenser, and Webster, to seek diversion from the present.

Except for music and painting, which are treated separately in this book, few areas of Polish culture are in the process of "awakening." Unlike Americans, who tend to think in terms of action, the Poles primarily think in terms of evasion; they avoid planning the future and concentrate on the past. It is incredible, for example, how hard World War II themes die in Poland. The Warsaw review *Zycie Literackie* admits that "there is a bad atmosphere of stagnation in our theater and drama." As regards the cinema, which was so prominent after 1956, one Cracow critic notes that the trouble with the Polish new wave is that "it does not exist." Like Zbigniew Cybulski, the actor with the dark glasses who symbolized a whole generation of young Poles, the new wave died prematurely. Cybulski portrayed the counterrevolutionary figure, in Wajda's famous movie "Ashes and Diamonds," who stood bewildered between idealism and disillusionment, whose insecurity and despair were masked by the mad, reckless streak of Polish humor.

The policy of Ulbricht's East Germany toward the arts is even narrower than Poland's and, like its goateed *Führer*, without a trace of laughter. Because of the regime's basic insecurity, East Germany's cultural policies have been much harsher than those of the neighboring regimes. Writer Stefan Heym wrote in 1965:

We expect our fellow writers in the West to raise their voices against tyranny and for human rights. Do we raise our voices whenever the great principles are violated, principles for which our revolution was made? We expect our fellow writers in the West, if need be, to give up honors, comforts, and life for so unrewarding a thing as truth. What have we ever given up when the occasion called for it?

Shortly thereafter, Heym was sharply reprimanded for publishing material in the West and deprived altogether of the right to publish his works in East Germany. The extremes to which convinced East German propagandists will go are astounding. When satirist and ballad singer Wolf Biermann (b. 1936) was accused of introducing pornography into his cabaret shows, the East German daily *Neues Deutschland* declared that "whoever is perverse politically must be perverse sexually." Biermann was promptly placed under a form of house arrest. Actually, Biermann's ballads had long been indigest-

21

ible to the East German officials. They had been particularly
nettled by the following lyrics:

> Those who once courageously faced machine guns
> are afraid of my guitar.
> Panic
> Is let loose when I open my jaws and frightened sweat
> appears on the trunks of the bureaucratic elephants.

By 1968 even Czech radio and television programs were being
condemned by the East German regime for their revisionism. And,
of course, the West Berlin television programs are regarded as
undiluted poison. An East German district court official has stated
that "viewing Western television" represents a fundamental reason
for the existence of crime in East Berlin.

Enrich Honecker, the number two man in the East German
Politbureau, claims skepticism and rising living standards are mutually exclusive in the building of socialism. Attacking those writers
who think "socialist education can be achieved only through a
massive recital of shortcomings and mistakes," Honecker protested
that such work, dedicated as it was to "abstract truth," could only
"retard and block the development of a socialist consciousness
among the workers." Honecker declared "unrestrained philistine
skepticism" as of no help to anyone.

Although in Rumania the artists, the writers, and the sculptors
are still suffering a hangover from the cult of personality, the
atmosphere is rapidly improving. After all, in the early nineteen-
fifties as many as thirty thousand books had been placed on the
Rumanian banned list, and there was a time when the transfer of
ownership of a typewriter had to be reported to the appropriate
ministry in Bucharest so that the police could trace the origin of all
carbon copies of manuscripts. By the mid-sixties, nationalist pride
was forcing the regime to recognize "our Ionesco" and "our great
Brancusi," who only a decade before had been unpersons. Even
Rumanians were aghast in the summer of 1966 when, at the conclusion of a gala performance by the visiting Peking Dance Ensemble,
the entire troupe turned their backs to the audience in order to face
and applaud a slide projection of the Great Mao.

Socialist realism in Rumania is now being replaced with national realism. The supreme test of any cultural activity appears to be: "Is it in keeping with the make-up of the Rumanian people?" The primary criterion is no longer whether a work adheres to the principles of Marxism-Leninism, but whether it serves Rumania's national interest. Naïve historical poetry, portraying the glorious deeds of brave Dacian warriors, the putative ancestors of today's Rumanians, is being officially encouraged by the state. The two recurring themes in these poems are the superiority of the Getae-Daci over the other peoples on the periphery of the Greco-Roman world and their characterization as the bravest and most righteous people among the Thracians.

Like Albania, Rumania still retains a centralized apparatus that controls all cultural manifestations. The Rumanians have discovered the value of art as a "cultural export item"; thus classified, it allows them to side-step the problem of freedom of artistic expression at home. One Rumanian painter, Ion Pacea, was permitted to exhibit both in Paris and at the Venice Biennale and the critical praise of his work was reprinted in the Rumanian press. At home, however, he continues to be severely chastised by the state for his abstractions. Similarly, the entire Rumanian press devoted lengthy articles to the Bucharest Biennale (January 1967). On view at this exhibition were the works of two hundred painters and a hundred sculptors, the latter mostly of the older generation. The show itself was a triumph of international epigonism and was devastatingly mediocre, but the Rumanian Communist Party was disturbed by the extent to which nonfigurative art had blossomed. Not without justification, the critics complained that, under the guise of folklore, the Rumanian painters had been introducing Cubism and primitivism into their work.

For years the Rumanian Communist Party has been asking the national dramatists to create realistic dramas, to write plays on themes dealing with the "new reality." The irony of it is that every time a straightforward play is written on the contemporary situation, it is viewed by the Party as being ideologically unsuitable. One frustrated author, Ion Baiesu, wrote that he had been writing a play for two years. "It is the only thing I totally trust, but it was rejected with a pitiful smile by three theater managers in Bucharest," claimed Baiesu. "Theater managers overwhelm us at meetings with declarations of love for original dramas, but when they draw up their repertoires, they are helpless before the theatrical administrators." However, even those authors whose plays are criticized are no longer subjected to "administrative measures." Speaking to an artists' and writers' plenum soon after his takeover of power, Party Secretary Ceausescu said, "We are for an art which by its optimism and vigor should represent our times and in which the life and aspirations of the Rumanian people should be vibrant," even though, in reality, their lives are drab. But the theater has fared far better than most of Rumania's other arts. Paul Everac, one of the most promising of the young generation of Rumanian playwrights, has noted that because the Bucharest stage is presenting all of contemporary Western drama—from Harold Pinter to Peter Weiss—Rumanian playwrights are forced to "compete" with them. That is, the audiences will choose only those plays that are most relevant or most entertaining. This is another illustration of the expanding cultural horizon in Rumania. On stage everything is permitted except the portrayal of contemporary political truths. It is even in fashion to play Shakespeare like Ionesco. In fact, director David Esrig's version of *Troilus and Cressida,* in which Patroclus is portrayed as an acerbic homosexual, earned high praise when it was played at the Théâtre des Nations in Paris. Esrig sees the Greeks as uncultured barbarians and the Trojans as overcivilized effetes. In keeping with this conception, he dressed the Greeks like Tarzans and the Trojans like Mayfair Victorians. Helen, whom he covered with a platinum-blond wig and a scruffy, black-bear stole, became a Greek "baby doll," all liberties being permitted except a show of modern liberty itself.

Hungary's cultural overlords have been practicing on-again, off-again tactics with the artists, poets, writers, and musicians ever since the 1956 revolution. (This wavering between hot and cold is not restricted to the Party's attitude toward the intelligentsia, but extends to the entire domestic situation.) Dwight MacDonald once made a distinction between *"cognoscenti"* and *"ignoscenti"* in America. Such a division is almost automatic in Eastern Europe:

The intellectuals view themselves as the *cognoscenti* and the party hacks as the true *ignoscenti*. The members of the Central Committee, on the other hand, usually consider the artists to be somewhat naïve *ignoscenti*, while they regard themselves—as the arbiters of power—as the only *cognoscenti*. In Hungary, this situation is confused by the fact that some members of the intelligentsia, such as poet Gabor Garai, are members of the Politbureau, while the intelligentsia is so infiltrated with agents, and even provocateurs, that all distinctions become blurred. This Byzantine power-labyrinth should not obscure the fact that Hungary has exceptionally talented creators: Szanto Piroshka is undoubtedly the most imaginative and fecund woman painter in any of the socialist states; novelist Tibor Dery continues to experiment boldly with the form of the novel; composer Sandor Szokolay (b. 1931) broke new ground with his avant-garde opera based on Federico García Lorca's *Blood Wedding;* and Istvan Szabo (b. 1938) placed himself among the best of the new directors with his two films "The Father" and "The Age of Illusions," both of which explored the disenchantment of young intellectuals with the outdated slogans of the past. An uneasy truce now exists between the regime and these intellectuals. The experiences suffered in 1956 are too bitter for either to forget. And, consequently, there is less militancy and far less hope among Hungarian intellectuals than among their Rumanian or Czech neighbors.

The Czechs enjoyed the most lively intellectual and cultural scene of any socialist country during the middle sixties. Their cinema, theater, sculpture, and music were of a truly international caliber. However, for centuries the Czechs have possessed a more cosmopolitan atmosphere than the other nations of Eastern Europe. Ever since the fourteenth century, Czechs have enjoyed meaningful relationships with the West, such as that between Jan Hus and Wycliffe or between John Amos Comenius and Messrs. Bacon, Pym, and Boyle. The Czech intellectual of today has a detached world outlook. His vision is far clearer than that of his Polish or Hungarian counterparts; at the same time, he passionately strives to cultivate his own garden, to develop his own style. Whereas communism has contributed little to the ways of human expression, unless it be a sort of shoe-thumping bravado, the moody, soft-spoken, melancholic *Weltanschauung* of the Czechs is likely to be of lasting significance. While the novels that exposed the horrors and excesses of Stalinism, such as Ladislav Mnacko's *Delayed Reports* (1963), were the ones that made headlines in the West, the really excellent works by Czech satirists Josef Skovorecky (*The Cowards*) and Bohumil Hrabal (*Closely Watched Trains*) went almost unnoticed. The subjects treated by the Czech novelists seemed to follow a definite pattern: After a wave of interest in the problems posed by World War II and the Nazi occupation, the writers turned to study the persecution of the Jews (as in Grossman's "Shop on Main Street"). Next, they occupied themselves with the cult of personality. By the mid-sixties, they were turning toward the present Kafkaesque unreality; they were beginning to depict the prevailing despair of the younger generation, the hypocrisy and compromise of the older generation, and the need for a new outlook, a fresh start. One Czech communist author explained that, to him, the principal question was, "How should my characters act in a truly socialist society? Which really means: How should I act in this society?" This Czech writer was even puzzled whether a "socialist style of life" exists or could exist—as opposed to the frequently condemned capitalist or "bourgeois" way of life. It seemed almost impossible for him to reconcile his humanist conscience with the deeds and everyday performance of the tiny, secretive, and isolated clique in the Castle which used to hand down all major political decisions.

One Czech writer, Gabriel Laub, presented a parody of the not too distant past in a satirical story entitled "The Intellectuals."

The Royal Procurator arrested a group of persons and charged them with being intellectuals.

There was no evidence and the Royal Judge consequently sentenced them to death.

The Queen did not feel like watching the execution because she was more amused—at the moment—by a pantomime. The King therefore promised the prisoners pardon, provided that they could prove to be useful to their monarch.

One of them worked out a stereometric equation that led to the conclusion that a gibbet can have as many as four arms instead of the original two.

Another calculated the amount of overtime that can be saved on the work performed by the executioner's assistants, provided that executions were held at dawn rather than early in the evening.

Yet another suggested that public executions should be held in the afternoon, so that even schoolchildren could attend them, in order to increase the educational effect.

The chemist compiled a technological process to manufacture synthetic hogwash; real hogwash—hitherto fed to prisoners—could be passed to the royal pigs.

The teacher, versed in music as he was, compiled a songbook of energetic and rhythmic songs for royal floggers.

The professional preacher of morality wrote a sermon against negligence and denounced in it his warden, who had knocked out two teeth fewer from a prisoner's mouth than prescribed by the norms of feudal justice.

It appeared that even intellectuals could be useful if they made the effort. In the crucial moment they all behaved as normal people do.

Only one behaved like a stubborn intellectual. He did nothing to win a pardon for himself. He only made it a condition that they should put an inscription on his tombstone to the effect that he disapproved of his own execution.

The Czech intellectuals try to create according to their beliefs. They call this "realism," in the hope of evading both official notice and Party condemnation. But in the face of bureaucratic tyranny, the Czechs have consistently shown remarkable courage. For example, rather than follow the "comfortable, but irresponsible and immoral" way of apology and repentance, the editors of the Slovak literary weekly *Knizhni Kultura* declared in 1965 that they would much rather "burn their fingers" than "sit on two chairs," and closed down their magazine. Similarly, the editorial board of *Tvar*, one of the best and most sophisticated cultural periodicals in Eastern Europe, folded in preference to changing either its policies or its editorial board.

No group in Eastern Europe of the sixties was more outspoken than the Czech and Slovak writers. Even when it endangered their careers to do so, many members of their Union protested vigorously against the prison sentences meted out in 1966 to Russian authors Yuli Daniel and Andrei Sinyavsky. Slowly the Czechs won the confidence of a large segment of the population through their honesty, forthrightness, and high principles. Tired of fighting for small concessions from the government, they actually came out for a form of "writer power" in 1967. They wished to create their own intellectual program and were fortunate to see a substantial part of their platform realized under Dubcek in 1968.

The Czechoslovak literary community has enjoyed a reputation for being in the political vanguard since the ninetheenth century: They greatly helped the Czechoslovak renaissance in the face of the Austro-Hungarian Germanization; they strongly came out for Czechoslovak independence during World War I; they were the most democratic and liberal element under Tomas Masaryk's Republic; they were in the forefront of the anti-Nazi underground during World War II. The democratic tradition of the prewar generation of writers is perhaps best reflected by Laco Novomesky (b. 1904), a Slovak communist poet and politician who was jailed at the time of the Clementis trial in 1950 and released and rehabilitated as a poet but not as a political spokesman. Although his large frame is now slightly stooped, Novomesky has retained all his ebullience. He is one of the truly great men in Central Europe. His lined Slavic face, his gentle eyes, his strong chin, and his sensuous mouth provide sculptural inspiration. "The culture of a country was seldom built by official writers," said Novomesky. "The issue is not merely what has already been written," he claimed; there are also "authors who should have written but would not write because they told themselves that they would not be published in any case." Novomesky said, even before Novotny's overthrow, "My purpose is to enable a Dostoevsky of today to become Dostoevsky, to allow him to have his say about people's gravest conflicts even in a socialist society."

Another Slovak writer, Ladislav Mnacko (b. 1919), author of the best-selling *A Taste of Power* and of *Delayed Reports,* felt he could not get his views heard in Czechoslovakia and fled to Israel in the summer of 1967. Mnacko represents the generation of Czech liberal intellectuals who have passed through all the phases: from wartime idealism, through the cult of personality in the early nineteen-fifties, and to the denunciation of the Stalinist system by Khrushchev. These traumas have left their deep scars. Once in exile, Mnacko pleaded that "this chaos, this elasticity of the law, this ability to circumvent the law, and, when it suits those in power, to use laws inappropriately, this arbitrary use of power must be ended." Mnacko was deprived of his Czech citizenship, expelled from the Communist Party, and stripped of all the state decorations for what the Czech news agency Ceteka called his "unprincipled" and "arbitrary" trip. Mnacko admitted his protest was of a "purely political nature," but he explained that "a literary person cannot be effective without taking into account the political factors of his environment." When the Slovak Writers' Association denounced Mnacko as an adventurer and anarchist, he replied that this was preferable to being "a publicist who receives instructions and writes what is demanded of him." Mnacko, in fact, called the Writers' Association statement "charming," and explained that the authorities must have applied much pressure on certain members in order to produce such a sharply worded denunciation.

Mnacko's one-man crusade was soon eclipsed by the stormy and dramatic Czech Writers' Congress in June 1967. The Czech writers seemed to sense that the people were ready for and wanted what poet Andrei Voznesensky has called "the naked truth, and not truth concealed beneath the fig leaf of censorship." They wished this Congress to serve as their chosen battlefield for an open confrontation between conflicting concepts of life and literature. It is difficult for Americans to fathom how a writer's congress could become the single most important and dramatic political event in Czechoslovakia since the communist takeover in 1948. But in Czechoslovakia all the writers' congresses have been forums of vigorous opposition. They have met with a positive national response. The Second Writers' Congress in 1956, for example, presented such a bitter denunciation of Stalinism that it deeply shocked the communist hierarchy. The Third Writers' Congress in 1963 heralded the wave of liberalization in the Czech intellectual community, which presaged the theater's rebirth. However, by the Fourth Congress, the platform was no longer in the hands of the middle-of-the-roaders;

the balance had now definitely tipped in favor of the younger rebels. The atmosphere at this congress of literati was heady. In fact, it was overly theatrical, too oratorical, like a poetry reading by Yevtushenko. To many of the more cynical generation, just graduated from the university, this effort by rebellious ex-communists to attack the Novotny regime for failing to appreciate the meaning of artistic freedom seemed, at best, superfluous. To them communism, as a system, was at fault.

Playwright Ivan Klima (b. 1931) felt that the question of the principle of "directing literature" had to be confronted directly. That is, he felt it unacceptable to place writing under the tutelage of officials who treated artists, "whose intellectual message is recognized by the whole cultural world, as citizens not yet fully in their rights." Klima said it was a disgrace for writers "to be admonished from time to time and enlightened by official intellect, which is recognized nowhere outside its officially designated area." But the strongest frontal attack came in the brilliant and protracted speech by novelist Ludvik Vaculik (b. 1926), author of *A Busy House* (1963) and *The Ax* (1966). His thesis was that in the face of a regime concerned solely with the perpetuation of its own power the artist and the citizen must seek stronger guarantees of their freedom than the mere benevolence of the nation's leaders. Vaculik outlined how "a totalitarian regime with an intact and functioning apparatus can, given time, turn an independent-minded nation into a herd of faceless, scared nonentities." This he believed was possible with "only a limited measure of actually exercised terror." Developing his thesis, he said that "just as I do not believe that the citizen and power can be identical, that the ruled and the rulers can sing the same song, I do not believe that art and power can ever feel well together." Vaculik further persisted: "Art cannot give up the theme of government, for governing means making continuous, direct and indirect decisions, through administrative acts, involving the life of man, his well-being, and his disappointments, everything he thinks about (and this cannot be dictated)." Although he demanded changes in the constitution, Vaculik concluded by saying that if the Politbureau of the Party came to the Congress and asked whether their dream of socialism was realizable, "they would have to take the following answer as the expression of our good will and at the same time of our supreme civic loyalty: 'I do not know.' "

The Party ideologist at that time, Jiri Hendrych, was particularly stung by Vaculik's statement that "Not a single important human problem has been solved in the course of the last twenty years." Hendrych purportedly blurted out to the Congress: "I have finally reached the end of my patience with you people." Hendrych maintained that "the great and concentrated endeavor of our society is being stabbed in the back by the preaching of freedom, democracy, and humanism stripped of their class and socialist meanings." As the Congress moved to a close, the speakers were aware that the hammer was just about to fall on their heads. Nevertheless, Jan Prochazka (b. 1929), an influential writer in the Czech film industry, said in the concluding speech: "If society wants to be heard, it must give a voice to its writer, because it is his privilege to be society's heart and to express its anger." Prochazka said that literature must be a dissatisfied voice, that it should be able to judge the size of the abyss between the ideal and reality, that it is an instrument through which humanity can talk in decisive moments. "The writer," said Prochazka, "will not be willing to subordinate himself to doctrines and dogmas and, on the contrary, will insist upon subordinating them to his will." In closing this audacious gathering Prochazka said, "We side with those who strive for a change in our unhappy age."

Although the Congress passed a resolution calling for "tolerance" of various aesthetic viewpoints and defined this "tolerance" as the "competition for freedom" and the "choice of alternatives," the Party responded with administrative solutions to this deliberate incursion of the writers into the political sphere. The Plenum of the Central Committee of the Party charged that *Literarni Noviny,* undoubtedly the brightest and most controversial publication in Eastern Europe, had gotten so far out of control that it had turned into a "platform of standpoints of political opposition." This weekly, with a circulation of one hundred and thirty thousand, was taken away from the Union of Writers and its management turned over to the Ministry of Culture. But these moves proved no solution and failed to neutralize the reformist spirit of the intellectuals.

31

Vaculik said that he would continue to "walk along the border between party discipline and revolution," and, in doing so, set the tone for the mass dissent that followed with the student demonstrations that autumn.

Fearing that the outspoken demands of these writers might well set off the sparks that could topple him from power, Novotny over-reacted: In addition to revamping the Writers' Union, curtailing its powers, and depriving some of its most outspoken members of their party cards, Novotny handed out prison sentences to some dissidents.* A young Czech writer, Jan Benes (b. 1933), was given a five-year prison term for "disrupting the Republic." (Ironically, Novotny's last act as President of the Republic was to sign his pardon.) These moves aroused within the ruling Politbureau exactly the type of opposition Novotny had so skillfully managed to avoid. Novotny's colleagues had long been dissatisfied with the way he had run down the economy and suppressed the Slovak minority. They seized upon his mismanagement of the intellectual dissenters as the excuse to oust him. Once outvoted in the Politbureau, he could not even be saved by a quick visit by Soviet Party Secretary Brezhnev. The small yellow-red-and-white standard bearing Novotny's motto, "Truth is Victorious," was lowered from the roof of Hradcany Castle, where it had flown for over a decade, and Novotny was expelled from the feudal manor of the Bohemian kings.

His successor, the restrained, soft-spoken Alexander Dubcek, said soon after taking office that he had decided to eliminate everything that had obstructed artistic creation. As a Slovak who did not enjoy widespread popularity with the Czech workers, he could find in Prague as his only allies the students and intellectuals. Dubcek, in his quiet, sensible manner, pronounced: "Democracy is not only the right and the possibility for expressing one's own opinion, but it

---

* Novotny's henchmen even went so far as to pass out a jail sentence to a twenty-five-year-old Prague Bohemian who staged a "happening," the principal offense being that seventy loaves of bread were used in such a way as to "insult the basic feelings of working people." Apparently, the hundred participants of this "happening" painted the loaves with water colors, used them as arm bracelets, and finally ended up throwing bread balls at one another.

also means how the opinions of the people are dealt with." At a ceremony marking the hundredth anniversary of the Prague National Theater, Dubcek said that "conditions must be created so that we may live in an atmosphere that would help the expansion of creative thinking, fantasy, artistic creation, and ingenuity, and would open the door to beauty." While Dubcek insisted that as a communist he would retain the various state committees that control culture, he did not want the artists to interpret this as an indication that "we want to issue orders on how and what is to be done." Censorship was quickly abolished and free speech permitted in all the mass media. A literary drive was launched to publish such previously forbidden works as Mnacko's *A Taste of Power* and Boris Pasternak's *Dr. Zhivago*. Films banned for years were suddenly released. When called by students at a spontaneous and quite unprecedented midnight rally in front of Communist Party headquarters in Prague to answer what guarantee there was that the old ways would not return, Dubcek retorted: "You, yourselves, are that guarantee."

Professor Eduard Goldstuecker, Vice-Rector of Charles University, was one of the true heroes of this civilized, calm, and star-crossed revolution. Imprisoned as a spy immediately following the Slansky trials in 1952, Goldstuecker was the man responsible for the rehabilitation in 1963 of Kafka's writings. Now, after some hesitation, he accepted the chairmanship of the Union of Writers. Goldstuecker said that the writers didn't want to be a tribune for professional exclusiveness, nor were they going to "behave like the *enfant terrible* of our cultural-artistic front." He emphasized that the Czechs had to "achieve what has never yet been done previously: produce a socialist society based on personal freedom." Goldstuecker soon announced that a new magazine of the Union of Writers, *Literarni Listy*, would "aid everything progressive, cultural, and enlightened in the life of our society." He claimed this periodical would not limit itself to literary issues. Quoting Bertolt Brecht, Goldstuecker said that "art without politics is unimaginable," and declared every effort to separate these two spheres as doomed.

Josef Spacek (b. 1926), who was appointed chairman of the

33

Party's ideological commission, dramatically pronounced, upon assuming office, that "anyone who attempts to fight art and culture is always the ultimate loser." As a fitting climax to the victory of the writers, Spacek added that he did not consider the Party could "set the tasks for art." Nevertheless, the writers remained on their guard. In the first issue of *Literarni Listy,* Prochazka, who had been elected vice-chairman of the Union of Writers, wrote: "If the state has until now been looking after its citizens with the results that we all know, then things should now be the other way around: that citizens look after their state."

The rape of Czechoslovakia by the Warsaw Pact nations in August of 1968 reversed this process again. The seesaw tipped the other way. I shall never forget the gray-haired editor of *Rude Pravo* who had come to talk to me at my Prague hotel in the spring of 1967. I had gotten to know him quite well over a period of several years, and during luncheon we discussed a wide range of topics, among them, Czech Catholicism. I asked if I could quote him on one or two points and he replied, "Why, of course." After lunch I returned to my room, where he phoned me. He wondered if I could again send him some books from Vienna, but when I asked him for the titles, he replied, "Could you meet me in front of the hotel so I can give them to you there?" When I came down some minutes later, he was waiting. He had already been cross-examined by one of the Ministry officials "tailing" me. This editor painfully pleaded that I not quote him or use his name, for he had not gotten official permission to talk to me. There were tears in his light-blue eyes as we walked into Wenceslas Place together. I tried to encourage him by saying that things had improved greatly over the past decade. "Yes," he agreed, "but that this still can happen *now* is so terrible; I am so ashamed. For twenty years we have had to put up with this, and I am getting old. I am almost sixty. I had hoped that the last years of my life would be different. I, like my entire generation, have been sacrificed. For us, it is almost too late." This editor enjoyed several deceptively free months during the first half of 1968. Then, just before the Soviet invasion of Prague, he was fired from *Rude Pravo.* For him the reprieve had been of brief duration.

French anthropologist Claude Lévi-Strauss has defined the despair accompanying the *status quo* of entrenched power as a phenomenon of what he calls the "cold society." The bloc communist parties, isolated and unresponsive to the process of historical change, have tried to prevent a multifaceted cultural evolution. Communists do not prize change in and for itself; they fear it. As opposed to the "hot" society, which throbs culturally and is susceptible to sweeping and revitalizing transformation, the regimes of Eastern Europe have been unable to accept cultural confrontation. Even so, they are aware that the popular and intellectual pressure to truly "humanize" Marxism-Leninism will be difficult to stem. With the widening of the Sino-Soviet rift throughout the past decade, the polarization between a regimented, dogmatic, Stalinist brand of communism in China and a more flexible, humane socialism in the Soviet Union and its former satellites has become pronounced. The guidelines to this new "humanist" socialism are not yet clear, but there is no other course open. The search can be seen in the endless debates on the nature of Marx himself, with scholars poring over Marx's *juvenilia*, in order to differentiate between the young, idealistic Marx—that is, the humanist Ur-Marx—and the old, constipated Marx. Even party-line intellectuals, such as Polish Central Committee member Adam Schaff, are openly examining the nature of this "humanism." Schaff, who suffered expulsion from his chair at Warsaw University in 1968 because of his Jewish origins, sees humanism as the belief that man has an intrinsic value and therefore must be treated not as the means to an end but as the end itself. Schaff believes that the Polish Communist Party, and the other communist parties as well, must change their outlook in order to accept happiness and well-being as the highest goal of all social endeavor. In his *Marx and the Individual* (1965), Schaff maintains that "he who fails to see that man holds the central position in the socialist idea disregards what is most important in it, and does not understand it at all." For the members of the younger generation, still in the university, there is the hope that what will develop in Central Europe is a humanism à la Camus: for they see the rats of *La Peste* as communists.

The younger generation believe in their capacity for self-realization through reason, not through party dictates or Marxist dogma. They have come to believe in the late Palmiro Togliatti's "unity in diversity." Their favorite quotation from Marx is: "Nothing that is human is alien to me." They want to be let alone and to live alone. The party reacts to this movement by trying to dilute the word "humanism" with adjectives, as in "class humanism," for traditional Marxists must reject any predominantly ethical approach to the problem of the individual. In the ensuing verbal tug of words, which is in the best Orwellian tradition, party ideologists present "socialist humanism" as the wave of the future, while the intelligentsia just shakes its head and drops the adjective.

From a historical perspective, the influence of the dictatorship of the proletariat on culture in Eastern Europe should not be regarded as an entirely negative occurrence: It has nurtured an exceptionally vital and virulent intellectual rebellion. The East European intelligentsia continues to voice its protest, testing how much it can get away with; the intellectuals are deriving an inner satisfaction from demonstrating to themselves, to their countrymen, and to the world that they are still fighting the discredited legacy of Marx-Lenin-Stalin. If examined with detachment, these intellectuals are, in a sense, fortunate to have such a real cause with such obvious villains waiting to be challenged—something Western authors in search of themes of protest often lack. Moreover, these East European intellectuals can feel the approval of the rising generation in a way that is not so different from the enthusiasm Paul Goodman or Jean-Paul Sartre once aroused in their admirers. And as the members of this new generation mature, they, too, are beginning to take up cultural protest. They, too, are awakening to the realization that only their ideas and their creativity will outlive them. Soviet apologist Ilya Ehrenburg wrote (in one of his more honest moments) that the whole world could be covered with asphalt, but that somehow, sooner or later, green grass would break through. That bit of green in Eastern Europe today is called "culture."

CHAPTER II

Oscar in a Shop

A cinematic *risorgimento* has swept Czechoslovakia. Its dimensions present a bewildering phenomenon to the West. How, it is asked, can a small communist state produce such an inordinately large number of artistically significant films? "Because we set out in 1961 to produce the kind of film that would make the Poles envious," quips one nationality-conscious Czech film official. But the true origin of this awakening stems from the reforms of a Czech bureaucracy haunted throughout the fifties by ever declining film revenues and a mountingly bored public. Faced with vast deficits, the Party decided in the early nineteen-sixties to loosen the controls and experimentally to permit young directors and writers freely to realize those films they wished to make. The consequence of this sudden and unprecedented cinematic freedom astounded the film-makers themselves. The Czechs, long accused by their Hungarian and Polish neighbors of being dullards trying to sublimate a national inferiority complex by overworking themselves, unexpectedly began collecting dozens of cinematic awards at the proliferating European film festivals. The winning of the 1966 Academy Award by "The Shop on Main Street" was a cause for jubilation in Prague. Huge billboards were erected on Wenceslas Place to announce the event to the public. To the Czech cineasts, it was a symbol that their films had finally shaken off socialist realism and were now reaching a global audience. As usual, Hollywood was late in recognizing talent. (I even heard bitter innuendoes in Prague

37

that the "Jewish lobby" in Hollywood awarded the prize to directors Kadar and Klos for political reasons.) Actually, the Czech film renaissance had begun back in 1963 with Milos Forman's "Peter and Pavla," Jaromil Jires's "The First Cry," and Pavel Juracek's brilliant short, "A Prop Is Needed." Symbolically, it seemed as if the young generation of Czech cineasts could build on the strong but little celebrated tradition of Czech cinematography* only after the huge bronze colossus of Stalin, on top of Prague's Summer Hill, had been ripped from its pedestal in October 1962. (The granite base of this monument remained intact, purportedly because engineers feared the city's water works might be damaged if it were lifted out of place—a typical Czech rationalization to muffle a delicate architecto-political issue.)

During the entire decade of the fifties, the Czech Communist Party regarded the film industry as a propaganda factory that could meet ideologic specifications. And, in fact, during the period of the cult of personality (1949–1955), the Czech film industry meekly prostrated itself to promote physical culture, heroism in the construction of steel foundries, vigilance against the class enemies, and the exceptional achievements of the dreary agricultural co-operatives. In these films, the hero held his fate and the destiny of Czechoslovakia firmly in his hands, while "history," usually represented as a collective of conservative views, capitulated and subjected itself to the hero's unbending will. ("But only after the chief exponent of the conservatives had been unmasked as a secret class enemy—a kulak, an intellectual, or a spy," commented one Czech critic.) During this black epoch, history was frequently falsified through gross oversimplifications. Socialist realism set out, after all, to show society not as it was, but as it should be. The favorite theme

* Suffice it to say here that this tradition, going back to 1898, began when an engineer named Jan Krizenecky brought back a cinematograph from Paris. The Czech film industry prospered after World War I and produced such outstanding films as Gustav Machaty's "Ecstasy," starring Hedy Lamarr. The Czech film studios were nationalized by President Eduard Benes in 1945, and a brief postwar Czech film boom culminated with Karel Steckly's "Sirena" (1947), which received the top prize in Venice. After that, Czech films entered the Zhdanovite Dark Ages.

of the filmmakers during those years was World War II. Nearly forty films describing the events between 1938 and 1945 were ground out during close to two sterile decades. It was this experience which enabled the middle-generation of Czech directors, as represented by Jan Kadar (b. 1918) and Elmar Klos (b. 1910), to produce the remarkable, in-depth detail of that exceptional war film, "The Shop on Main Street." Kadar emphasizes that his picture, produced after the government relaxed its control over the movie industry, is not merely a historical film, but one that "depicts everyday weakness in the face of authority." Although no Jews were actually shown being tortured or beaten and no brutal SS men were characterized in it, "The Shop on Main Street" proved an eloquent portrayal of the oppressive stupidity of a political dictatorship. In fact, when it was shown in provincial Slovakia—where audiences are still virulently pro-Catholic and anti-Semitic—the film was booed and hissed. To the Czech intelligentsia in Prague, however, the film represented a turning point for the entire cinema. "The Shop on Main Street" asked the basic questions most disturbing them: How is man to decide between the authority of the state and his own rights and self-respect? When must even the simplest individual stop and protest? Instead of providing hackneyed responses, the film made the audience stop and think. Here, indeed, was innovation! But Kadar's generation of film directors, including Zbynek Brynych, Jiri Weiss, and Voytech Jasny, was quickly left behind by the pace of events, by the vigor of youth. A rapid crystallization of generations took place, in which the younger directors, turning the cameras on the present and on themselves, assumed the role of judges. The younger group—some fifteen directors who produced their first film between the years 1962 and 1965—was no longer interested in presenting the broad scope of human relations. They emphasized the specific apposition of a couple or the interplay of a handful of individuals. Ideology, fame, power, the acquisition of capital, greed, religion, patriotism—subjects concerning the middle generation—were leapfrogged by these newcomers. For example, little importance was attached to work as a theme. Rather than being portrayed as an end in itself, work was presented as inevitable drudgery. The teen-agers pictured on the screen were

39

essentially nonheroic, antiromantic, and sober. While the political attitudes of these young directors were rarely, if ever, expressed directly, their hostility was largely conveyed in the form of a defense of fundamental human rights against bureaucratic deformations. This new cinema was neither one of pessimism nor of overt opposition. Pavel Juracek (b. 1935) explained, "Our nonconformity is no cultural revolution, because it does not reject the ideas of socialism. It only rejects the difference between theory and practice."

Jaromil Jires (b. 1935), director of "The First Cry," claims that, while the films of his generation possess many similarities, he and his colleagues never thought out a program for their creation. "The only thing we had in common was that we disagreed with the old ways, and that provoked us to search for something new." Jires says, "We had a feeling while in school that some things were not filmed truthfully; we did not like the academic, pseudo-historical approach." Negation was the premise on which these young directors created the greatest revolution in the history of Czech cinema; they knew exactly what they did not want to make, but were not certain of what they did want. Alois Polednak, Director General of the Czech Film Corporation, explained that, after years of cinematic dullness and mediocrity, "Our art of the cinema strives to address itself to the present day. It does not evade classes and problems." And his words were echoed by the directors themselves, who feel it is absolutely essential to believe that truth has no limits. Jires said, "One must believe in the power of truth. The first sign that a society is in good health is when it does not attempt to limit the truth, when it does not fear certain truths for being dangerous." In "The First Cry," for example, Jires shows numerous illuminating sidelights on Czech life, such as the speed with which a black African student can stir racial prejudice in Prague by talking too long in a public telephone booth. Socialism theoretically had eliminated such prejudice, and it took courage on Jires's part to present the truth. "We hope that our problems are other people's problems," Jires confided, adding, "It is no good to make a film which is not on *our problem.*" What is their problem? Self-examination, self-discovery. The new Czech generation is obsessed by the need to explore its conflict with the adult world, the nature of love, the struggle to live.

Everyday Czech life, and it was fairly grim, formed the setting for these new films. Fortunately, there was no hankering for Western-style sophistication in these movies—although such superficial manifestations were much admired by the new generation of socialist youth. Jires, like most of his colleagues, did not want to reproduce life—he wanted to make films that were more real than life itself. Because every statement these directors made was interpreted symbolically as a comment on socialist existence, the directors were careful in their use of metaphoric and allegoric language. Most of their films were intentionally left open to a variety of interpretations. Jires and Juracek confessed there was much disguised criticism in their films but immediately interjected, "Metaphoric language is the language of art." The thin, frail Juracek, who so superbly adapted Kafka in his film "A Prop Is Needed," said, "For us, Kafka is reality; it is not the influence of Kafka that affects us so deeply, but the reality of our surroundings that pushes us toward the Kafkaesque."

The genuine belief of these directors in the possibility of communicating—especially through the use of symbols—originated during their training at the Czech Film Faculty in Prague (FAMU). This school, which opened in 1945, instructs students in five principal "disciplines": film history and criticism, dramaturgy and writing for the screen, production, camera work, and directing. Since the late fifties, the Faculty has placed equal emphasis on freedom and on practice, and this has played a vital role in the resurgence of Czech films. The mistakes made during the decade of the cult of personality rendered all rules suspect for the students; so much so, in fact, that even the Faculty claimed, "We must err on the side of freedom." Evald Schorm (b. 1931), whose film "Courage for Every Day" won him an enviable reputation among his colleagues, admits that "running after truth generally leads to defeat, but it is a defeat we must learn to tolerate in school." Milos Forman (b. 1933), who began his career as a scriptwriter, acknowledges that at the Faculty he had been able to work "all the stupidities and crazy things" out of his system. Forman feels that in making their thirty-minute diploma film (which costs the state some ten thousand dollars in materials alone), as well as their other training films, the three dozen students who graduate every year are able to exorcise those cinematic devils that might otherwise have haunted them for a lifetime.

At the school it has become the practice for students to form functional groups of producer, director, writer, and cameraman. These teams will have worked on twelve short films by the time they have finished the four-year course. Graduates of the Faculty are immediately employed either in the Barrandov Studios, on the outskirts of Prague, or in the regional TV centers. There is a security and continuity between school and work that does not exist in the West. In the United States, film unions virtually exclude young directors and cameramen from employment. The advantages of putting graduates to work immediately are considerable. By the time they get their first lucky break, many American, Italian, or British directors have lost much of their vitality; in Czechoslovakia, most of them have made their first full-length feature by the time they are twenty-seven. Financially, however, the Czechs do not live in paradise. Salaries of about a hundred dollars per month make it necessary for directors to fill the role of writer, actor, and director simultaneously—as did Jiri Menzel (b. 1938)—in order to earn more money.

At a group interview with Jires, Menzel, Juracek, and Ivan Passer at the Prague Film Club, it came out that the directors did not want their cinematic practices frozen into convention. They preferred a free, antitraditional approach to everything from film sequence to film dialogue. They enjoyed intertwining tragic and comic scenes with the same abandon as they did in film school. "We refuse all stickers," said Ivan Passer (b. 1933), the director of "Intimate Lighting," "especially *cinéma-vérité.*" Passer refused to see himself and his colleagues as part of any movement, and consequently rejected the label of *"nouvelle vague."* While many of the directors used free cameras and nonprofessional actors, no one wished to form a theory out of this. As to the authenticity of the settings, including the soot-covered, antiquated industrial plants of Czechoslovakia, Passer said he wanted to make "the viewer see the facts with all possible lucidity—but this does not make *cinéma-vérité.*" What quickly impressed me with these directors, as a group, was that they were all such close, intimate friends. "The most important thing for us is the continuation of our friendship," said Jiri Menzel.* "The success of one of our group enlarges the possibilities of the others," said Menzel. "If one of us has a failure, it represents a danger for all of us." "We are not running after Mammon," interposed Juracek, who felt there was little currying for favor or jockeying for position among his contemporaries.

Milos Forman, perhaps the most promising phenomenon of his generation, emphasizes the experimental nature of his work. "I never consider my scenario finished before I have completed the film," he said. Forman frequently uses amateur actors who are urged to improvise before the live camera in order to show what he calls "the matter-of-fact acceptance of the human condition." He believes that, while preparation is crucial to improvisation, one should not give amateurs a chance to edit themselves. In "Loves of a Blonde" (1964), Forman kept the amateurs in the famous three-in-a-bed climax cooped up in an apartment for an entire week. When he felt the mother, father, and son were so involved with each other that they were capable of working out the scene by themselves, he told them a few lines important to the script and turned on the cameras. They fumbled for the covers and exchanged insinuations, stale moral slogans, and insults. "They act the whole scene much funnier than I could write," said Forman in his unique English. "It is like your happenings, no?"

Forman says, "Hypocrisy existed so long there is now a need for an emphasis on sincerity." Indeed, Forman's sincerity is in the humanist tradition of Griffith and De Sica. Forman concentrates affectionately on the open-eyed aspirations and the bewilderment of

* Menzel, a shy, oddball type, affects not to like "Closely Watched Trains," which won the 1968 Academy Award. Menzel's great charm is that one never knows when to take him seriously. Even the Party bigwigs were highly puzzled by his ambiguous desecration of the legend of Slovak wartime resistance.

Upon accepting the Oscar in Hollywood, Menzel flew immediately back to New York. When director Jan Kadar and his wife brought champagne and flowers to Menzel's Chelsea hotel room, he uncomfortably tossed the roses on his bed and said, "I don't drink." Somewhat taken aback, the Kadars then asked if Menzel had cabled his parents (with whom he lives) back in Prague. After much discussion, he reluctantly sent a wire that said: "Mr. and Mrs. Menzel. Please ready place on mantelpiece for Gold Dummy. Jiri."

the long-haired Czech teen-agers. Forman's first two films, "Black Peter" and "Loves of a Blonde," explore the entry of teen-agers into adulthood. Peter, for example, has to find a job and, like most youths, he knows exactly what he does not want to do, without having any clear notion of his aspirations. In the process of floating between odd jobs, he is overwhelmed by sermons and lectures of his very upset and bewildered father. "Why do I make films about teen-agers?" rhetorically repeats Forman. "I suppose it is because I don't understand the world of the older generation, or even of my contemporaries." The father of preschool twins, Forman went on to explain, "I like teen-agers, I understand them, I know them, I am even, perhaps, biased in favor."

In Forman's "Loves of a Blonde," a teen-ager working in a shoe factory searches for love and engages the viewer's sympathy by the discomfort she faces in the process of growing up. Forman manages to catch simultaneously both the extraordinary humor and the pathos of this girl's predicaments—particularly when she goes to bed with a boy some fifteen minutes after she first meets him. Sex is presented honestly, without cruelty or cynicism, as in the scene where the factory girls—led by the party leader—formally take a vote on the question, "Should girls be moral?" Slowly, reluctantly, the blonde (played by Hana Brejchova—then Forman's sister-in-law) raises her hand to vote in favor. But being honest about sex is not easy, even under socialism. Some of the more prudish Czech mothers reacted hysterically to a scene showing the blonde naked in bed with her boy friend. Forman said he was pestered by crank calls and anonymous letters, "some of which were written on toilet paper," for several months. When attacks against the morality of the movie appeared in the press, a group of cinematic artists felt obliged to make a public statement in the magazine *Literarni Noviny,* attacking those "who pretended to protect public morality." The cinematic presentation of a nude boy and girl in bed was not easy to accept for such a long-repressed society.

Director Pavel Juracek takes a more literary, poetic, and symbolic approach to the film. Juracek is at his best when developing dream-like sequences, suspended between reality and fiction. His first film, "A Prop Is Needed," runs for only forty minutes, but it entirely succeeds in capturing the psoriasis of Czechoslovak socialism. Juracek presents a bewildered, isolated seeker of truth in an incubus-ridden society. The hero rents a cat from a pet shop, which vanishes when he has satisfied his whim and wishes to return the cat. Cat hire costs more than two dollars per day, and he has been warned that "the misuse of cats loaned is punishable by law." Because of the dire penalties facing him if he fails to return this state loan, he begins a frantic search in the proverbial bureaucratic labyrinth for a record of the transaction. "What do you mean that this couldn't happen anywhere else?" demands one official. The state insists that it is his fault for wanting to hire a cat. The hero always hopes to find the man with the answer around the next row of filing cabinets, but the elusive Dr. Josef Kilian is not to be found. There are no answers in this anonymous Czech bureaucracy. Even the small, shaggy black-and-white cat, whom the hero feeds canned mice, peers with bewilderment over the briefcase in which it is carried.* The nightmare that was so often reality during the Stalin era in Czechoslovakia comes terrifyingly back to life. Juracek says, "We ought to get rid, once and for all, of the specter of the cat, and think!" In the film, Juracek has two beer drinkers completing a crossword puzzle. One asks, "What is the quality that differentiates man, in nine letters?" The other answers, "Obedience." Juracek maintained that the Czechs were still dragging the cat with them in their minds, unable to find a place where it could be deposited for good. He shows symbolically in the film that this way of thinking must be discarded with the old pictures of Stalin, the empty slogans of the past, and the meaningless propaganda placards.

Evald Schorm's "Courage for Every Day" (1964), perhaps the first real socialist tragedy, is prologued by a long passage from Kafka's fable "The Vulture." Schorm says, "The Vulture stands for a whole complex of destructive traits that threaten and attack a human being and that have to be driven out if man wishes to·

---

* It was my privilege to watch the film "A Prop Is Needed" at a private screening in Prague attended only by New York *Times* film critic Bosley Crowther and his wife. Crowther, whose naïveté and lack of comprehension amazed the Czechs, asked me in the darkness of the projection room, "What does he borrow a cat for? Are there cat rental shops in Prague?"

become more humane." One of the boldest films, in the ideological sense, ever to be produced in a communist state, "Courage for Every Day" illustrates that a devotion to Marxism-Leninism can alienate a man from society. The film opens as two lovers meet on a hilltop —the grass is waving in the summer breeze, but right below them lies a soot-covered industrial town. Jarda, a former shock worker and Youth Union official, is in trouble. He continues to perform heroically at the factory, but the revolutionary acts of the Stakhanovite days are now outmoded—even for a man of thirty. He tries to live as if the old slogans were still true, but because of his willingness to serve the system, he loses his cheeky blond mistress and disgusts his fellow workers. Director Schorm contends that "a hero is able to gain everything only when he has lost everything; that before a person can come to grips with a conflict, he must plummet to the lowest depths." His blockhead hero, Jarda, is left crying on the ground at the end of the film, to all appearance a broken, bewildered man, but Schorm maintains, "If a man perseveres in his search to the end, if he can bear to look the truth in the face and still find the strength to go on, then he has discovered something of value." The Kafka quote introducing the film says, "We must always retain a little hope and say that this time we have lost." The Czech viewers saw the fate of their nation in these lines.

"Something is lacking in Czech society," says Schorm. "People are living, earning, buying what they want, and suddenly we find that we have one of the highest suicide rates among minors and among those who earn the most." This is the subject of his second full-length feature, "The Return of the Prodigal Son" (1966). The hero is a successful architect, the father of a lovely little girl, the husband of an even lovelier wife. Superficially, his life is no different from that of other Czechs. Slowly, and imperceptibly, he has lost his self-preserving immunity against everything that is false, immoral, and unprincipled in his surroundings and he begins to regard himself as abnormal. Because of this he attempts suicide and winds up wandering in and out of mental hospitals. (After all, suicide is even more of an offense against the state in a socialist country than it is in a capitalist one.) There is no solution, no resolution to the problems or to the film.

Schorm, Juracek, Forman, Passer, Jires—all espouse a positive form of humanism. However, they condemn political polemics of any kind on film. This they regard as journalism, not art. Instead of attacking frontally, these directors often attack the meaning of life through satire. "From the point of view of Marxism-Leninism, there can't be a ghost," says one member of the communist municipal council in the satirical movie "The White Lady." Using fantasy as a means of criticizing reality, the directors show how a well-intentioned phantom, who paves roads and installs plumbing, causes Party officials to lie and cover up in the face of public opinion. Film boss Polednak said he considers "The White Lady" an attack on the local National Committees. "It is an attack on narrow-mindedness, sapheadedness, and stupidity, in which the world around us is often abounding." Defending the film against Party critics, Polednak insisted: "A satirical film cannot help showing our defects as inflated, exaggerated, and shocking."

The social discontent and malaise of the young filmmakers came out in their frequent stress on absurdity, but they were well aware of the limits. "We know we can't do everything," said Ivan Passer in 1967, after having had a screenplay that criticized Czech teachers approved, only to have the head of the studios veto the film. However, Passer's "Intimate Lighting" shows how much could be done even then, if one did it with wit and finesse. "Intimate Lighting" is devastatingly sharp in its commentary, although it only portrays the Sunday hours of the city branch of a musical family visiting its country cousins. The revolutionary phase has passed for these country people, and the lethargic, jovial, beer-drinking rhythm of Jaroslav Hasek's *Good Soldier Schweik* has been resumed. The family members—and they are normal, average Czechs—regard socialism as only the latest name for authority, which must be carefully circumvented. After all, there have been many such alien systems in Czech history. With great humor, Passer shows how this family divides a chicken for Sunday dinner—the point being that the regime has not succeeded in making its people any different from the bourgeoisie of any other country—a message that was anathema to a system continuing to pay lip service to the creation of the "new socialist man."

Getting a scenario accepted for production in Czechoslovakia remains a tediously bureaucratic process. The young writer-director presents a synopsis of his idea for a film to one of the five creative teams constituting the Barrandov Studios. Each of these five groups has a budget of about one million dollars per year, with which it must produce five movies. If the idea is approved, after lengthy discussions and conferences between the members of the creative group, the writer, and the head of the studio, the synopsis is developed for treatment.* Eventually, after the scenario hurdles even more intense bureaucratic obstacles, the director receives full economic and artistic liberty to create his film. Once he has the go-ahead, he can do as he pleases. Nobody looks at the director's rushes, for example. The film remains entirely in his hands until completion. Alois Polednak, the Czech film czar, said, "The Party accepted the principle of confidence in, and responsibility of, the filmmakers." There were numerous Party officials who naturally felt hesitant about granting such leeway to the directors, but this is the way the system worked after the "artistic council," which controlled Czech films until 1961, was abolished.† Polednak tried to reassure the doubters by explaining "that a filmmaker has the right to put forward questions to himself and society which neither he nor society are as yet capable of answering." Writers, producers, and directors "must explore new avenues," said Polednak, and "this is where the art engenders a risk not everybody understands correctly." Polednak convinced the Party that the hard currency returns made the risks worth-while.

---

* These teams are headed by intellectuals, not technicians or Party hacks. One of the groups is headed by a poet, one by a music critic, one by a dramatist, and two by screen writers. These group leaders choose their own consultants, who are not paid, but who try to advise the authors and directors on the artistic as well as commercial merits of their projects. There are also four writer-editors associated with each group who advise on the professional and technical aspects of every scenario.

† In the sixties these teams were freely constituted, but Forman wrote for the *Saturday Review* that "It is almost beyond belief what can happen if you put together a group of outstanding individuals and force them to make collective decisions on the fate of art." Forman concluded that the inevitable "result is that mediocrity and naïveté become supreme virtues."

The freedom of the young directors remained circumscribed between 1964 and 1968. Group decisions meant months of waiting, and, sometimes, years could pass while the completed film was weaving through the web of bureaucracy. For example, "The Party and the Invited Guests," directed by Jan Nemec (b. 1936), was not released for showing until two years after it was finished. The screenplay, written by Nemec and his wife, Ester Krumbachova, is guided by Francisco Goya's words: "The world is a masquerade, face, clothes, and voice being make-believe. Everyone trying to seem what he is not; everyone cheating and none knowing himself." The themes are universal: popular indifference to human dignity, the desire to enjoy oneself and forget the past, the incapacity of man to accept nonconformity, the gusto with which man sets about hounding and torturing his fellow man, the collapse of the democratic ideal in postwar Eastern Europe. The movie is as harsh and as brutal as its crisp, staccato black-and-white photography. And, of course, what irked the top Party leadership in Czechoslovakia was the uncanny, uncomfortable resemblance of the mustached, goateed "leader" in this film to Lenin—or could it possibly be to Klement Gottwald (now posthumously discredited Czech Party leader of the Stalinist era)?

Jiri Hendrych, Czechoslovakia's former ideological boss, cited "The Party and the Invited Guests" as a result of the ideological confusion that exists among Czech filmmakers. "The latest films by director Jan Nemec openly advocate the lack of communication," said Hendrych. "They are abstract allegories open to a multitude of different meanings void of human and social activity and full of incomprehensible mystic symbols in which the author critically dissociates himself from reality." Hendrych went on to deplore the "too frequent use of themes dwelling on abnormal people, whose extreme behavior is explored for answers to questions of a general social importance." Hendrych concluded that "this orientation reveals the old existentialist tenet that man can find freedom only in himself, in his loneliness." But progress has been made. In the Stalinist era, such an attack from the number two man in the Party would not only have meant the end of the career of Jan Nemec as a filmmaker; it would, in fact, have made him an unperson. But even

49

before the 1968 revolution, such negative criticism no longer constituted a physical threat to the artist or to his ability to earn a living.

In time, every film movement is challenged by new forces and by its own growth. This was true of the neorealistic school in poverty-stricken Italy following the end of World War II, and of the series of heroic Polish epics in the late fifties. Forman, Passer, and Menzel succeeded—through simple narrative—in making ordinary people fascinating. They portrayed humans as they are. These directors captured delicate common sensibilities, as well as the tragic and comic human extremes. What they said was understood by the entire world. But another of their group, Vera Chytilova (b. 1929), asserted that "what we say is too obvious—we must become more subtle and imaginative," and she consciously initiated a more "artistic" cinema with her film "The Daisies" (1966).

Vera Chytilova began her career as a model. Then she became, in turn, a clapper at the Barrandov Studios, a continuity girl, and an assistant director. Blocked in her ambitions because of a lack of education, she enrolled in the Film Faculty and, as her graduation picture, made a semiautobiographical documentary about a fashion model who chooses the easy life, from bed to bed. This was followed by another documentary, "A Bag of Fleas," which depicted a group of fifteen-year-old inmates in a residential vocational school. Like Forman, she portrayed the relations among the girls with insight and warmth, and sided with them against those grown-ups who do not understand youth. Her first full-length feature, "Another Way of Life" (1963), realistically drew a parallel between the lives of two women—Eva, a gymnast, and Vera, an ordinary housewife. Both are confronted by the question of the meaning of their existence. The famous gymnastic champion sacrificed her youth, strength, and happiness to a rather vacuous career. "But her rigorous training seemed no more nonsensical than Vera's unproductive drudgery at home," said Chytilova. "The two women led similar lives: unvarying, stereotyped, monotonous. Theirs is the philosophy of human sacrifice."

Chytilova's second full-length film was "The Daisies," which she wrote together with Ester Krumbachova, whose pronounced penchant for philosophical abstraction has made her one of the key figures of modern Czech cinema. This story is again a history of two girls, Marie I and Marie II, but this time their lives are chaotic, wild, and reckless. Theirs is the outlook of modern hedonism. Filmed by Chytilova's husband, Jaroslav Kucera, in brilliant and audaciously kaleidoscopic color sequences, the film opens as the two Maries are debating the meaning of life.

"Have we any parents?"
"Not really, if they leave us to look after ourselves like this."
"If it is true that everything in the world gets spoiled, why shouldn't we?"
"So let us be spoiled."
"Do you mind?" [*Slaps the face of the other.*]

Then, as a succession of dazzling overlays of colors and polarizations succeed one another, they ask themselves: "Does it matter, or doesn't it?" This question becomes the yardstick for all their iconoclasm. The game, "does it matter or not," develops. It certainly does not matter that they cut each other's dresses to shreds or tear out each other's hair; they make up again and again, and call it all tremendous fun. They stand boys up, run up restaurant bills for old men, take a bath in soup—none of it matters. Finally, they end up in an orgy of gluttony—eating, drinking, and smashing their way through a sumptuously laid-out banquet table. They throw creamy layer cakes at each other, shatter the crystal, and tear down the magnificent velvet curtains, while screeching that it doesn't matter. Suddenly the girls find themselves drowning in a pool, and are told that unless they mend their ways and make good they will drown. Patiently—with all the irony and sham of the classic, posthumous socialist rehabilitation—they try to set the banquet hall right again and tidy up the mess. They tell each other how lucky they have been, but that really doesn't matter either, for the movie ends with the solarized colors of Armageddon.

"The Daisies" is not presented in the classic, narrative fashion, but in a succession of sharply cut frames and scenes. It should not be misunderstood as a realistic story about two teen-agers. "Their psychological development did not concern me," said Chytilova in

51

her intense, high-pitched voice. "They are only puppets, human puppets." Not only are they parasites (that is, nonbeings in the socialist order of things), but they also feed on their own substance. In their curious imitation of life, they begin playing a game that concludes with their ultimate self-destruction. "In this strangely detached existence away from the past and without a future, life becomes not a continuation of acts and experiences relating to the personal ego," says Chytilova, "but a succession of unrelated chance events." What these two teen-agers regard as happiness, depravity, and morality are empty terms—proof, says Chytilova, "of a life spent on the fringe of fact." The director feels that the reason for portraying this pseudo existence on the screen is to force the viewers to recognize the sham reality within themselves. The film in no way criticizes Marie I or Marie II; instead, it attacks the destructiveness, the illusions, and the sham "inherent to a smaller or greater extent even in the most humdrum and well-ordered bourgeois existence."

"Why do we so much like to see things breaking?" asked Chytilova—who is known in real life as an expert heartbreaker. She feels man is tantalized by destruction—whether it be the destruction of a relationship, as in "The Daisies," or the devastation of war. Chytilova explains that it is natural for man to wish to create something, and that those lacking creative ability (presumably, the members of the Communist Party) create antivalues. So, she says, "you might sum up this film as a necrologue about a negative way of life, about the dangerous hunger for prestige, which entails maintaining a posture all the way to death."

Chytilova sees "The Daisies" as an experiment with film language. But she recognizes this "farcical, philosophical document," as she calls it, as "only a beginning." Chytilova rebelled against film always being literature, or theater, or sociology—"all that is too formal, too superficial." And, she noted with a sigh, "It is so very difficult to get away from past experience and cinematic conventions." Expounding her ambitions with a masculine directness, while her husband (a cameraman) listened passively to her monologue, she said, "I see movement as a continuation of time, and, in this sense, the film has not yet developed its full potentialities." However, in "The Daisies" Chytilova was boldly experimenting with the state's money, and the state, even when it is a communist state, seeks a return on its investment. "The Daisies" was banned for more than a year before being released in Czechoslovakia—and abroad it failed to draw crowds. The attitude of Hendrych and other Party ideologists was that "The Daisies" was incomprehensible to the average working man and could at best sow confusion in the minds of the masses. When I asked Chytilova for her reaction to this criticism, as well as to the interpretation of twenty-one deputies in the Czech National Assembly who disapproved of the production of such "objectionable films," she answered angrily that "the masses should not be the judge of what is created; the creator cannot wait for the masses, but must proceed." In school, she had felt that authenticity, unmarred by artificial sets and props, could provoke and stimulate the viewers. Her object then had been to force the audience to become actively engaged through a process of identification. Now, she feels such authenticity is insufficient to "fulfill the process of self-realization," and despite all the dangers her experiments imply for the entire generation of new Czech film directors, she is determined to continue on her post-Dadaist way. Perhaps, as she herself remarks about the antiheroines of "The Daisies," "Man's desire to destroy is only because he has not been able to satisfy his idea to create."

Some Western movie moguls are amazed and rather horrified to find that, despite Party supervision, the Czech film industry is almost entirely in the hands of intellectuals. These tycoons, accustomed to thinking in terms of returns on investments, consider there is little hope for an industry that specializes in symbolic films. The Czechs, naturally, disagree. Director Ivan Passer says, "If the film industry belongs to the state, the only reason is that it should produce art." Another director, even more outspoken, states, "Our movies are, in a sense, guilt-money for the bad conscience of the state."

It is true that Czech films were not subject to the dictatorship of the box office, but not even a state-owned cinema could afford to neglect the questions of attendance and profitability indefinitely. In 1967 Czechoslovakia's film imports versus exports showed a surplus of several million dollars. Significantly, the proceeds from showing Western films in Czechoslovakia were almost twice as large as the proceeds from domestic features. Like other audiences, the Czechs want to be entertained. Consequently, of the forty-odd films produced each year in Czech studios, only six or seven are so-called "intellectual" pictures; the rest are bad musicals, tasteless comedies, and stereotyped copies of American westerns. Another threat to good Czech cinema has come from the invasion of American, British, Italian, French, and West German TV producers anxious to make films with cheap Czech labor. "These capitalists are eating all our good technical people," warns Forman. In 1967, for example, seven American and West German "westerns" were turned in the Barrandov Studios.* And Forman has already had his troubles with Carlo Ponti, who concluded a ten-million-dollar coproduction deal to make seven films in Prague using Czech directors and personnel. There is even some concern that Forman and others might eventually be drawn to the West, as were Poland's Roman Polanski, Andrzej Wajda, and Jerzy Skolimowski. One cannot but wonder whether success may not spoil Czech cinema. As director Passer anxiously warns: "The worst thing for us would be if we were to become film laborers, rather than creators."

Whenever freedom is granted after a prolonged period of suppression, art blossoms like fruit in an irrigated desert. But the water may be cut off at any time. Although cinematic art is no longer synonymous with propaganda, Lenin's words continue to ring in the Party's ear: "For us, the cinema is the most important of all the arts." In most of the socialist states, films are commissioned on an assembly-line basis. One could claim that the majority of Soviet films are still prefabricated, as it were. The lack of good scripts on contemporary themes forces Russian directors to turn to such adaptations from the classics as the grandiose, four-part, eight-hour-long "War and Peace" by actor-director Sergei Bondarchuk (b. 1924) or Aleksandr Zarkhy's gigantic version of "Anna Karenina." The spectacle of these films is so lavish that most Rus-

---

* This represents more than fifteen per cent of the total capacity of the Barrandov Studios, which is a factory, with some three thousand employees, consisting of eleven indoor studios with a total floor space of over twelve thousand square yards—ideal for TV westerns.

sians, who are much more avid moviegoers than Americans (some eighty-four million persons go to the movies every week in the U.S.S.R.), feel compelled to see the diadems and ostrich plumes of the czarist era but are generally bored by the new pretentiousness. The post-Khrushchev spirit has manifested itself much more timidly on the Soviet screen and stage than in the letters.

In Poland, on the other hand, the puddles from the post-Stalinist thaw have frozen. What has happened in Poland is a warning to both the Czech Party and the Barrandov Studios. After producing a series of meritorious films—among them "Ashes and Diamonds," "Eroica," "Man on the Rails," "Kanal," and "Eva Wants to Sleep" —the best directors gradually went to work abroad as the opportunities at home dried up, leaving the Polish film industry a backwater ruled by bureaucrats and impotent directors. Andrzej Munk, the sharpest critic of Poland's romantic historicism, died in a car crash. Aleksander Ford, often referred to as the "father of Polish cinema," was expelled from the Party in the spring of 1968 because of his Jewish background. Accused of coresponsibility for "politically incorrect" coproductions with West German film studios, Ford was, in effect, placed on pension. Disenchantment seems to have overtaken Skolimowski after he had overwhelmed Poland with his vital braggadocio in "Walkover" and "Barrier." Now he seems preoccupied with filming the groovy curves of the Porsche.

One Polish critic, writing in the weekly *Kultura,* said in 1967 that the three main symptoms showing the "diseased state of Polish movie-making" were: First, there were too few films that "in a direct and lively fashion corresponded to those feelings, thoughts, and ideas which troubled our society"; in other words, that the contact between film and reality has been broken. Second, the directors seem to have forgotten that films include the subtle art of observation, not just the development of story lines. Finally, in "watching our films, one gets the depressing sensation that the majority of the people in this field are convinced they live in a vacuum, hermetically sealed off from everything that goes on in the world of cinema." Apparently the Polish directors have reached what has been called by them a "threshold of conscience," beyond which they cannot advance. But it is unfair to place the blame on the directors, who are accused of being afraid to expose even a glimmer of the depressing reality that is Polish life today. Except for the nonideological arts, such as painting and music, Polish culture is generally stagnating because of the narrow, limited, and repressive policy of Wladyslaw Gomulka's clique. Gomulka's attitude toward the written word is that criticism of the regime, or of socialism, or of Poland, should not appear in print. And when writers feel they can't express the truth, they don't produce film scripts; they just manufacture stereotyped evasions. A sample of the unreality that surrounds the Polish cinema is Roman Polanski's experience with his film "Knife in the Water." The Polish censors initially refused to allow the film to be viewed because the Party official in it was driving a Mercedes—that revanchist, West German automobile. Polanski had to retake the scene showing the functionary driving a Peugeot 403, although actually many officials can be seen driving Mercedeses every day.

The Poles have noted that the successful Czech films, which make them seethe with envy, almost always border on sociological studies, social journalism, or the documentary. "The documentary flavor of these movies," notes one Polish film critic, "is so authentic that we are sometimes surprised that this is actually fiction. The actors act naturally. Act is the wrong word. They live on the screen. We believe in their real existence, unfalsified by the interference of a director." This same Pole thinks Czech films go beyond mere naturalism, that while they document life in present-day Czechoslovakia, they are also an artistic condensation of Czech feelings and atmosphere. That is, "they offer a profound aesthetic experience." It is not by accident that the concept of man as a victim of history, as an individual accepting injustice, unable to make more than a ritual gesture of heroism, dominates the Polish cinema. The atmosphere of historical fatalism and resignation hovers over Poland as well.

Director Passer insists that "The state closes doors, art opens them." What neither he nor any of his colleagues dares ask himself is: "How long will the door remain open?" Most of the young directors keep their fingers crossed; they can hardly believe their good luck thus far. Reviewing the film year 1966, Miloslav Bruzek, then

Vice-Chairman of the Czech State Commission for Culture, wrote: "The search for and the discovery of new artistic approaches led to an exaggerated emphasis on technique, on the extrinsic expression of novelty and modernity." Continuing in the same vein, Bruzek said, "The lack of communication between art and society is felt by creative workers themselves, and they are beginning to disown the view that the artist should create only according to his inspiration, for art only, regardless of the public for whom he is creating." But there were also strong pressures for this freedom to continue, fostered principally by the hunger of the regime for foreign currency as well as by greed for international prestige and acceptability. Hoping not to shake the Party's "sensitive and scrupulous cultural policy," the Praesidium of the Film Artists' Union stated: "The prevailing spirit of individual creative freedom and tolerance, which is not understood as lenience in the face of ideologically hostile attitudes, must be maintained."

The most frequently asked question today is: "How long can the Czechs continue their streak of good films?" Historically, the prospects do not look good. The lifespan of the classic Soviet school was six years: from "The Battleship Potemkin" in 1925 to Dovzhenko's "Earth" in 1930. The Italian postwar school lasted about eight years. The Polish school (1955–1963) survived an identical period of time, and then both public and directors became bored with the dashing heroism and isolation of the historic principals.

"When we left school," said Menzel, "everything was open to us. We were the first generation and were allowed to do as we pleased." But after the best and most courageous of the new directors had finished their first or second film, the bureaucracy began to block their completed scripts. Sometimes three or four years passed in which they did no work. After editing "A Capricious Summer" (after a novel by Vladislav Vancura written in 1920), Menzel said he was not interested in tackling serious problems. He claimed he wanted to make films that flow like a song: easy, amusing, and sometimes melancholy. The puckish, eternally turtle-necked Menzel said, "We all know that life is cruel and sad. What's the point of demonstrating this in films? Let us show how brave we are by laughing at life." But most of the directors, who could not tell

57

whether Menzel was talking tongue-in-cheek, felt this was taking an easy way out.

Although Forman finished "On Fire, My Love," which satirized the venality and incompetence of local communist officials, about half of the fifteen directors who produced their first full-length feature in the early nineteen-sixties were unemployed in 1967. This outcast group included Juracek, Chytilova, Schorm, Jires, and Antonin Masa. Jires, for example, had not been permitted to shoot a full-length feature after "The First Cry" and had three scenarios rejected in succession. Juracek wanted to shoot a contemporary adaptation of the third section of *Gulliver's Travels*—but also failed to get approval. In the eighteen months before the overthrow of the Novotny regime, the Czech film industry was turning out empty comedies and stale crime films. Then the flood gates were thrown open. Everyone was given the green light in January 1968, and, until that summer, they were all shooting their long-cherished dreams. Whether these films would ever be completed or released remained problematical. What worked in favor of the younger generation was that they made only those films which they truly felt; they were driven by a compulsion to tell the truth as they saw it. The hope was that somehow they would be able to continue in this uncompromising fashion even after the Russian invasion.

CHAPTER III

People Who Live in Glass Wedding Cakes . . .

I have always harbored the rather childish illusion that, under socialism, city planning—free from the restrictions and greed of private enterprise—would take on new, more rational dimensions. My initial view of Belgrade and Bucharest in 1964 shattered this naïve anticipation in the most shocking way: These communist cities were brutally bereft of fantasy. There is nothing original, not to say revolutionary, about any new socialist city I have ever visited. The futuristic vision of a communist metropolis, as developed by the early Bolsheviks, has long since perished. And there were great visions in the early twenties: In their aspiration to make Moscow a showplace of socialist architecture, the more idealistic commissars asked world-famous architects to contribute wild and sundry ideas. Frank Lloyd Wright suggested razing much of Moscow and turning it into a garden city. Le Corbusier, who built a distinctive green-glass-and-brownstone structure in Moscow (which still houses the Central Statistical Administration), proposed to clear the center of the city of all automobile traffic. And then Stalin burst in upon the scene, and the Russian architects are still in the process of recovering from the impact. The new curved façade of the thirty-two-story Comecon skyscraper may offer a welcome change from the past, but even this building smacks of the tentativeness of group architecture. The fact is that Soviet architecture today is nothing but an unstifled yawn. As elsewhere in the communist world, one has the distinct impression that rather than explore new possibilities, the Russian architects are intent on catching up with Western styles of a decade ago. In contrast to Philip Johnson's "International Style," there is no such thing as a "socialist style" (unless that be undisguised drabness). While the medieval church developed the Gothic, which was in harmony with its spiritual purpose, and the capitalist system developed the aluminum-and-glass skyscraper, the socialist system thus far has only plagiarized concrete monotony—which is, perhaps, an honest reflection of its current bureaucratic outlook. The uniform rectilinear package has become the trademark of what is fashionable in communism. It is almost as if the thinking were: "If it has no character, how can it be criticized?" The cause of such a disaster undoubtedly is that a state-controlled bureaucracy will not tolerate more than one style at a time. Consequently, there is at present no room to maneuver; Russian architects cannot even resume the modernist experiments that characterized the early twenties.

Socialist architecture is currently enslaved to such construction-related demands as the availability of time, material, and labor, and is further limited by lack of funds and overhelming demands for space. The needs of society are so truly desperate that architecture under much of communism is not considered as an art but as production on an immense scale. The consequences are tragic. Dreary, grimy, monotonous blocks of brick or concrete are bereft of spiritual feeling or human content. Their almost penitentiarylike order consciously ignores the multifaceted nature of man. Row upon row of apartment slabs, set just far enough apart so they don't cast shadows upon each other, destroy any semblance of intimacy. There is no familiar human scale in the modern sectors of Belgrade, Warsaw, Bucharest, Budapest, or Moscow—only sterility.

Until the early fifties, innovation in communist architecture came from above—from Stalin. I have been accused of being a crypto dogmatist, an eccentric, and even a Stalinist for my admiration of the monumentally grotesque wedding cakes imposed on Moscow with its seven swinging pseudo-Baroque towers, and on Warsaw (Palace of Culture), Prague (Hotel International), and Bucharest (The Scintea Publishing House). My impression is that the corniced piles, frosted with pediments and irrelevant, almost rococo ornamentation, have a distinctive period flavor. But the Poles, Czechs, Rumanians, and even the Muscovites are all repelled by the style because these wedding cakes, erected with their own slave labor, conjure the most sinister associations. Nevertheless, Stalin's historicism in decoration—which was presented at the time as the only acceptable architectural approach—has its own readily definable spirit. The style combines Victorianism, corn, and black humor. It is Soviet camp. However critics may ridicule them, the seven Stalinist spires in Moscow seem far more in keeping with the character of the city than the new glass-and-steel backdrop of the three-thousand-room Hotel Rossiya, which has just been erected behind the Kremlin's St. Basil's Cathedral. This hotel, reputed to be the world's largest (and among the worst), smacks of an iconoclasm that reveals the ignorance and pretentiousness of the modern generation of architects. Similarly, Warsaw's Palace of Culture (which was Stalin's "gift" to the Polish people and which, characteristically, was built entirely with Polish labor and materials) is a more arresting phenomenon than the ludicrous glass matchboxes that now surround it.

Polish architects are particularly concerned that the industrialized, standardized cities they are helping to mass-produce totally lack that natural sparkle which characterizes the Polish people. The result is that the good Polish architects try to pass over the current desecration and immerse themselves in grandiose planning for the year 2,000, or in glorious recollections of the eighteenth century. Boleslaw Malisz, Director of the Warsaw Institute for City Planning and Architecture, hopes that residential construction will soon become so industrialized "that buildings will be traded in as they are used up—in the manner of automobiles." Only such construction, Malisz feels, would be able to keep up with the rapid changes in the demands made upon the contemporary human habitat. Only such construction could cater to the Polish sense of the unique.

Nowhere is the obsession with historical novelty, with architectural reminiscence, as distracting as it is in Warsaw. And no building in the communist world presents such a grotesque ensemble as its megalomaniac "Grand Theater" (Teatr Wielki)—as Warsaw's Opera is called. This structure, with a staggering volume of two hundred and fifty thousand cubic yards, is nicknamed the "Polish pyramid of extroversion." Actually, it is more like a Pentagon of bad taste. The Opera manages to embody just about every conflicting historical style. This feat seemed less incredible when I was told that it was constructed over a twenty-year period and that most of the decisions regarding the finishing details were made by different committees. When World War II ended, all that was left standing of the Teatr Wielki was the scarred nineteenth-century colonnaded façade of the Italian architect Antonio Corazzi. (This Italian had worked on the extravagant, imperial-style exterior, as well as on the far less grandiose interior, for some twenty-five years at the beginning of the nineteenth century.) The rest of the opera house was in total ruin. But the love of tradition prevailed here, as elsewhere in Warsaw, and it was decided to enlarge upon the Opera's former glories. Polish impresario Arnold Szyfman, who, like so many of his countrymen, wanted to reconstruct the Warsaw of his dreams, was placed in charge of the project in 1950, and Polish architects scoured the world's opera houses for ideas to incorporate into their own. This was going to be the opera house to end all opera houses. "If Royal Poland and the Poland of the insurrection could permit themselves the luxury of a Grand Theater, then, in the second half of the twentieth century, People's Poland could afford it even more," said the eighty-five-year-old Szyfman to me shortly before his death in 1966.

The vast extension of columns on the façade of the reconstructed Teatr Wielki now strike the viewer as incredibly pompous; after all, this is not the Louvre. But upon entering the theater itself, I was treated to a saturnalian concoction of bad taste: The glistening floor of the entrance is patterned into huge multicolored marble snowflakes and flower bouquets. Overhead, the opalescent coloring of six surrealist glass flowers, each about seven feet tall, would make even the most enthusiastic Art Nouveau fan blush. Two gigantesque broken-mirror mosaic clocks top the Doric mock-marble columns on either side. Chandeliers glisten overhead. In fact, the chandeliers are scattered like Cocteau Christmas décor all over the Opera; in the principal hall alone I counted twenty-five. It would be needlessly unkind to describe in detail the hideous thirty-two-foot-long tapestries of flowers and birds that decorate the foyer, or the parquet of black, gray, and white hardwood stars. Suffice it to recount that the pale, shellacked plywood snack bars, with their baby-pink artificial marble surfacing, resemble the luncheon counters of a prospering Polish ham-processing plant.

Szyfman, who, as an octogenarian, looked like a cross between Thutmose IV and Konrad Adenauer, personally took me around the two-thousand-seat Opera hall in 1966 to show off its splendors. Szyfman was particularly anxious to point out that the eight-, twelve-, and eighteen-ton blocks that formed the ceiling of the Opera were impervious to orchestral vibrations. The fact that the acoustical loud-speakers which had been inset into these blocks made the ceiling look like a simulated Lunar staging area for NASA hardly bothered Szyfman. More important from the aural aspect, which still counts in opera, were the abominable acoustics. It is difficult to hear anything in the minister's loge without the aid of a special amplifier; but then, perhaps it is fitting to create an isolation booth out of the place of honor. However, the acoustical control room— built in the West—is the only truly modern aspect of this Opera. It looks like the control center for a jet airport, with panels flashing myriads of red and green buttons. In this wonder house of modern electronics the engineers can make such delicate manipulations that sparrow chirpings can be heard on stage before they are heard in the hall. They can make church bells peal with the flick of a button and thunderstorms can shake the hall by increasing the volume up to one hundred times.

Just as poor old Szyfman was explaining that the fundamental concept of his edifice was identical to Lincoln Center's—that is, he intended it to be an artistic center for opera and the ballet—he stumbled on the stage and fell flat on his face. Fortunately unhurt, Szyfman continued the backstage tour to take in the shower rooms of the ballerinas. "We have showers. Men's showers, women's showers . . . water, hot water, cold water," Szyfman proudly explained. With the people's money he had built, he implied, an "artistic paradise" for the twelve hundred workers, technicians, dancers, singers, and administrators who made up this new house of Polish opera and ballet. An irate Polish critic, lamenting this fantastic investment of funds, said, "Our opera is yesterday's music in the theater of the day before yesterday." The true pity of it is that, like nearly all new socialist buildings, the Teatr Wielki represents a lost architectural opportunity. It is, of course, true that the craftsmanship, the materials, the designs of such buildings as New York's Ford Foundation headquarters or the Chase Manhattan tower are far superior to anything that could be commanded in the socialist states.

The completion in six months of a new forty-story New York office building no longer provokes any interest; in Belgrade, Warsaw, or Sofia, a twenty-story glass-covered hothouse (which would take several years to build) is regarded as a sign that communism is up-to-date. Like an ineffectual virility symbol, the low-rise skyscraper is regarded by the local architects and by the people as proof that they have "arrived" as a city. What initially struck me in visiting these depressing capitals was not the existence of these very scattered and infrequent high-rise buildings, but the fact that the size of the cities had already exceeded the capacity of the urban planners to cope with the transportation, shopping, and entertainment needs of the inhabitants. Let me cite a few examples:

● Shopping centers are inadequate in almost every city. Not only is their layout such that queues are inescapable, but also the location of these centers has little relation to distance from the housing developments, and even less to bus or trolley lines. Usually there is even no provision for customer parking (bicycle, scooter, or automobile). Instead, such a shopping center may be graciously surrounded by strips of mud and cinder.

The streets in socialist capitals (washed at night by teams of gypsies, old women, or people with an unreliable political past) are exceptionally clean, but it is quite hopeless to try and find a really well-kept lawn. Landscape gardening under socialism is unseemly. Contracting teams usually leave hideous gashes of soil tissue untouched after they have bulldozed the clearance for a housing project. Topsoil and the successive layers of clay or sandstone are usually left uncamouflaged in the environmental massacre. If there was a large tree standing on the site—well, that was usually the first to be chopped down as an obstacle to speedy construction. Almost every new housing project I visited was littered with scraps of bricks, rusting steel rods, chipped concrete blocks, and other rubble. Even after a number of years, the landscaping around these apartment dwellings looks as scrawny as sumac on a vacant Harlem lot. For example, Mosa Pijade University, in Zagreb, has been touted as one of the best of the new Yugoslav buildings. However, the high weeds that were growing in profusion all around the property bestowed an abandoned, desolate look hardly in keeping with one of the most frequented university structures in Yugoslavia. (Unfortunately, the cracks on the exterior of the yellowed structure, which appeared only six years after completion, made the university look as if it had been damaged by an earthquake.)

• Air pollution is not a matter of civic pride in the communist capitals, but each of these cities would willingly exchange their winter rates of air pollution with that of New York City. In Belgrade the smog turns so soupy every fall that at times it is impossible to see twenty-five feet ahead. And in New York there are complaints when the visibility is down to a mile! The socialist smog is caused by the many diesel engines and trucks using low-grade kerosene, by steam locomotives run on inferior-quality coal, by home-heating units that use sulphur-rich brown anthracite, and by the factories that discharge uncontrolled amounts of soot and chemicals into the sky. Legislation to combat any of these sources of air pollution has proven completely ineffective. Should a man stop heating his house when he cannot get any other fuel? Should an important factory stop production when reliable purification equipment is unavailable? No. Factories have been penalized for failure to arrest pollution, but the factory managers quickly calculate such fines into their production costs. In fact, in Czechoslovakia factories were given subsidies to pay for their air-pollution fines. Instead of going to the source of the problem, communist states concentrated on the end results: the human beings who inhale the toxic brew. Budapest residents, for example, now are all subjected to frequent X-ray examinations for lung cancer. The Yugoslavs will soon have to adopt a similarly callous approach.

• Under socialism, Louis Sullivan's maxim that "form follows function" has been badly misinterpreted. Today all the emphasis is being placed on mechanical forms that are too advanced for the capabilities of those erecting the buildings or even of the people maintaining them. The result is that heating plants, elevators, garbage chutes, and electric systems are frequently inoperative.

● Industrialization has generally wreaked havoc. One Czech critic, after having taken a walking tour of Bohemia, found that his homeland had decayed more than an old woman of easy morals. He wrote in the Czech review *Literarni Noviny:* "Village squares are full of dirt, mud, and rusting machinery. Waste and rubbish is dumped in any place. Deserted houses dilapidate and grow over with weeds. New houses have skipped good taste, order, and style, as if the craftsmen lost their sight; they shamelessly lay bare the *ersatz* nudity of after-work hastiness. New utility premises that cost millions and could have been built in harmony with the surrounding landscape stick out like sore fingers; far from crowning the country, they implant artificiality on it. He who does not believe me should measure them against the proportionality of old barns, game-keeper's lodges, or iron mills."

What is the Czech Communist Party's retort to such accusations? Ex-President Novotny said, "In architecture, both the economic and the ideological missions of the building industry find expression"— a fact, Novotny insisted, that was not always appreciated. "The housing development," he said, "has a solid standard, but its sometimes dull nature and lack of a finishing touch do not correspond to our ideas of socialist and communist living conditions." Industrial architecture, on the other hand, is supposed to rely on "structural sincerity." If a factory is an unadorned eyesore, no matter; it is fulfilling its socialist function.*

To the casual observer, city planning under communism might appear to be a suppressed science. If housing projects are not built right next to chemical plants, it is frequently just as much a matter

---

* Perhaps the most functional and least attractive structure in Eastern Europe is the Berlin Wall. Huge, undecorated slabs of poured concrete were just dumped one on top of another and topped with barbed-wire netting. If Ulbricht had any feeling for aesthetics, he would at least have planted geraniums in flowerpots along the middle of this cold, Germanic monument.

of accident as intent. But even the communists are becoming aware that functionalism must eventually come of age and be projected into the future. The Czechs have been planning a utopian city, Etarea (Aetas Aurea), on the outskirts of Prague. Etarea, which is being envisioned as a sort of semienclosed, artificial biological circuit, would maintain a balance between urban and rural living for its one hundred and thirty-five thousand inhabitants: Instead of first building homes, as is common in Czechoslovakia today, the architects have submitted blueprints that call first for the building of communication and transportation facilities and the erection of a dam, then for the construction of community centers, and last of all for the building of apartment houses and factories. Wherever possible, the housing units would be surrounded by green fields and trees and would not be subjected to the usual overcrowding. The buildings themselves would be extremely varied in style, but by American standards the quarters would be small: An apartment for four people would have a total floor surface of only sixty-five square yards (equivalent to a living room of thirty by eighteen feet!). However, Etarea, if it is ever built, will include such novel ideas as the introduction of food, mail, and services (such as washing and dry cleaning) directly into each home by means of pneumatic tubing. The use of underground transport channels would also help cut down on the problems of air pollution and traffic congestion.

But generally there is a vacuum of intelligent planning for the future. Westerners should not be surprised that Poles, Hungarians, Czechs, and even Russians prefer to exhibit their antiques—ranging from the onion domes of the Kremlin to the Gothic spires of medieval Prague—rather than any of the existing modern structures. This refuge in the past is reinforced by the incredible investment the communist parties have pumped into the preservation and restoration of the past. The old Fort of Belgrade, Buda Castle, Old Warsaw, and most of Dresden have been reconstructed according to antique pictures and plans. In the United States, if a building is destroyed, it is almost never replaced with a replica; in the socialist states such reconstruction is a true obsession. The Poles are almost maniacs in their passion for reassembling and glorifying ancient history. In the twenty-odd years since the end of World War II, more than eight thousand historical monuments have been restored. Hundreds of millions of dollars have been spent on the dubious enterprise of sifting the bricks and rubble of the "Old Town" of Warsaw in order to rebuild it with the maximum number of authentic stones. This devotion to tradition and history seems rather pathetic when one walks past a reconstructed medieval building into whose chipped and worn marble lintel is engraved in old-style lettering: 1956. The result is particularly lamentable because Warsaw, which was eighty-five per cent destroyed in 1945, is an incongruous hybrid of reconstructed feudal palaces, gray boxlike tenements, and granite office buildings with secretive miniwindows, as well as curved-glass shopping centers and postwar red-brick ruins. I admire the Poles for the energy that went into resurrecting their devastated capital within a generation, but I also blame the city planners for having failed so conspicuously to integrate their architectural ideas.

The frustrations of the city planners under socialism have been compounded by the approach of those cost accountants who long ago computed that repetitive patterns save money and by those party hacks whose adherence to their deficient Marxist training caused them to rule out all but the dullest architectural schemes. Everything must conform to the plan. Unfortunately, even the rare, unconventional designs for opera houses, museums, theaters, fair grounds, and circuses look far more promising on the drawing boards than when they are realized. An exception is the Museum of Modern Art in New Belgrade. It stands out as a white whale in a sea of gray, mediocre government buildings. Thus far, this museum is the most original and provocative structure to be erected in a socialist state. That such a daring multimillion-dollar structure should be built first in Yugoslavia is no wonder. Only the anarchy that prevails in the socialist thinking of this Federal Republic would permit such a free-flowing, nonschematic museum to be conceived in the first place. The museum (finished in 1965) stands on the plain of New Belgrade close to the point where the Sava and the murky Danube rivers merge. In the daytime, when the bright sun is reflected from the sparkling white-marble-and-glass exterior, the six identical tetrahedrons, interlocked at forty-five-degree angles, look deceivingly simple. Ivan Antic (b. 1930), the architect of the museum, told me he thinks of the repetition of these solitary geometric forms are "like trees in a forest . . . independent and yet intertwined."

The shimmering white marble facing of the museum continues to the interior and helps break up the very notions of "interior" and "exterior." In fact, the forty-five-degree slant of the pillars and horizontal beams gives the impression of the molecular structure of a crystal. On the inside, the tetrahedrons are connected by two concentric staircases that give access to the five exhibition levels. Here, undoubtedly, the architect was influenced by Frank Lloyd Wright's Guggenheim Museum, except that in the Belgrade Museum the visitor can get an over-all view of the exhibits from the staircase and can then select those he would prefer to see. "The Guggenheim is a machine one must follow," says Antic, "but I did not want people to walk into the Belgrade Museum like cattle going up a slaughterhouse ramp." Since the paintings and sculp-

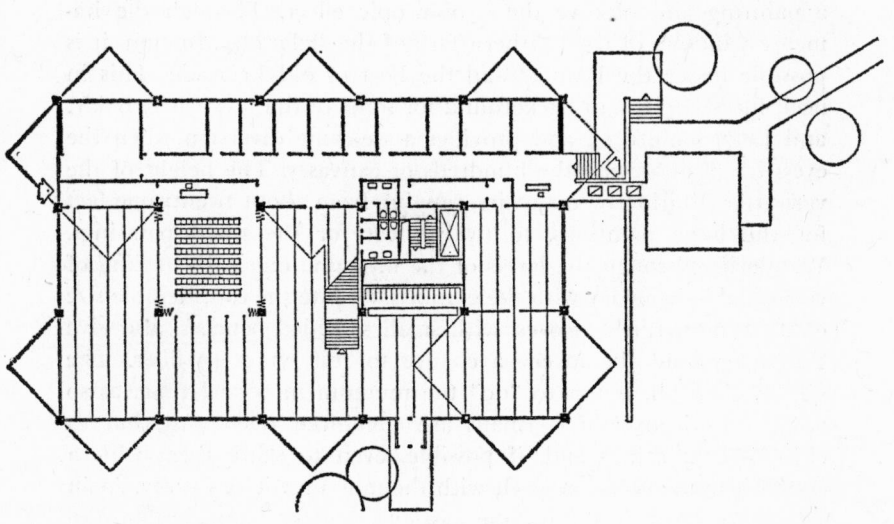

Floor plan of first floor of the Belgrade Museum of Modern Art

69

tures in the Belgrade Museum are exhibited progressively according to three historical periods (up to 1914, up to 1945, and post-1945), this is particularly agreeable for those visitors interested in a particular field. The permanent collection itself is fascinating because it demonstrates, with resounding finality, the failure of socialist realism to exercise any lasting influence on contemporary art. (As far as this collection is concerned, there never was a Zhdanov.) Antic won an open competition for the best design in 1959 and then spent an entire year in working out the details of his conception, together with architect Ivanka Raspopovic. The result is a minute realization of the interior finish, which is most unusual for Yugoslavia. Daylight enters all the exhibition rooms of the Museum of Modern Art in Belgrade. This is no small accomplishment in itself, as compared, for example, with the new all-artificial lighting of the Whitney Museum in New York. Looking at the Op and Pop Art in the Whitney, I have the distinct impression of facing television art: The flickering of the lights at thirty impulses per second only becomes obvious when you move a finger in front of a painting and observe the stroboscopic effect. Through the immense windows of the northern face of the Belgrade Museum, it is possible to see the Danube and the Fort of old Belgrade. This in itself forms a pleasant background for some of the Mestrovic, Bakic, and Logo sculptures, and provides a welcome diversion when the eyes tire of absorbing the hundreds of canvases. The height of the various exhibition rooms varies, ranging from about twenty-one feet for the large paintings, to twelve feet for the small paintings. Wandering through the levels of the museum, one has a feeling of comfortable intimacy with the exhibits, despite the considerable size of the rooms. Little alcoves, with small secluded benches, also give the weary—and the lovers—a chance to rest on every floor. The object, after all, is not to "do" the museum in record time, as so many Americans and Germans are convinced they must, but to enjoy the paintings and, if possible, even to share them with a friend. I found only one fault with the museum: it was stuffy. As in so many socialist buildings, the passion for glass is greater than the ability to construct and maintain a functioning air-conditioning system. The windows are all hermetically sealed. It is quite possible

70

to enter the museum in the early morning, before the sun really has had a chance to warm up the interior, and find that either the air conditioning is not working, or that some easygoing Serb superintendent forgot to turn it on. Only a handful of engineers know anything about the operation of air conditioning in any socialist capital, and, because there are few repairmen and no instruction books, one comes to expect the stale carbon-dioxide-rich interiors. That is the museum's principal drawback. But this is not Antic's fault. At night, when the interior and exterior of the building are illuminated, his work is revealed in full splendor. One has the impression of looking into a phosphorescent beehive. Considering the obstacles Antic faced during the five years it took to execute his work, it is difficult to overrate his achievement.

The contrast between the architecture of the city of Belgrade and that of the museum could not be greater. Despite its beneficial location at the confluence of two rivers, and the fact that it has existed as a town for almost two thousand years, Belgrade gravely lacks charm. Like Canton, Ohio, it is an industrial bog. In the winter months Belgrade is enveloped in noxious layers of anthracite smog; in the summer, the monotony of the architecture makes one wish for the balmy Adriatic Coast. Except for its many outdoor cafés, Belgrade has few amenities. It has been too busy to create them. Although the growth of Belgrade, like other socialist cities, was originally neatly pigeonholed in a five-year plan, the dynamic attraction of the city has overwhelmed all the foresight of the planners. From a sleepy hollow of about a quarter of a million inhabitants in 1945, Belgrade has expanded into a capital of a million people. This has produced incredible dislocation. Motorized traffic now clogs the center of the city. It would seem as if the ideal of the communist parties were to copy the nightmare of massive motorization in order to prove communism is on a par with the much envied "advanced capitalist states." Everyone agrees that the lethal exhaust of the semicombusted diesel fuels is noxious, yet no one does anything to control fumes from public conveyances or state-run trucks. And the human dislocation is equally critical, if one can judge by the newly urbanized farmers who still plant onions in city parks.

The New Belgrade building site is reputed to be the largest such construction project in southeast Europe. But, like Americans, Yugoslavs are much obsessed by exaggerating size and understating quality. One Serbian city planner actually displayed a sense of civic pride when he explained to me that in this new development they had succeeded in housing one thousand people per acre—and this in spite of the fact that the buildings were all relatively low, that is, under fifteen stories. Driving through this huge project, which probably will have to be torn down as a slum by the turn of the century, I saw only two or possibly three structures that did not reflect compromise and fatigue. Only the wash drying on some of the balconies broke up the monotony. But the interiors of these new structures are far more depressing than their shells. The first impression I received upon entering the apartment of a respected Serbian film director was one of Kafkaesque claustrophobia. The ceiling was very low (about seven and a half feet), the inside corridor leading into the living room was dark and narrow, the bathroom was no more than a windowless cabinet, the partitions between rooms seemed flimsy and cracking, the kitchen was hardly large enough to prepare a hot meal in—the reasoning being that the liberated socialist housewife should spend an absolute minimum of time in the kitchen. The soundproofing of the apartment was such that I could hear the rock-and-roll beat from the apartment below and the loud dispute that was being conducted in the apartment to the left. It seemed hardly conceivable that the building had only been finished six months before because there were already cracks in the concrete—yes, in reinforced concrete walls. None of the concrete seams on the ceiling appeared properly caulked—or, perhaps, the stress had been such that cracks had developed. In the bedroom—for by this time my jovial host had decided to show off all the main defects of his apartment (appropriate entertainment for a capitalist visitor)—he quietly placed a marble at one end of the bedroom and it rapidly started rolling toward the opposite side of the room. This was only a one per cent inclination, perhaps, but enough to remind one of a ship. Antic later tried to reassure me that this is not the fault of the architects but that the laborers and supervisors were not paid well enough to care about a one per cent error. This became apparent as I observed "progress" on various construction projects. Not only was the rusting equipment on the site an indication of the indifference of the workers to "people's property"; a fairly common sight was a bulldozer pushing bricks—causing an exceptionally high percentage of breakage. To prevent such carelessness, Antic said, the architect must go to the working site every day to supervise everything that might go wrong. When fifteen identical tenements are being constructed on a prefabricated basis, however, even the architects stop caring, so sloppiness—not to mention fraud—abounds. Private houses are being built not only in Belgrade, but in Warsaw, Budapest, and Sofia out of the bricks, cement, glass, and tiles stolen from these large public developments. There are two hundred and fifty-five "luxury" co-operative apartments in a new twenty-four-story "skyscraper" on Marszalkowska Street in Warsaw (in Poland, as in Yugoslavia, it is now possible to "buy" co-operative apartments from the state), and complaints by the tenants do not seem to differ from those in any other socialist capital. The owner of Apartment 47 said, "The finishing is criminal. The storage closet is unplastered. The window catches were broken and had to be replaced. The kitchen is too small and there is no room for an oven. . . . The woodwork must have been done by apprentices, for the doors and the windows are crooked." Farther up, in Apartment 81, the water heater in the bathroom was leaking, the garbage chute had clogged, and the tenant complained of loud noises in the water pipes at night. On the top floor, in Apartment 186, the tenants said that it was impossible to arrange the furniture because the radiator stood in the middle of one wall—although there was enough space for it under a window. The lady of the house claimed that the walls in the kitchen were crooked and the window sills had cracked, and that the difference in size between one end of the bedroom and the other was five centimeters. "I don't know what experts adjusted the wooden doors in the steel door frames," she said, "but the results are scandalous; those twisted door latches look awful." No one is more aware of all these deficiencies than the Polish satirists. Poles are estimated to live 1.57 people to a room, so this opens abundant opportunity for humor.

If the living do not exactly reside in splendor, the dead do. The most modern designs in Yugoslavia—as in many other socialist countries—are reserved for memorials to fallen World War II heroes, for the sites of concentration camps, and for cemeteries. Bogdan Bogdanovic, a bright, charming, and articulate Yugoslav architect, has become a specialist in creating Partisan memorials and is, in fact, completing a cycle of park cemeteries dedicated to the primeval elements: fire, water, earth, and air. At Jasenovac, an SS slaughter site in Serbia, Bogdanovic has created a huge concrete flower in the form of a crypt. The petals of this concrete flower, which appears particularly striking at night when the reflection in the artificial pool resembles an hourglass, are themselves twenty-four feet high. However, most of these memorials are more akin to sculpture than to architecture.

Television towers, perhaps the other outstanding example of imaginative socialist design, are, on the other hand, much more the product of engineers than of architects. Without any doubt, the ultra-short-wave and television tower constructed at Avala, a mountain south of Belgrade, is the boldest such structure in any socialist state. The reinforced concrete section of the tower rises some four hundred feet and is remarkable for the harmonious transition from the triangular base of its trunk to its well-proportioned tripod. The glistening white concrete of the tower is capped by a one-hundred-and-seventy-five-foot spiral steel antenna, making the whole structure resemble a huge rocket resting on a launching pad. Designed to perform a twentieth-century task, it is bare of unnecessary embellishments and looks truly modern. The fact that this six-hundred-foot tower rests in a reinforced concrete base that extends only ten feet beneath the surface reveals imaginative, nonconformist engineering and thinking—so lacking in the construction of the human habitation.

In many ways the socialist societies, in their greed for foreign currency, have been parodying the capitalist system. Top priority in construction is given to the tourist industry. Tourist hotels along the Adriatic in Yugoslavia, and along the Black Sea in Rumania and Bulgaria, take precedence over domestic housing. When funds ran out in Croatia, the framework of the new Concert Hall in

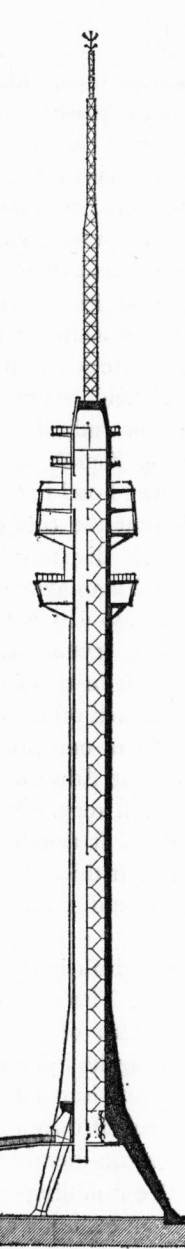

Zagreb had to be covered with tar to protect the metal parts from exposure to the elements. But while the squeeze was being applied in Zagreb, a luxury hotel was built in Split and finished in a year—a Serbo-Croat record. To its credit, the Marjan Hotel is one of the few socialist structures snuggled into its surroundings. Its base is a two-story glass-and-steel quadrangle that serves as a restaurant, foyer, and reception center for tourists; over this, in Lever Building fashion, an eleven-story hotel, accommodating close to five hundred people, rises. The Marjan Hotel is not startlingly new in its conception. However, its execution proves that even East Europeans can build adequate accommodations without Western help—something I had begun to doubt when the Hilton and Intercontinental chains first started to expand their operations into Eastern Europe. That the beds are hard, the shellacked plywood furniture awkward, the metal bucket chairs uncomfortable, and the factory-loomed carpets simply hideous is quite another matter. In the lobby, the violent murals by Zagreb abstract expressionist Edo Murtic (b. 1921) are tasteless. Murtic has consciously imitated Jackson Pollock since 1953, when he staged an influential one-man show entitled "Experience from America." Murtic has succeeded in placing his dribbling gestures everywhere along the Adriatic Coast. (He owes this strategic placement to the fact

Line drawing showing section of TV tower at Avala, near Belgrade

75

that he was a high-ranking Partisan during the war.) But one should not take Murtic seriously; most of the tourists who visit the Yugoslav coast have never even noticed his works.

South of Dubrovnik, at Kuparim, the Yugoslav Army hired architect David Finci to design what is perhaps the most imaginative of the Adriatic Coast hotels. This five-story structure, whose concrete face is of the same ochre shade as the jutting rocks that surround it, is built in the form of a quadrangle with a court in the middle. Each floor juts out about four feet beyond the preceding one, developing the idea of a truncated and inverted ziggurat. Even more imaginative plans are being made in the hotel field, where architects feel more confident of receiving support for radical projects than they are in the area of public housing. Zagreb architect Vojtjeh Delfin has finished blueprints for a floating hotel to be built of reinforced concrete floats. His argument is that the cost of the infrastructure—that is, the land, roads, sewage disposal, water supply, and so forth—of a Category A hotel in Yugoslavia is now about fifty per cent of the total cost of the project, so why not build luxury hotels that can be moved through the crystal Adriatic waters at will? Delfin's floating hotel is to be built in the shape of three aerodynamic inner tubes welded on top of each other, so that in a strong wind the hotel will not slant or tip to one side. The hotel could be moved like a barge up and down the Adriatic Coast. Delfin, who drew up his first plans for the project in 1963, is hopeful that by 1971 such a hotel will actually be afloat. It usually takes close to a decade for radical projects to come to fruition in Yugoslavia; in the United States these same projects would require a few years at the most.

It is regrettable for Yugoslavia that Marshal Tito's influence in the arts has not been of a more refined nature. Tito's taste, unfortunately, borders on the flamboyant. "The Last of the Hapsburgs," as he has been called by A. J. P. Taylor, regales himself with resplendent military uniforms, chrome-plated American and West German limousines, and diamond rings. However, if only through his choice of court architects, Tito has exerted a considerable influence on the course of Yugoslav architecture. The rambling Federal Executive Council building in New Belgrade is an example of what

happens when an individual with little taste but with vast preten-
sions to modernity comes to power in a semideveloped country. The
seven-story, white-marble-faced mammoth, which took some twenty
years to complete, now houses the burgeoning Yugoslav bureaucracy
that has grown around the President's office. This is by far the most
luxuriously appointed official structure in the socialist world. Its
cavernous entrance and oversized reception halls are now used for
official state functions. Other socialist leaders, such as Poland's
Gomulka, have frankly expressed their disapproval of this royalist
style of ostentation. Everywhere there are immense abstract murals
and large, nonfigurative sculptures by Yugoslavia's leading artists.
If these works had been chosen and placed with greater selectivity,
the overwhelming impression would not be one of parvenu vulgarity. Tito's intended palace of retirement at Pantouscak (near
Zagreb), where he has built a glass-and-steel mansion closely resembling Belgrade's new airport, shows how consistently "off" his taste
is. This pretentious villa, built by court architect and designer
Vjenceslav Richter (b. 1917), exudes a sterile, nonlivable, office
ambiance.

No city anywhere had a greater opportunity to show imagination
and a radical approach to its reconstruction than Skoplje, Macedonia, after its great earthquake. And yet today the city sprawls
over miles of formerly fertile valley land and is totally lacking in
structural integration and architectural tension. Perhaps the person
most to blame is the charming Polish city planner Adolf Ciborowski, who had gained great experience in the reconstruction of
Warsaw. Ciborowski was unable to resolve the conflict between
diffusion and concentration. In the center of Skoplje today there is
a collection of fissured matchboxes—strategically placed for maximum effect. (I was never quite certain whether the cracks in the
walls resulted from the earthquake or were just the natural consequence of inexperience in casting reinforced concrete.) On the outskirts of Skoplje there stand, mile upon mile, small, prefabricated
boxes, each with its own garden, which represent gifts from the
entire Western world: Finnish bungalows, white and blue corrugated fiberboard huts from Italy, pink metal barracks from the
United States, wooden cottages from Norway. Here individualism

77

has suddenly run rampant, regardless of the expense of providing water, electricity, roads, and other improvements for all these homes. But the co-operative facilities for washing, drying, and even child care are far better in the nonsocialist communities on which suburban Skoplje has patterned itself. As seen from the air, the Skoplje conglomerate, sprawled along the winding Vardar River, leaves an impression of overwhelming confusion. As seen from the ground, nearly all the buildings appear half finished—as if Skoplje, too, had suffered from the Yugoslav disease of starting new projects without a penny in the till. And the decision to build a huge steel complex, which will prove as much of a health hazard to the two hundred and fifty thousand inhabitants as a source of jobs, reveals the industrial ambitions of this city which used to be admired for its minarets and rustic charm. By the year 2,000 Skoplje will undoubtedly have doubled in size and will be a city without a soul. Like Galati (Rumania) and other monotonous planned cities of the communist world, Skoplje is ignoring the natural process of architectural accretion.

The younger Yugoslav architects are the sharpest critics of the parsimonious system that uses the same blueprints over and over again. Not only are they dissuaded from presenting remedial critiques of new housing projects (possibly costly in execution), but their architectural imagination is also stifled by the socialist system. The great majority of the five hundred to six hundred architectural students who graduate each year from Belgrade and Zagreb schools emigrate to France, West Germany, and Canada—to join the East-to-West brain drain. They are casting their votes against the lack of opportunity at home and against the bureaucratic system that has prevented socialism from developing a new style, creating a new architecture, or really planning new cities. In Yugoslavia only a few really good structures, like the Museum of Modern Art and the Avala tower, have appeared, and they are notable exceptions. However, even this modest achievement is more than the other communist states have been able to boast of—for theirs has been a long-abandoned promise.

CHAPTER IV

The Sniping Szinpad

Political satire is a cunning scalpel; it combines, usually in an aggressive manner, the reality of a beauty mortician with the incisiveness of a clinical diagnostician. Plato was well aware of the danger such humor presented to the state more than two thousand years ago. Dissertating upon abuse and ridicule in his *Laws,* Plato asked, "Do we admit into our state the comic writers who are so fond of making mankind ridiculous if they attempt in a good-natured manner to turn the laugh against our citizens? Or do we draw the distinction of jest and earnest and allow a man to make use of ridicule in jest and without anger?" Plato had no second thoughts about earnest ridicule—he forbade it. Plato decreed: "a comic, poet, or maker of iambic or satirical lyric verse shall not be permitted to ridicule any of the citizens, either by word or likeness, either in anger or without anger." To punish the lawbreaker, the judges would impose a large fine or expel him from the city-state. Plato's thin-skinned attitude toward satirists has been adopted by most dictatorships. This makes it particularly surprising that Hungary's Janos Kadar, one of the anorchous dictators of history, actually pays to have the state satirized. Perhaps this is not only because Budapest, the home of Franz Lehar and Ferenc Molnar, has a reputation for laughing in the face of misery, but also because Hungarian communists regard satire as a sophisticated way to let off steam. Kadar, who himself occasionally visits the Vidam Szinpad (Merry Stage) in Budapest, reportedly once said, "What the people laugh about on stage, they won't whisper behind closed doors."

Although there is absolutely no mimicry of the contemporary leadership on the Merry Stage, and little, if any, parody, Marxism is considered fair game. Indeed, few subjects are more vulnerable than the system Marx conjured up one hundred years ago. Perhaps the most brilliant critique of the gap between socialist reality and socialist theorizing ever presented on any stage enjoyed more than a year's run at the Vidam Szinpad in 1966–1967. The Merry Stage skit, by framing Marxism in a thoroughly anachronistic context, accentuated the incongruous and made the Hungarian application look supremely risible.

A bald, cross-eyed manager of a socialist factory, brilliantly portrayed by actor Laszlo Kazal, is walking home, slightly tipsy after a night on the town with some French trade negotiators. As he strolls through the dark Budapest park, stumbling along the way, he passes a marble bust of Marx. Suddenly, he does a double take. Perhaps it is all part of a dream—just like the favorable contract he has signed with the French? (Rarely does any Hungarian State exporter conclude an advantageous agreement.)

"Well, well, good evening, Comrade Marx," he bellows in a drunken voice. "Ah . . . it is a wonderful coincidence that I, a simple enterprise manager, have just bumped into you and have the chance to tell you my problems. . . . Now that we meet here, let me tell you quite sincerely that you didn't realize how things would work out. . . . You didn't have plans to fulfill, or people who came to you with technical complaints. You only had Engels to argue with, but me, I have to argue with all the ministries." (Burps.)

"The simple enterprise manager knows best how difficult it is to translate theory into practice, so that all index numbers are correct, that everybody is satisfied, and all this without getting an ulcer. Because if he fulfills the quantitative plan, productivity will decrease, if he tries to prevent the decline of productivity, the quality will be inferior, and if he tries to maintain the quality he will miss the export deadline. But if he manages to fulfill all export requirements, he cannot supply the domestic consumers. Well, Comrade Marx, you could say that all these are professional questions which are none of your business. Why should I ask you about these problems? It would be better to ask the competent ministry. Well, you are right to a certain extent. I will admit that the complaints about our export articles, which Western customers return to us time and again, are never from the ideological, but always from the technical, point of view." (The quality of Hungarian goods is unusually shoddy.) "Still you can't leave me alone with my problems, Comrade Marx, after you helped me this far. But for you, I wouldn't be a director today. I would still be a warehouseman working for Cohn & Sons. . . ."* (Burps, then continues the inebriated soliloquy.) "To be honest, I have profited from your *Kapital,* Comrade Marx. I actually made a profit out of the misery of the British working class. You wrote that a specter haunts Europe. Well, do you know who was visiting Europe? I was, from Amsterdam to Athens . . . at public expense. In London the taxi driver, who knew that I came from a socialist country, could not believe his ears when he heard that I did not want to see the Marx-Engels memorial, but the pajamas at the Marks and Spencer department store. It really is so, Comrade Marx. You forgot to figure only one thing in your theory—that is, man is greedy, selfish, and narrow-minded, even if he is not being exploited by anyone. He takes care of the official business as soon as possible, Comrade Marx, and then he runs to buy some pullovers, Comrade Marx, just as you can see on the list which his wife gave him at home, Comrade Marx. Life passes among these things just as it is written in the book—I don't know which one of you wrote it—*Origin of the Family, Private Property, and the State,* because I will be very honest with you, just between you and me . . . not everything came out the way you imagined it would." (Kazal hiccups, grows slightly red in the face, staggers around a bit.)

"Well, did you ever learn historic materialism, Comrade Marx? Oh, excuse me, you were the one who invented it. . . . You wrote a hundred years ago that I had nothing to lose but my chains. Well, what about my Trabant?" (A two-cylinder East German model.) "It is almost as good as a car. And what about my weekend house in Visegrad? Well, why do you look at me askance? And yes, I have a refrigerator, too, but I'm not the only one; almost everybody in the factory has one. Well, are we soft and petty bourgeois because of this? I know, I know that in the last century the British working class had no refrigerators. But they didn't have anything to eat either . . . Comrade Marx. A worker who does not have anything to eat can easily exist without a refrigerator. But what happens after the elimination of exploitation? There are no capitalists any more. There is more and more food which will spoil overnight without a refrigerator. This is not nonsense, Comrade Marx, if somebody says A, he should say B, as well." (Burps.)

* In a radio version of this program broadcast for a wider audience, the name was changed to Sernwart & Sons—in order not to feed the Hungarian penchant for anti-Semitism.

"Well, now that I have started I might as well continue: Everybody saves for something. Were the working class in an easy position when they lived in slums like cattle? They did not have a chance to save anything. But what happens after the elimination of exploitation? Ha, ha . . . then it comes: The socialist house is a blessing: an apartment with parquet floors. A parquet floor needs a carpet. And where there is a carpet there must be a vacuum cleaner, and where there is a vacuum cleaner there must be a TV, and where there is a TV one should save for a car to get away from the TV—it is so terrible! Well, is this my fault, Comrade Marx? I know, I know that one can work hard for mankind in a well-furnished house as well." (Leans against marble pedestal.)

"What is going on at home? The TV blares in one room, the cleaning woman squabbles with my wife in the kitchen, in the other room the children are recording the 'Teenager Party'" (a Radio Free Europe program from Munich) "and I should sit alone on the floor and fight for world revolution? Then there is my daughter. Well, how can I explain to her, Comrade Marx, that, because her grandparents were unemployed in 1930, she should be the only one in her class who doesn't wear a miniskirt? And, after all, I am here, too. I would like to allow myself some things, too. You, Comrade Marx, were a married man and cared very much for your children. But, on the other hand, Comrade Engels found his happiness not in family life, but in bachelorhood. Well, I would like to follow the example of both of you, which is terribly expensive. Do you know how difficult it is to earn a lot of money?

"In my factory the work discipline is just miserable. You didn't even dare to dream of such skulking when you were studying classical capitalism. You wrote that the worker is always threatened with something so that he will do his job: in slavery, with the lash; in feudalism, with hunger; and in capitalism, with unemployment. Well, there is neither lash nor hunger nor unemployment in socialism. . . . What can the worker be threatened with? The trade union? All right . . . I heard it. . . . I am the manager, I should threaten them. But even this is not as easy as it is in theory. Well, whom will I harm when I fire one of my foremen who is a miserable worker? Him? . . . No, the people's economy. Because if I do fire him, his brother-in-law at the Ministry will not settle with the cooperative enterprise to deliver the spare parts that are vital to the fulfillment of the plan. . . . Well, there are dialectics, too, in the world, Comrade Marx. The same goes for patronage. It is true that I have given an extra pay raise to one of my departmental managers, but he deserved it because he has connections. You said, Comrade Marx, that the building of socialism in every country will take place according to the traditions of the country. Well, it seems that these are traditions in our country." (Burps.)

This devastating critique is superior to anything an American or French or English humorist could write about applied Marxism. It overemphasizes the incongruities of enforcing ideology. To produce first-rate satire, a certain patient, reflective resignation is necessary. Because of this, Hungarians in the mid-sixties could be wittier about communism or about their own living conditions than Americans in the mid-sixties could be about Vietnam.

While barbs are flung like sharp porcupine quills into the audience, satire in Hungary is a curiously passive phenomenon. It is also unique: Plato suggested that people laugh at the misfortunes of others because they are relieved that they do not share them. This is not the case in the humor of the Budapest theaters—much of the public is suffering privation. Hazlitt ventured that satirists gain the applause of others through fear. Again, the problem of fear is not primary in Hungarian satire. Voltaire thought satire could play an integral role to further change, but again this is not uppermost in the minds of Hungarian scriptwriters. What Hungarians laugh at is the perfect mess in which they find themselves and the contradiction between state promises and actual accomplishments. Polish novelist and social critic Leopold Tyrmand contends it is "a cardinal error" to think such satire represents anything more than "the mocking ambivalence and opportunistic attitudes of the upper class." Tyrmand is right in saying that "if such skits were dangerous, they would not exist," but, basically, Hungarian satire is not an upper-class phenomenon, nor is it merely a manifestation of ambivalence or opportunism. Groups of soldiers or collective farmers from the sticks laugh just as hard at the skits as the Jewish intellectuals and other Budapest sophisticates. When the lines are funny, they laugh. When the laughter ceases, the program is changed.

The short life of the scriptwriters and directors proves satire is not entirely in the hands of collaborationists. From time to time a government newspaper will even complain that these little theaters (none of which can seat more than a few hundred) aren't "constructive" enough, but mostly they are left alone. Istvan Fejer (b. 1911), until mid-1967 the director of the Vidam Szinpad, told me that once a Party member had warned him "to take it easy with the jokes or he would get into trouble." Fejer, who has a large, hooked nose (although he claims he is no more Jewish than an Irishman), answered: "Why trouble? Look at Khrushchev. He kept on playing jokes and nothing happened to him. He now has a state car and several assistants." The official laughed. Fejer discovered by a process of experimentation that what makes Hungarians laugh most is telling the truth, and that is what he did.

Before the war, humor in Budapest concerned politics, politicians, and parliamentary life. "However, you can't make a joke about someone you don't know," said Fejer, remarking that under socialism nobody knows very much about the character, the taste, or the preferences of leading politicians. "We used to know whether the Prime Minister kept a mistress or preferred boys," Fejer jested, but not any more. Many topics have also become taboo: It is no longer permitted to satirize Jews, Czechs, Rumanians, gypsies, policemen, or even the fire brigades. It is no longer possible to caricature the Hungarian Church or the aristocracy (because both have disappeared from power), and Fejer said that it is no longer even possible to be spicy, because the "proletarian audiences tend to be prudish." Under such tight restrictions, Fejer's great contribution was to take the cabaret out of the coffeehouse atmosphere, in which the skits had previously been written, and into the street. The man in the street, in fact, became a common figure in his programs.

The first program to set the new tone for political satire was "We Speak Different Languages," which had its première in 1964. It was the first show in Hungary that dared to utter the name of Kadar publicly. This program also asked where the "Hungarian Stalin," Matyas Rakosi (actually living in exile in Russia), was hiding out. And the MC immortalized the saying, "One shouldn't be afraid of communism; after all, it doesn't move so fast." Most of the subsequent productions spoofed the Hungarian tourist industry, bureaucrats in agriculture, the obsession with soccer, the sad state of television, the sagging birth rate (the main point of the skit was that the state only gives apartments to young couples if they have a baby, but without a flat and without a car, there is nowhere for them to procreate) , and the housing shortage. Here is an example:

"What are our apartments like?" asks the teacher of his pupils.
"Cultured," responds one student (a man in his fifties dressed in short pants) .
"We often use this word without defining it," says the teacher. "Tell me, if that is possible, what is the Hungarian synonym for the word 'cultured'?"
"Small," responds the student sitting on his dunce's stool.

Fejer pretended to me in 1966, with what turned out to be sheer bravado, that things were relatively easy for him, politically, because "Nobody in Hungary says 'no' to anybody." This, he explained, "would be regarded as the suppression of criticism." However, Fejer admitted he occasionally inserted provocative jokes that he knew would be censored, just to protect the rest of his script. But the course of censorship was so erratic that sometimes the provocations were left untouched. One sketch that had been censored depicted an organ grinder below a window marked "Ministry of Culture." The Minister, who never could bear Fejer, took offense at the grinder's explanation that he stood there because "they throw more money out of this window than anywhere else." In general, Fejer explained, the more sophisticated Hungarian audience no longer laughs at open criticism. "For the past ten years the mistakes and the reactions to these mistakes have been the same," he said, "namely, there has been no change." Consequently, no Hungarian audience is going to laugh about traffic problems, dry cleaning, service in restaurants, Hungarian films, incompetent plumbers, or TV repairmen. "We must be like Menippus, the cynic who joked about serious things," said Fejer.

Fejer explained that the word "satire" does not derive, as he once had hoped it did, from the Satyr who was always ready to insert himself into every cranny, goat, or human, but from the word "satur," meaning "sated." This culinary expression takes on a special meaning in socialist countries, where no one is ever sated with the indigestible, inelegant, starchy fare. Fejer explained that to be successful, satire must appear to be light and spontaneous; it must spring from a casual occurrence or a sudden impulse. And, of course, the tone must be totally inappropriate to the gravity of the subject. For example, in one of Fejer's famous scenes, an old charwoman goes to the Ministry of Foreign Affairs to apply for a visa to visit England. The officials don't want to grant her a passport but she argues that it is going to be a study trip. "I want to study cleaning work in the West, doing it with modern methods," she says. "Well, what would be the use of it?" asks the passport official. "You would come back and would do the same cleaning work as you did before." So the old biddy retorts: "And the managing director? And the chief engineer? And the other comrades? How many times were they on Western study trips? And what changed after they came back?" The logic is overwhelming. Her visa is granted. But the old charwoman almost defects. "In England they offered me the salary of a university professor," she says. "I mean, the salary of a Hungarian university professor."

During his tenure, Fejer presented political satire on the stage of the Vidam Szinpad that, if it had been presented on American television, would have drawn strong official protests from the ruling communist parties. This is probably one of the principal reasons why Fejer eventually fell into disfavor; there was too much heresy in his satire. In one of the skits, "It Is Difficult to Vote," the speaker explains to the audience that in Hungary voting is a formal procedure. Everything that the people want is decided on beforehand and then voted upon in an absolutely democratic fashion. The speaker explains one can choose between two kinds of democracy: one that is always "perfect," because it is talked and written about as such, or one that has many faults, which can be written about and discussed. The Vidam Szinpad is a democratic institution, the speaker explains, and therefore, the public will be permitted to vote on the program, the price of admission, and even the MC. Four members of the audience propose a candidate, a comedian named Alphonzo. The speaker says, "Who agrees with our candidate for *conférencier* should remain seated. Those who don't agree should take out their typewriters and write out a protest, which they can send up to the platform. There are no protests? Alphonzo is unanimously accepted." Alphonzo then steps on stage and takes out a

prepared statement from his pocket, just as most newly elected
Hungarian politicians do. "This honor is bestowed upon me quite
unexpectedly," he reads, "and, of course, I am not at all prepared
for this part. . . ."

An intermission follows, during which the audience has a chance
to nibble away at some *perec,* the Hungarian version of stale,
warmed-over bagels. When the curtain goes up again, the speaker
steps up and reads a statement: "Owing to his bad and declining
state of health, the MC you have elected is to be released from his
difficult duties and given another function of appropriate importance. Alphonzo has been appointed doorman at the Vidam
Szinpad."

The public is then informed: "Until now, who was given the post
of Master of Ceremonies? . . . Only a man of the privileged class,
an actor. But to show how utterly democratic a theater we are, an
ordinary man will fill the post, even though he doesn't know anything about it." The new *conférencier* is the former tailor of the
theater, who unfortunately turns out to have a bad stutter. When
an actor rises from among the public to demand his removal because of incompetence, the speaker retorts, "My God, if everyone
was removed who was incompetent, where would Hungary be?
Politically, this man is okay, his working-class background is okay,
so what can we do with him?"

"Recommend him to another theater," says a critic in the audience.

"Send him to TV," chimes in another.

"Don't you think he is too good for TV?" asks the speaker. "A
place more appropriate for his talents will be found: our Parliament."

Fejer's humor, for all its disjointedness and occasional bitterness,
was refreshing because it was never official. The trouble with satire
in Bucharest, Sofia, East Berlin, and Moscow continues to be that it
is government humor—the jokes serve a purpose that is obvious,
unspontaneous, and occasionally even crude. Official humor cannot
be funny, because it always strives to score a point in promoting a
particular aspect of foreign or domestic policy. The removal of Jews
from the satiric theaters in Russia robbed the Soviets of most of

their best wits, leaving only such cautious humorists as Arkady Raikin. With sharp sarcasm, the Hungarians relate that the Soviet Central Committee organized a nationwide contest for political anecdotes—first prize, twenty-five years of forced labor. Lord Shaftesbury stated, "Ridicule is the test of truth," and that is one test the Soviets reject. On the Budapest stage it is possible to tell such jokes as: "In 1972, one out of every five Russians will have a car, one out of every three a television set, and one out of every two a pair of shoes." In Moscow it would be censored. Even now, individuals caught spreading political jokes in Russia are liable to be sent to Siberia—unless they already happen to be living there—for a prolonged stretch.

The Novosti Press Agency printed a little booklet entitled *What Is Communism?*, which was distributed at the Russian pavilion of the Montreal Expo '67. One of the questions this booklet attempted to answer was, "Will political jokes be allowed under communism?" (Not, mind you, "Are they allowed under socialism?") The authors admitted that there are Russians who are against satire and humor, but stated: "Laughter is killing, but it cannot be killed! People were tried as counterrevolutionaries for jokes during the Stalin personality cult period. But the Soviet people's sense of humor could not be subdued. The people have always laughed and continue laughing at everything that is funny or absurd." The approach to humor and satire in the Soviet Union is very different from that in Budapest. First of all, the Russians have gone in for elaborate theorizing on the nature of satire. One Soviet pseudo philosopher, Elsberg, maintains that "Satire derides and scourges the social system (or its remnants) and its representatives, who have already revealed their impotence and feebleness in the course of historical destiny." Elsberg considers only the "bourgeois system" a fit subject for satire. One denominator binds all of the aspects of comic satire, writes another philosopher. "At their root lies a common law: the contradiction between outworn, outmoded forms of life and new and revolutionary forms." In practice, only "vestiges of the past and of "outgrown modes of life and thought" in Soviet society may be the object of satire. The party and contemporary Soviet society are automatically exempt from satiric attack because they represent what is "new, revolutionary, and progressive." With such restrictive ground rules, it is small wonder Russian humanists keep their jokes to themselves. Even the leading Soviet caricaturist, Boris Efimov, claims the "path of our political satire" is to unmask and deride "citizens who have no wish to be heroes, that is, militant philistines and trashy persons indifferent to everything in the world but their own selves, overweening potentates and grabbers who place their self-seeking interests above all else." If it were not for the fact that he applies his theories by making all Germans look like Nazis, or all Americans like murderers, dollar-mad capitalists, and enslaved Negroes, one could regard Efimov's outburst as a parody on the linguistics of the Soviet system itself. However, the Soviets do apply their theory of satire. All through the mid-sixties, for example, attacks were directed against Plutschek and Lewinsky, the directors of the Moscow Satiric Theater. The result was that the productions there became progressively more vacuous, as they had during Stalin's time. Until the communists abandon the notion that satire is "a work of art that openly rejects an unjust social system as a whole," there will certainly be no satire worthy of the name on the Russian stage.

The wry, sophisticated satire of Poland has also faced mounting tribulations during the sixties. Humor is one commodity that the Polish government would like to believe is produced at home and abundant enough to export. This is only partly true. Polish humor magazines are banned in the Soviet Union, for example, but are available in France. (The Russians didn't appreciate such barbs as: "Q. What is the latest discovery of Soviet agronomists? A. How to sow wheat in Russia and harvest it in Canada.") But while the student theaters, cabarets, and clubs in which satire flourished in 1956–1957 formed one of the more promising intellectual movements in People's Poland, by the early sixties the seesaw had tipped the other way.

Janusz Szpotanski (b. 1932), a writer and translator, was sentenced to three years in prison in early 1968 for his satiric operetta *The Quiet and the Honkers.* Although his satire was never performed or even published in Poland, tape recordings were discovered by the secret police. The operetta, whose music was entirely plagiarized from Lehar, Verdi, and Puccini, satirized, by means of thinly veiled allusions, such readily recognizable figures as Gomulka and Stefan Cardinal Wyszynski. The judge, in condemning Szpotanski's operetta, said it contained "false information on the social, political, and economic conditions in Poland that could do harm to the interests of the state and could lower the prestige of state authorities."

If a Polish cabaret is too daring, the government simply replaces the director or writer responsible with someone "more constructive." On the other hand, if the performance isn't caustic or sharp enough, the theater will soon lose its public and go bankrupt. For the satirist it is a heads you win, tails I lose proposition. For example, at the famed Student Satiric Theater in Warsaw I saw a stagnant revue featuring the slow hotel service under socialism, the good life in a socialist jail, and the loss of idealism among the students. It concluded with a skit about state production of macaroni. A decade ago a factory started producing good macaroni with four eggs, but the state soon discovered that macaroni could be made with three eggs, in order to export the fourth. Soon macaroni was being made without any eggs, was as tough as wood, and was lying unsold on grocery-stores shelves. Mercifully, the audience did not laugh.

Krzysztof Teodor Toeplitz, one of Poland's best-known journalists, recently wrote a long essay analyzing satiric writing in Poland, explaining why it had become too tame to be even mildly amusing. The reason, Toeplitz believes, is that satire is no longer mirroring life—it is mirroring the propaganda system. The course of satire in Poland is contrary to nature, as if a water faucet were to suck water in, instead of spouting it out. In other countries, Toeplitz maintains, satirical magazines, cabarets, and TV shows produce new jokes, which are then repeated by the population. In Poland, on the other hand, the satirical clubs repeat, with some delay, jokes that have first made the rounds of Poland and that have then been adjusted and prettied up for redissemination. Further proof of the sad state of Polish satire is evidenced by looking through old copies of satirical magazines. The caricatures of the lazy waiter, the helpless bureaucrat, the unfaithful wife, or the delinquent youth are so immortal that they cannot really be identified with any particular period of history. Anonymity, which is one of the basic characteristics of a system where no one likes to give his name on the telephone, is also crippling to good satire. "I believe that the anonymity in our satire is the fruit of apprehensiveness on the part of both the satirists and the middle-level officials and civil servants who invariably see in satire a threat to their jobs . . ." writes Toeplitz. Any mention by name results in such an "avalanche of letters, *démenti*, official writings with all the requisite stamps and signatures," he reports, that it ceases to be a paying proposition.

Toeplitz observed that, throughout history, satire has been one of the most libertine and trenchant forms of writing. "Sullying all that's sacred" was almost the professional duty of the satirist. In Poland all this has been reversed. "If satire shows any interest in youth, it is only to preach at it; if it mentions miniskirts, it is only to brand them as immoral; any spirit of anarchy is totally absent, and in this way it is more reminiscent of a fault-finding old maid than of a playful satyr." Satire becomes as bland as the moon displaying its half-smile, and the authors who invent threatening phrases about "certain people," "highly responsible officials," and "powers" only puzzle or bore their readers. Toeplitz gave a good example of what he thinks satire should be like, by attacking the Polish government for promoting the "cult of the dollar." Toeplitz writes that the average Pole who switches on his TV set continually hears how the government has managed to sell hams, timber, skis, boats, and vegetable produce for foreign exchange. When a Pole opens his newspaper, he reads what new measures the tourist agencies or the Ministry of Trade have taken in quest for precious hard currency. (For example, they exported a number of pigeons from Warsaw's Old Town for "precious currency.") And when he puts his hands in his pockets and touches the worthless Polish zloty, he begins to feel uneasy. Is this why he has toiled during the day? No. He, in turn, also begins to look for "the green stuff."

Polish satirists have been noted for their subtle understatements. Slawomir Mrozek, one of the best playwrights and satirists, claims in the preface to his play *The Police* that his works have absolutely no meaning. But Mrozek, who lives in the West most of the time, continues to pour out a blistering torrent of absurd comments on Polish life, and tries, through satire, to show the complete subjugation of the ordinary citizen to the all-powerful state. In his one-acter, *Striptease,* Mrozek lets his two actors be imprisoned and then stripped down to their shirttails. All the while the one tries to blame the other for their bad luck because he wasn't satisfied with "inner freedom." The point is, of course, that those who constantly take refuge in their famous Polish "inner freedom" only allow themselves to be tyrannized to the point where they become accomplices to the despotic system. Such satire, however, should not be confounded with the theater of the absurd. Mrozek's heroes are tormented by the absurdity of "being" but are unable to propose a solution. The world is askew, and there is no way to restore its balance. In his play *On the High Seas* Mrozek creates a grotesque parody of the mentality that induces a whole people to be cultivated as cannon fodder. A well-educated Pole is being persuaded to sacrifice himself for his two shipwrecked companions. When this pompous victim has finally been talked into being eaten and is delivering his farewell speech in acceptance of this great honor, one of the three castaways finds some cans of veal and peas.

"Psst! Hide them quick," says the first.

"But to be honest, I would rather eat the peas," says the discoverer, who does not particularly look forward to cannibalism.

"I'm not hungry for peas and besides . . ." says the first.

"What, besides?" says the second.

"Can't you see how happy he is?" (pointing to the victim, who is still delivering his acceptance speech) .

Like Mrozek's cultured, considerate cannibals, East European satirists are always uncertain of their fate. Up to the end of 1966, Hungary was producing the finest humor in the communist world. Then inauspicious changes began to appear. Fejer, the director of the Vidam Szinpad for some ten years, had during the course of numerous encounters explained to me that "the comic writers who combine political knowledge, humor, a familiarity with music and verse are a lost generation—the generation of Hungarian Jews who had a monopoly of prewar Hungarian satire either were killed, fled in 1956, or are now in retirement." During the course of my interviews with Fejer, I noticed that even he was becoming progressively more cautious. The last time I saw him, in the spring of 1967, he seemed exceptionally reticent to give a straight answer. He side-stepped my questions with oblique *non sequiturs* until I finally felt obliged to ask him if he was feeling all right. He side-stepped this question, too, and told me that he had just finished a book on behavior. "I can't live on the salary of a director," he complained. This book was not about socialist manners, he said, but about good manners in general. It was inspired, he claimed, by a work, written around the turn of the century, in which it was stated: "It is most indecent for a lady to skate backwards. . . ." Fejer predicted the book was on its way to become a Hungarian best seller. I hope that it has, because a few weeks after I last saw him, Fejer, although only in his early fifties, was "retired" and placed on a pension. Apparently, the Minister of Culture had not appreciated Fejer's irreverent insights for some time—and so Hungary lost one of its brightest and most witty humorists.

Fejer told me, "In Hungary, changes are seldom for the better." This is a depressing comment for a satirist to make. But I soon discovered that he was right. Fejer was replaced by a journalist and public relations man, Tibor Rona, who refused to see me, talk to me, or let me read the script of Fejer's skit on Marxism. Rona, who claims he is not a member of the Communist Party, was quite unexplainably placed in charge not only of the Vidam Szinpad but also of another satiric theater, the Kis Szinpad. Soon the entire press was propagandizing Rona's incredible wit and acumen, Fejer having meanwhile become something of an unperson. Seen in the context of a general hardening in the approach of Kadar's regime, Fejer's dismissal means that "The public will be permitted to laugh . . . as long as the jokes are government-sanctioned."

CHAPTER V

A Night at the Opera

Thanks to Walter Ulbricht, the crossing from West Berlin into East Berlin has become one of the world's great tourist attractions. "Checkpoint Charlie," bristling with armed guards, concrete barricades, and competing East-West propaganda placards, serves as the entrance to that corrective institute known as the "GDR" (German Democratic Republic). Those who cross the border to catch the seven o'clock performance of the Komische Oper (only a few blocks beyond the Wall, on Friedrichstrasse) are treated, like all other tourists, to a desultory spectacle. While waiting for the East German bureaucratic machinery to process the passports and count the *valuta,* one can leisurely ponder the discrepancy between the communist banners, which proclaim peace, freedom, and democracy, and the goose-stepping guards whose Russian-made submachine guns are mostly pointed against their own people.

East German communism, one soon remarks, is like no other. It is regimented, efficient, and preposterously pretentious. The combination of Prussian demands for efficiency and communist proclivity for dogmatism results in an awesome product. Spade-bearded Walter Ulbricht presents one of the most ludicrous portraits of political history (his high-pitched voice and Saxon accent inexorably bring to mind the parody of a Nazi on the old Sid Caesar show). Ulbricht insists, with Teutonic fervor, that every aspect of a communist society, including art, must be amenable to rationalization. This would-be *Führer* somewhat dubiously proposes that society is con-

94

sciously able to determine how art is to reflect life. Artists are to be told exactly what to paint,* composers what to compose, and philosophers what to write. When Robert Havemann, formerly professor of physical chemistry at East Berlin's Humboldt University, courageously advanced the notion that "human beings can be told to do many things, but not what to think," he was promptly silenced and deprived of his chair.

Germany being the home of Marx, the East Germans have seen to it that their state is being fashioned into the most consciously thoroughgoing example of applied political science in Europe. (Even the Russians find the spirit unpleasantly didactic; Soviet philosophers abhor being told they are subverting Marxist strictures by some ultraorthodox East German Marxist.) When Ulbricht visits an art exhibit, he asks, "How will this show help our working class in their struggle?" It is consequently small wonder that the GDR has no daring composer, no abstract painters, and no published rebellious writers.

If the East German regime battens down the cultural hatches, it is only because the Party is almost paranoid with fear of subversion from all sectors. The Pankow government even bans certain Soviet reviews and periodicals for fear these might pervert its own communists. In music the situation is no better. A Central Song Commission has been established to popularize "socialist songs" that simultaneously promote group consciousness while undercutting so-called "decadent influences." This Commission passes judgment on new songs and controls their dissemination over the mass media. The East German "purists" are fearful of any form of musical disengagement. They distrust everything from twelve-tone music to rock, but they have nothing to put in their places. The Party organ,

---

* How do you tell a painter what to paint? I was told members of the East Berlin Painters' Union must prepare a sketch of any painting they would like to execute and submit this "draft" to an exhibit committee. If the committee approves the motif, a contract is signed and a percentage (about twenty-five per cent) of the price set on the painting is advanced to the artist. While the painting is being completed, a committee member will come by to judge whether the painting is being realistically executed according to the sketch. If it is, the painter will receive some sixty per cent of the agreed contract price, but if it isn't, the painter must return his original advance to the Union.

Neues Deutschland, with habitual and resounding Teutonic harshness attacked the admiration of certain East Germans for the Swingle Singers. Nowhere else, except in Albania, would anyone care about who listened to jazzed-up Bach, but in East Berlin a number of musicology professors and conductors signed an article early in 1967 that methodically dissected the Swingle heresy. "No true Bach interpretation should deviate from the original score," they insisted. "No invented voices should be added to a genuine Bach interpretation." In sum, they decreed, with obvious Party approval, that the revamping of classical works for the purposes of musical entertainment should be limited.

Given such a sinister cultural context, it seems odd that East Germany should have such a thriving operatic life. Why should this half-country of some seventeen million people have close to thirty-five opera houses? Somehow, unbelievably, the East Germans pretend that opera can help to produce the unified musical culture that is supposed to be a natural phenomenon in the classless society. But if opera is among the most liberal facets of East German culture, this is partially due to the residue of the postwar influence of Bertolt Brecht. It takes more than one decade, even in East Germany, to kill the experimental genius of the Berliner Ensemble. Today the outstanding theatrical performances no longer are to be seen in the Deutsches Theater, but in Felsenstein's Komische Oper —undoubtedly East Germany's finest cultural ornament.

Standing amidst the crumbling shells of buildings destroyed more than a generation ago, the new house of the Komische Oper (reopened at the cost of some twenty million East German marks in 1966) looks every inch like the showcase it aspires to be. Its glistening façade of simulated limestone clashes with the surrounding rubble much as the sparkling Lincoln Center collides with its brownstone and red-brick environment. The white-and-gold, pseudo-Baroque auditorium of the Komische Oper, with its heavy crystal chandeliers, is garishly nineteenth-century (like the Prinzregenten Theater in Munich). However, when I visited it, the musty stench of a Lysol-like disinfectant instantly overwhelmed all my other senses. Either the Germans feared an epidemic from their Western visitors, or East German operagoers have fleas; there could be no other explanation for such a massive overdose of fumigation. (The disinfectant left my larynx seared after I sat through a performance of *Don Giovanni*.) But the public just didn't look like the flea-scratching type; about half had come across the Wall for an evening's entertainment, and the rest were fat-necked East German bureaucrats and their dumpling-filled wives.

Surprisingly, even the Komische Oper's director, Walter Felsenstein (b. 1901), must come through the Wall for every performance and rehearsal he wishes to control. An Austrian by birth, Felsenstein is one of the few inhabitants of Berlin who is allowed to commute freely between his home in West Berlin's residential Dahlemdorf district and the Komische Oper in the center of East Berlin. But this is only one of the many extraordinary privileges Felsenstein enjoys as the despotic general manager of the Kollectivoper Company. He is also granted a two-and-a-half-million-dollar subsidy each year to dispense with as he sees fit. With this wad in his pocket, Felsenstein manages to ignore the inconveniences of communism, the box office, and even the twentieth century. Felsenstein, whose thin pursed lips, stern blue eyes, and autocratic mien give him the appearance of a Prussian colonel in civies, does not believe time is of the essence. Felsenstein stages an opera only when he thinks it is ready, making a première something of an impromptu occasion. No other opera company in the world could afford the lengthy and meticulous rehearsals to which Felsenstein subjects his singers. (Eight months is not unusual when Felsenstein is rehearsing a première.) In fact, he is so fanatical in demanding theatrical perfection that until 1966 he altogether rejected the well-established practice of double casting. Felsenstein simply would not tolerate the smooth surface of one of his productions being marred by the intrusion of an outsider who had not been trained with the entire cast. If a singer fell sick, the performance was canceled and the evening's program was left empty unless it could be filled with another opera. (The long illness of tenor Hans Nocker in 1963 removed three operas from the repertoire, delayed the opening of both *Così fan tutte* and *Tales of Hoffmann,* and set back the entire schedule many months.) Such a self-willed and eccentric approach would be completely unthinkable in a Western company. But the

East Germans—who admire impetuosity—are willing to tolerate Felsenstein's capriciousness for as long as Felsenstein manages to attract tourists to the only world-famous opera house that does not have world-famous singers.

Felsenstein is a drama fanatic who has worn political blinkers all his life. Born under the Hapsburg monarchy in Vienna, he was musically and artistically uncompromising from the start. When his father, a civil servant, gave him a violin of inferior quality, Felsenstein insisted on a true instrument. When Papa Felsenstein didn't give in, little Walter smashed the violin on the ground in a fit of pique. Never again did he pick up a musical instrument. Although he was graduated from the Burgtheater School in Vienna, Walter despised the stilted atmosphere of this famous theater and always sneaked out after the first act. He did the same at the Vienna Opera, whose romanticism and false convention nauseated him.* Finally, Felsenstein left Vienna altogether and spent three years as an actor in Lübeck and Mannheim. In 1927 he became *"Ober-spielleiter"* (producer of plays, operas, and ballets) at the Stadtheater in Basel, Switzerland. Then, under Hitler, he went to work as head stage manager at Cologne's Municipal Theater and during the war years as guest director at Berlin's Schiller Theater. The Nazi era past, he switched to the American Zone's Hebbel Theater before moving on to become musical director of East Berlin's Komische Oper in 1947. "My first goal as director," he said, "is to produce only works without which I would not care to live." Felsenstein's first performance in the two-thirds-destroyed Metropol Theater was Strauss's *Fledermaus,* and he quickly delighted the public with his superb dramatic staging under the most trying circumstances.

Whether it be under the Hapsburgs, Hitler, or Walter Ulbricht, Felsenstein has devoted himself to his own ideas of the theater and has tried to avoid the political realities. In fact, he has adopted the moral, self-righteous attitude toward the presentation of an opera that others assume toward political candidates. Only on rare occa-

---

* He also walked out on *La Gioconda,* after two acts, at the new Metropolitan Opera in 1967.

sions has Felsenstein ever uttered anything that might be interpreted as having political overtones. During the height of Stalin's control of the arts, Felsenstein declared: "It is extraordinary how many of the people who stand on the stage, and so many more who don't, today are familiar with realistic stage production, with critical realism, and with socialist realism. All of them think they have something to say. However, it is also shocking when people employ valid and important theses of this kind without feeling anything about the way these insights were developed or without knowing how to use them. That is why they talk of a lot of dung and do a great deal of harm." But this tastemaster has also frequently warned against "erudition becoming dry and dialectic driveling." Felsenstein is not really interested in what Marx, Lenin, Stalin, or Ulbricht thought of opera. He is guided by his own instinctive inclination to verisimilitude, the sense that what is happening on the operatic stage could be happening in real life. That this might be a naturalistic demand, in a medium that has seldom been open to naturalism, hardly concerns him. Felsenstein is annoyed that Western critics suspect this longing for verisimilitude might be ideologically motivated. It is difficult to prove Felsenstein makes neo-Marxist concessions to the East German regime. I did feel he makes the most of class differences and that his tendency is to overdo the misery of the proletariat. In the group scenes of Mozart's *Don Giovanni,* for example, there is an olive-brown-gray cast in the costumes of the hoi polloi. To me, there seemed to be a resemblance between the drabness of the East German collective farmers and that of Masetto's friends. Felsenstein contends that this is a close approximation of what domestics and peasants really looked like at the time Mozart composed the opera. To distinguish between a socialist production of a classic opera from a capitalist production seems a dubious venture. Felsenstein claims he purged *The Magic Flute* of its usual "pyramid style" because such interpretation is nothing but "hypocritical pseudo romanticism." Religion has been conveniently de-emphasized in *The Magic Flute,* he said, because "one must reject every conception whose prime purpose it is to achieve an interesting performance, without having most carefully investigated the intentions of the author and of the composer and without

99

having tried to carry these out." Felsenstein dropped the mystical ideals of freemasonry from *The Magic Flute* and translated these into the humanist ideals of fraternity, liberty, and equality, which, he said, "unite humanity." Brushing aside Mozart's own involvement with freemasonry, Felsenstein insists that the triumph of love and light are what inspired Mozart to compose *The Magic Flute*.

As a dramatic disciple of Stanislavski, Felsenstein abandoned the traditional "Germanic adaptions" of what he likes to call "music drama" (*i.e.*, opera). When he opened the Komische Oper in 1947, he said, "One thing I promise here and now: We are going to perform only that which we are able to perform as it should be performed." Immediately, it is asked: Is there any absolute standard by which to judge how a work "should be performed"? Yes, answers Felsenstein. "One should attempt to raise the most valuable works of the classical musical theater to the interpretative level of their original creation." And he will go back to Ottavio Rinuccini and Jacopo Peri (the two Florentines who developed the operatic medium in the sixteenth century) to justify his theory of opera as heightened drama.

Only after Felsenstein has thoroughly researched the original text does he go about reconstituting a model for each scene as he believes it should have been performed. When he has finished with all the parts, he tries to put the whole opera into perspective during the rehearsals and to unify the scenes. In this process, the music assumes only situational relevance; for Felsenstein, it is only one of the multiple dramatic manifestations on stage. This is one of the reasons why Felsenstein rejects Wagner and his conception of opera as a *"Gesamtkunstwerk"* (a unity of creation). Wagner actualizes the dramatic power of his operas almost entirely in the music—leaving very little for gesture, movement, expression, or even speech. (Theatrically, Wagnerian opera results in unbelievable tedium. Tristan's tortured, hour-long death in the third act of *Tristan and Isolde* would be unbearable without Wagner's music.) Likewise, Wagner's habit of musically anticipating actions by the use of leitmotifs is anathema to Felsenstein, who wants the music only to intensify or elaborate what is happening on stage at any particular moment. Sad music must be sung by a sad person, says Felsenstein,

and his sadness must be accompanied by other dramatic manifestations of this mood—ranging from handkerchiefs to dimmer, bluer
lights. Instead of sweeping the audience away in thunderbursts of
emotion, as Wagner aspired to do, Felsenstein tries to appeal to the
understanding as well as to the feelings of the public. The individual in the audience cannot be content with emotion; he must
confront the dramatic situation in which it appears. In other words,
instead of being a captive to the musical sweep of the opera, the
individual must also think along with the play. Felsenstein claims it
is the director's duty to make "the visible become music and the
audible become action." The music must always have accompanying dramatic significance, and the action should always be as carefully conducted as the music. One of Felsenstein's greatest problems
is to co-ordinate the flow of the music with the flow of the operatic
action. When a singer commences an aria, the public should not
sense that the action is being abruptly halted and a lyric moment
thrust awkwardly into the course of the opera. Neither should the
public feel that the dramatic sections of an opera are meaningless
connectives for the music. Felsenstein's goal is for the actor of his
"Musiktheater" to create the impression "he cannot give vent to his
feelings in any other way than through music." Felsenstein's idea of
approaching opera by way of drama is his personal resolution to the
question of the unity of music and action in opera. All too frequently in the mid-twentieth century the director's penchant has
been to concentrate on the music and to emasculate the drama by
converting opera into a spectacle with plush scenery, dazzling
costumes, and exaggerated choreography. But one of Felsenstein's
many compulsions is to go against the trend of the times.

Felsenstein scorns operatic prima donnas, nor is he willing to pay
for top talent. The result is that he is engaged in a relentless struggle between the theatrical ideal and the vocally possible. Felsenstein's endeavor is to create real people on stage who can act and
sing with genuine expressiveness. For example, Felsenstein cautions
Pamina in *The Magic Flute:* You may imagine that you hate
Sarastro, "but that is not the point. You must REALLY HATE him," he
yelled. "Sarastro should not be the conception of your fantasy, but a
reality you have lived with."

101

Those interpreters who only concentrate on their vocal cords Felsenstein brands as "vocal imbeciles." He says, "Potbellied lovers and corpulent heroines can no longer enthrall the public." The trouble is that most outstanding singers are not good actors—it is overly demanding to concentrate on both a high note and a real embrace. Because the most common and the most justified complaint against the Komische Oper has been the mediocrity of the voices, Felsenstein has primed his demanding repertoire with singers from nine different countries. Nevertheless, basic difficulties remain. Felsenstein so overrehearses his singers that, in my opinion, they tend to become somewhat robotlike in their so-called "expressive movements." "Emotion on stage should originate from a *Lebenslust* (a lust for life), from true emotion," says Felsenstein. But his characterizations tend to be on the hammy side. In *The Magic Flute* he presents the Queen of Night as a demonic, icy, calculating bitch— the incarnation of the hysterical female. Her role is consequently overplayed. But this is Felsenstein's way of emphasizing his belief that Mozart created more than enthralling melodies, that he created real characters with intense and complex feelings.

Felsenstein has said the public wants to believe the story they are being told. "The plot presented to them must be plausible . . . the most beautiful chords, the most subtle harmonies, the most seductive melodies can no longer delude the audience about the incredibility of the action." If Felsenstein can be accused of preferring the letter of the dramatic action to the spirit, it must also be admitted he has removed a multitude of operatic clichés from the stage. The old bromides long ago lost their dramatic value and have degenerated into mere stage gallantry. At the Komische Oper, each singer is integrated into the single-minded movement. Felsenstein does not permit the singer's vanity to seduce him into playing to the gallery. In sum, Felsenstein has transformed the snobbish wet rags of the operatic stage into competent actors and he has stripped them of their coquetry.

Felsenstein tends to be conservative in his choice of operas. But his assistants staged such seldom-heard works as Paisiello's *The Barber of Seville* (a Baroque predecessor of the well-known Rossini opera), Carl Orff's *Die Kluge* (The Wise Woman), Arthur Kusterer's *Was ihr Wollt* (As You Like It), Robert Kurka's *The Brave Soldier Schweik,* Carl Zeller's *The Bird Dealer,* Albert Lortzing's *The Czar and the Carpenter,* and Ermanno Wolf-Ferrari's *The Curious Women.* Since the Opera House opened in 1947, Felsenstein has personally staged only nine productions. The most famous of these have been his *Magic Flute, Carmen, The Cunning Little Fox, Don Giovanni,* and *The Tales of Hoffmann.* There is a good measure of Teutonic pedantry in the way Felsenstein has rewritten and researched the librettos for all of these productions. Susan Sontag has noted that "the modern style of interpretation excavates and, as it excavates, destroys; it digs 'behind' the text to find a subtext that is the true one." It is against this type of interpretation that Felsenstein fights. He considers opera too often interpreted at the expense of being carefully researched or even read; before imagining a subtext it is essential to study the text.

Because no authentic version of *The Tales of Hoffmann* existed (it had been destroyed in a fire at Paris's Opéra Comique), Felsenstein was led by long investigations in the French archives to conclude that "the tales" had been written as a "series of musical numbers with long dialogues in between." Felsenstein saw the puppet Olympia, the courtesan Giulietta, and the singer Antonia as three sides of Hoffmann's "muse," Stella. So one actress plays all the roles. The logical result of this conclusion was for Felsenstein to rewrite the text, to expurgate the recitatives, and to revert to Offenbach's original duets, arias, and ensembles. With fanatic ruthlessness, he combined portions of the original Jules Barbier–Michel Carré play with Offenbach's unfinished score and interspersed an aria from Offenbach's *Maître Peronilla* into the Olympia act. Felsenstein, already conscious that this extraordinarily individualistic production had been nicknamed "The Tales of Felsenstein," expressed regrets in his program notes that he had cut out the usual introductory chorus, but claimed this was necessary to the interests of cohesion. However one might object to such musical anacrostics, "The Tales of Felsenstein" were highly popular. Olympia performed like a true automaton; nothing about her seemed human. The production truly captured the phantasmagorical, somewhat maniacal character of E. T. A. Hoffmann's tale. When in the last act

103

Coppelius in a vengeful moment tears off Olympia's head, the bolts and springs pop out of her neck. The effect is deeply shocking to a public who has heard her sing a few moments previously.

Another of his more remarkable productions was Janacek's *The Cunning Little Fox,* an opera so fragile that it is rarely attempted in the West. Basically, the plot is an inconsequential assembly of scenes that Felsenstein has managed to integrate into an opera. Approaching the production entirely by way of the text, Felsenstein managed to re-create the primeval, sylvan atmosphere of the forest. Leos Janacek (1854–1928), who wrote the work when he was seventy, took many of his characters from La Fontaine's *Fables,* but the ability to present these animals convincingly on stage had eluded every director. Felsenstein succeeded because he made a precise, almost zoological study of animal characteristics. Eventually, Felsenstein's forest really was populated by little human beasts. The fox's cunning, revealed in her preference for the freedom of the woods to the embrace of the tame, overcivilized life promised her by the romantic forester, is convincing. At the end of this carefully costumed production one believes the little vixen really prefers her own kind. Felsenstein triumphantly approximated a synthesis of nature and art. Refusing to create an esoteric experience for a few musical connoisseurs with a special store of knowledge, he sought a much wider public. Not that Felsenstein would turn down the chance to select his audience if he could. The Komische Oper director even disclosed in one of his more uncompromising moments that he did not want to let anyone into his theater who was not capable of being naïve. However, even his regimented mind could not find the way to bar the ultrasophisticated who might pretend to naïveté.

Doctrinarily, Felsenstein approaches every opera by way of the text. Like his acknowledged precursors, Brecht and Stanislavski, Felsenstein believes the "event" is the key to singing, acting, and directing. Only if the director minutely examines and truly grasps the role of the central "event" can he block the action. This single-minded concentration also serves to steer the director clear of such pitfalls as letting the opera be engulfed by secondary sequences. The libretto of *Don Giovanni,* which Felsenstein regards as "a faultless, unplayable" masterpiece, is not seen as the skeleton of the opera, but as a matrix out of which innumerable interpretations can be drawn. After studying the libretto's descent from Tirso through Molière, Goldoni, Bertati, and Da Ponte, Felsenstein decided the "key event" in the opera is Donna Anna's relationship to Don Giovanni. Donna Anna is promoted from her usually secondary role and turned into the focal point of Giovanni's downfall. For Felsenstein, the clue rested in her very first words: "Till you show me who you are, sir, I shall never let you go." (Giovanni had come to her masked and, after imposing his impersonal lust, left without revealing his identity.) Donna Anna is therefore portrayed as the antithesis of Giovanni in her insistence on faithfulness and morality. To emphasize this contrast, Giovanni himself is no longer a swaggering hero, a demigod, but has been retouched by Felsenstein into a depraved, wretched woman-chaser whose neurosis has overwhelmed him. Felsenstein's Giovanni, to be sure, is a believable villain, whose "hang-up" rather convincingly is his infatuation with his own seductive powers. But this new Giovanni has entirely shed his traditional Casanovian romanticism. In keeping with this new character casting, Giovanni's servant, Leporello, is transformed by Felsenstein into a timid servant who remains in his master's clutches solely on account of the ducats. Donna Elvira is presented as a somewhat gauche and melodramatic bourgeoise whose libido thirsts insatiably after Giovanni. Those many Giovanni fans who are accustomed to the more traditional interpretation of the opera may find this performance a travesty; and, indeed, it becomes painful to see the transmogrification of this superman, who defied the gods themselves, into a rather insecure neurotic.

In his usual, ruthless manner, Felsenstein has resolved the inner contradiction of this *opera buffa in due atti*" (as Mozart and Da Ponte titled this masterpiece). Felsenstein opts for the serious, moralistic, nonromantic course and plays down the comic character of Leporello, Masetto, and Zerlina. *Don Giovanni* becomes far more tragic than one can conceive Mozart of having wished it to be. Only a monomaniac like Felsentein could ignore the conventions of the traditional *opera buffa* of Mozart's period and persist in over-emphasizing the tragic trappings. The *buffa* duet (*"Per queste due*

105

manine"—Leporello and Zerlina) Mozart tacked on to the end of the opera is an indication he himself wished it to conclude on a blithe note.

In keeping with this heavy atmosphere (and the gray and olive-drab costumes) the sets of *Don Giovanni* are structured around cumbrous Renaissance oak beams. Felsenstein is against "abstraction" in stage design and says that "the viewer must always know where something is being played." Too often, he maintains, the modern avant-garde stylizations distract the public through attempts at "originality." While scenes of *Don Giovanni* are skillfully changed by moving various balconies, columns, and furnishings in and out, the heavy beams remain in place, casting a depressingly dark mood over even the lighter outdoor scenes. To my mind, a courtyard or a cemetery confined by oak beams is unbelievable.

As in his other productions, Felsenstein was particularly intent that the action of *Don Giovanni* be wholly comprehensible to the audience at all times. To this end, he worked on the standard German translation for months to ensure that all ambiguities were expurgated from the text, even if this meant sacrificing traditional verse. Felsenstein also spent weeks working out ingenious connectives that would hold the action together. For instance, in the finale, he leaves a charred table in the middle of the stage with Donna Anna, Octavio, and Donna Elvira, as the last remainder of the conflagration that had engulfed Don Giovanni and his house. During one of Don Giovanni's arias (as he is drinking wine) there are a number of flashbacks enacted on a balcony in the rear, first of a ball and then of a man assaulting different women. This sacrilegious intrusion, which entirely confuses the brilliant euphoria of Mozart's music, is supposed to clue the audience in on what might be passing through Giovanni's mind (or what Felsenstein thinks ought to have passed through Don Giovanni's mind) at that moment. However, this was one of Felsenstein's many interpretative tricks I failed to understand at the time of the action. No wonder that after four months of steady rehearsals, fourteen hours per day, sometimes seven days a week, Felsenstein still felt his *Don Giovanni* was not ready for the public.

While the changed emphasis of the *Don Giovanni* production

may have suited the Ulbricht regime, art in the Komische Oper transcends the not so comic opera that East Germany remains today. It is quite impossible to prove that politics have corrupted Felsenstein's outlook on *Don Giovanni*—even if the most was made of the ball scene at the end of Act I, where the proles waltz, the bourgeoisie does a *contredanse,* and the aristocracy minuets. However, it is not without significance that, while in the West producers will take Hamlet and make a modern farce out of it, in East Germany Felsenstein tries to submerge man's most vibrant music with rationality and psychologism. It is revealing for a producer to attempt to fashion a sociotragedy out of a semicomedy.

The facts are that Felsenstein is very much of a dramatic moralist and that the East German regime gives him a free hand to restructure operas as he will. Curiously, Felsenstein has little appreciation of such honors as the East Germans bestow on him (*e.g.,* the East German National Prize and the East Berlin Goethe Prize). He is far too knowledgeable of the vicissitudes of the arts to fall for this type of propaganda. Instead, he esteems the less-biased critical reviews and commentary in the Western press. (By and large, he is praised for his audacity, his unorthodox insights, and his deep comprehension of drama.) Felsenstein's propaganda worth to Ulbricht is to demonstrate to the outside world the high cultivation of the arts in East Germany. This is window dressing. As Ulbricht's cultural drawing card, the Komische Oper is regarded as a sound investment, despite its exorbitant cost, but it would seem doubtful this anomalous status will be prolonged into the nineteen-seventies. When Ulbricht passes from the scene and the arts in East Germany are liberalized, the pressure for a "show piece," such as this opera, will vanish. Despite this continuing rear-guard action, this era of cold-war cultural extravaganzas is now rapidly drawing to a close.

CHAPTER VI

"Lavdi Marksismi Leninismit!"

The best way to appreciate the extent to which controls in Czecho-slovakia, Hungary, Poland, and even the Soviet Union have been relaxed since Stalin's death is to glance at Albanian "culture" in 1968. While the rest of Eastern Europe has carried out a program to cast off the more nightmarish aspects of the "cult of personality," in Albania Stalinist norms are preserved in their maiden form, as if in a Madame Tussaud's on a national scale. Albania, a minicountry of some 1.8 million people living in a mountainous Adriatic enclave, remains Big Brother land. Five-year plans, a vigilant secret police, and a tight party dictatorship are prominent features of the land-scape. Bronze colossi, vaguely resembling the mustached Dzhugash-vili, can still be seen in all major Albanian cities (*i.e.,* towns). To the Russians, this post-mortem faith smacks of ludicrous heresy. In his political poem, "Stalin's Heirs," published following the Twenty-second Party Congress, poet Yevtushenko wrote: ". . . I fancy, there is a telephone in that coffin: / Stalin instructs Enver Hoxha." But the Albanians are no supernaturalists. Their Red line is not hooked up to the Kremlin but to Peking. Party Chief Enver Hoxha (b. 1908), who founded his country's Communist Party and has been its top leader since 1941, is ever on the prowl against the infiltration of Soviet heresy. "Cosmopolitanism is alien to Marxism-Leninism," he shouts hoarsely at Party rallies. And in the summer of 1967, Hoxha cautioned would-be Albanian intellectuals that "Calluses on the hands are an invincible barrier to revisionism."

This is a most fitting reminder of the simple-minded absurdity to which Albanian communism has plunged.

Hoxha's watchfulness has not exactly spurred the arts in the capital of Tirana. In the recently completed pink-and-white Palace of Culture, naturally built in the Stalinist tradition, one can see touching ballets about the unrequited love of a sexy bricklayer for the local bulldozer driver. One can hear poetic monologues on stage of "How Khrushchev unfurled the banner of discord and betrayal." Ballads are sung by "enthusiastic" school children to celebrate the arrival of new seed potatoes from Red China. And for those who still don't know how to applaud a speech, the text is marked with such appropriate hints as: "Applause . . . Prolonged applause . . . Tumultuous applause . . . Ovation . . . Rousing cheers . . . All rise!" No effort is spared to maintain the "crystal clarity" of Albanian culture. Even Hoxha's wife, Nexhmije (whose name is genuine onomatopoesy), contributes by attacking the parasitic, opportunistic tendencies of Albanian youth. "The danger of foreign influences through radio, television, movies, literature is under-estimated," she noted recently. As a former Partisan heroine, Nexh-mije warned the people not to underrate the danger of copying anything from the outside that might be new and that would there-fore be "foreign to our ideology and our national traditions." Nexhmije, whose ascendency curiously paralleled the rise of Mao's own wife, regretted that Communist Albania no longer provided those "special sacrifices" that fired and tempered the elder genera-tion. Albanian youth, she proclaimed, was in danger of decadence because of the current "alienation of schoolwork and education from life."

Few outsiders understand why Albanian novels are almost always directed against the bloodsuckers of the working class, or why Albanian writers must keep on spouting invectives and venom at the "war-mongering, imperialist boa constrictor." The explanation is fairly simple. Hoxha, who is an unrepentant Stalinist, would probably lose his head as well as his historical role should any new dictator or "revisionist collective" come to power. He therefore makes certain that anyone who doesn't follow his policy in Albania is promptly liquidated. While this black-and-white hypothesis may sound simplistic, so are politics in Albania. (However, conditions really were not much better in the golden era of King Zog.) Hoxha feels that while he has continued on the correct internationalist path of Lenin and Stalin, all the other parties but the Chinese have sold out to revisionism. When he was invited by the "Moscow renegades" to attend the fiftieth anniversary of the Bolshevik revolution, Hoxha said: "Our party has rejected with contempt this dirty invitation of the Soviet revisionists. We are going to celebrate the great October revolution in our fatherland in the midst of happiness."

Hoxha's deputy and Anabaptist henchman, Mehmet Shehu, boasts that, after putting in a revolutionary ninety-hour week, he is translating Victor Hugo's *Les Miserables* into Albanian. One can picture this Balkan Balzac drinking cups of powerful Albanian coffee at four in the morning while perusing his French-Albanian dictionary. Translator Shehu claims, "Our party has become a shock brigade." His motto is: "What the people want, the Party does; what the Party says, the people do." In consequence of this democratic routine, Shehu purports the proletarian dictatorship has been continuously strengthened. "Our socialist democracy for the broad masses has been developed, deepened, and perfected with each passing day; our fatherland's defensive might has been increased and has become invincible." Shehu and Hoxha may seem like a good comedy team to Americans, but the nerve endings of East Europeans are still too raw to appreciate such macabre humor.

To Albanians, what is happening to the arts from Prague to Moscow is nothing but decaying revisionism. Albanian leaders reiterate that the other communist parties are using art as a tool of ideological diversion away from the class struggle. To this end, Hoxha and Shehu shout that the revisionists have "opened the doors wide to decadent art and to mystic and bourgeois ideology." One Party stalwart, writing in the revue *New Albania,* said Albanian artists and writers discard "with disdain" all those theories according to which they should be "free, aloof from politics, above classes, and nonaligned." "In Albania," continued this ideologist, "every writer is free to choose the themes he wants to treat in his work, to militate against the negative aspects of the past as well as

110

those which still survive in society, to exalt what is positive and progressive in life—laying special emphasis on the high virtues of the vanguard men and women." The result is the creation of pure socialist-realist prose, such as the following short gem, written in the mid-sixties:

OUR TRACTOR DRIVER!

This was a very dry summer. The earth had cracked and seemed to be complaining to every passer-by of this. It was midday and the sun's rays fell obliquely on the "Maja e Gjate" [collective] hillside covered with vineyards and olive groves. . . . A large assembly of young volunteers coming from work centers of the city alight from buses down at the foot of the hill and betake themselves to the hilltops. They start watering the trees with unparalleled enthusiasm. New life is brought to the young trees which were on the point of fading away.

Agim, the tractor driver, hauls the water up in his "Zetor" tractor. Although it is hard work driving his tractor up and down, he seems not to mind at all. He drives his tractor carefully up the road, towing barrels of water. The volunteers admire the tractor driver for his perseverance, for his good conduct and cheerful temper. Every time he arrives, they greet him, crying out, "Here comes the mountain eagle!"

Agim has to work harder today for more volunteers have come to help than expected. The suggestion was made that another tractor be brought from other sectors to help the work of irrigation. Agim heard of this and said to the man in charge:

"I hear that you intend to bring another tractor to help me. This is not a good idea. All the other tractors are busy working in other sectors; therefore, I will try to do this work all by myself. Please don't bring any other tractor. . . ." And he started driving his tractor.

Those present looked at him with a feeling of admiration. The man in charge smiled and, turning to those present, said:

"What a wonderful fellow. No job is too hard for him. This is not the first time he has volunteered to do extra work."

The volunteers were admiring him for his speed at work and his good qualities. Every time he was coming up they used to shout: "Here is the mountain eagle!"

The tractor driver came up again. He unloaded the barrels of water and loaded the empty ones and then drove down again. The road was rough. All at once the brakes on his tractor failed him. The tractor ran down with accelerated speed. The man wielded his steering wheel with his tight grip.

His very life was at stake. The volunteers shouted to him to jump off his seat and save his life. He wavered at first but then came to himself again and stuck to his steering wheel. He steered his tractor looking for some safe nook, for if it toppled over it would be ruined.

Olive branches scratched his face. His flushing and perspiring features were covered with white dust, making him look like a man aged before his time. He came to a sharp turn of the road. The back wheel of the tractor slipped away. It looked as though the whole body of the tractor was toppling over, but he skillfully wielded the steering wheel and got the tractor safe. He felt somewhat relieved when he had passed the corner. Sweat ran down his face and eyelids. He brought his tractor to a stop. He set to work to repair the defect.

Somewhat later the batch of volunteers who had watched all of his gigantic efforts came to him. They embraced and raised him up in their arms.

A man approached him and said: "Agim, why did you endanger your life, and why did you not jump off the tractor?"

Agim smiled and replied, "How could I leave it! This was our tractor." His eyes sparkled with joy. Not very long after this the "Zetor" was again towing the barrels of water for irrigation.

"Our Tractor Driver!" typifies the verbal sludge that used to be smeared over the pages of countless magazines and newspapers throughout the communist states in the years 1949–1953. The romance between the driver and his tractor, the emphasis placed on overtime and Stakhanovite labors, the role of the willing "volunteers"—all come from an era that is happily past everywhere but in Albania and Red China. The ties between these two disparate states are based on Peking's extension of aid to Tirana and the mutual suspicion of both parties of Soviet "revisionists." So close were the bonds in the mid-sixties that Albania appeared to be on the threshold of a Chinese-style cultural purge in the summer of 1966. Mehmet Shehu delivered blistering attacks on writers whose ideas about physical work were created in their offices and painters who were afraid of walking on unpaved roads. The official Tirana daily, *Zeri i Popullit*, picked up the ball with exceptionally harsh assaults on young writers who had "fallen prey to bourgeois and revisionist literary currents" and who were trying to destroy the hero image of the Albanian worker. Some forty artists and intellectuals were dispatched to the country in order to be "closer to the masses." Simultaneously, Chinese-style wall-posters appeared on prominent billboards in Tirana. Chinese movies began to be shown in the local theaters,* and in July 1967, the Chinese Red Guard sent over visitors to Albania in order to help the Shqiperi (as the Albanians call themselves) preserve the cultural purity of their revolution. The Albanian leadership seemed quite pleased with this course of events. The "revisionist blockade" in the fields of culture, education, and science only served to prevent any crumbling of the "monolithic" unity of the Party. Hoxha had no intention of establishing closer relations, even in the arts, with any of the other Eastern European regimes. In fact, he supported a Stalinist Polish government-in-exile in Tirana. On the other hand, Hoxha also wished to prevent the Albanian cultural revolution from getting out of hand. Hoxha's harshest measures were taken against the church. *Zeri i Popullit* announced in 1967 that "As a result of the sharp class struggle initiated by the youth against everything foreign to the Party's culture and ideology, and with the full support of the population, religion was forced to turn over to the young people 2,169 churches, mosques, monasteries and other religious institutions." Purportedly, these religious buildings were being turned into cultural centers for the Albanian youth.

Literature suffered most from the new, Chinese-influenced cultural line. (The little red book of Hoxha's thoughts became a Tirana best seller.) A prominent writer, Razi Brahimi (b. 1931), was one of the exemplary victims of the cultural purge. Brahimi had started his literary career at the age of nineteen by writing prose and literary criticism. For a time he worked on the editorial board of the weekly organ of the League of Writers and Artists and then was promoted to editor-in-chief of the Naim Frasheri publishing house. It was in that capacity that he published a short story, "Those Hands," which showed that, as far as the cultural revolution was concerned, Brahimi was definitely not with it. The story starts as a

---

* One curious visitor, actor Peter Ustinov, reported that Chinese toothpaste, combs, writing pads, cosmetics, and shopping bags were available in the hinterlands.

shy university student, Hekuran, meets the girl of his dreams, Lili, but he is so flustered that for many months he cannot even talk to her. Finally, she makes the first move, and shortly thereafter they have a proletarian rendezvous in his bedroom.

"Since you like it let us sit here!" and she dropped carelessly on the bed. Hekuran closed the door and sat to her left.

It was the first time they were alone in a room and so close to each other. He felt the warmth of her body whereas his arm, which he had pulled as near to his body as he could, touched the forepart of her shoulder and her taut and compact breast.

"Shall we begin?" he asked lest his emotions betray him.

"Let us begin!" she answered.

He took up Engels' book on *The Origin of the Family* . . . and turned the pages to find the chapter on classes.

"Wait a moment," and she snatched the book from his hands. "Congratulations! You read Russian. A lucky fellow! I, to tell the truth, have no patience to learn this language; it seems hard. . . ."

"It is not too easy but it can be learned."

"It may be so, but I lack patience. . . . Why, if that is not Engels!" She was surprised at seeing the portrait of Engels. "What a large beard he had! A real scientist! . . . But why did he have such a large beard?"

Hekuran was both amused and angry at her conduct and the naïve questions she asked. She gave him the impression of a spoiled child who never goes deep into things but finds her greatest satisfaction in the color and shape of the playthings that Father has brought with him from the market.

"Well, it is not the beard that counts, it is the work."

"Yes, that is true. But . . ." and she made a half-turn toward Hekuran. "I wanted to ask you a question but I want you not to take it amiss and to answer it frankly."

"I will not take it amiss and I will answer it frankly," repeated Hekuran, trying to give it the tone of a vow.

"Well then, the question is this: Do you like classes?"

They were so close together that they felt the warmth of each other's breathing. They looked at each other eye to eye.

"I do not understand you. . . ."

"Really? You do not understand me?" the girl wondered. "Why, the question is very plain. Are you or are you not fond of classes?"

"Well, I do not know what to say, for, after all, it does not matter

114

whether I like them or not, inasmuch as they have historically existed and still exist today. Naturally, the day will come when they will cease to exist. . . . This too, will occur regardless of the subjective wishes of people. . . ."

"That is exactly where I wanted to come to: They will cease to exist, but in what way? Let us suppose, for instance, that I am a bourgeoise whereas you are a proletarian. Which one of us will cease to exist?"

"Neither the one nor the other of us two may cease to exist, but the classes will eventually go. . . ."

"What about the bourgeoisie?"

"Some will die off, some have already been proletarized and now are gradually being transformed into simple workers who live by the sweat of their brows like everybody else. . . . Let us suppose your father has been a capitalist."

"Yes, that is true."

"In the beginning he was expropriated, is that not so?"

"Yes."

"After a certain period of time during which he got used to the new climate, so to speak, he now lives like all the rest—utilizing not the labor of others but that of his own, while you attend the courses of study at the University and are considered a transformed bourgeoise. Do you understand me?"

"Perfectly. But you, as a proletarian, what attitude will you adopt toward me?"

"If you like me, I like you. If you do not care about me, I do not care about you either," Hekuran took heart to say, pleased that the conversation proceeded on that line.

"You seem to be well versed in Marxism." She laughed and added, "This is what I did not have clear in my mind. Did you have anything else to tell me?" And although she tried to utter these last words in an unconcerned sort of way, yet she blushed.

Hekuran looked at the books he had opened and the lessons he had got from them ruefully and was at a loss as to what to do next. He was at times at the point of speaking, but his tongue was tied. The thousand and one words that whirled in his brain but a little while ago seemed to have fled from him and had left him helpless before that proud girl, who looked straight in the black of his eyes in a hypnotizing way. He found no place to hide his large sinewy hands, which embarrassed him every time he found himself humiliated. . . . He feared lest something out of the ordinary would happen if those large rough hands touched the brittle arm of

115

the girl with black eyes, which she constantly kept half shut, as if in ecstasy.

"In other words, you have nothing else to say to me?" and Lili rose to her feet, straightened the end of her skirt and combed her hair and said:

"Shall we adjourn?"

Hekuran came out with her, blaming himself that he had had no courage to tell her:

"I love you."

With such a heretical approach to Marx and Engels, it is small wonder Brahimi was soon sacked from his job. In the summer of 1966, he was relegated "to work in the fields" for publishing a book by Dhimiter Xhuvani called *The Tunnel*. This novel, which described in the bleakest terms the disregard for human life in the construction of a nine-thousand-foot railroad tunnel, was attacked by *Zeri i Popullit* as "an entirely negative work, with serious political-ideological distortions which are a reflection of the influence of foreign esthetic bourgeois-revisionist concepts." What upset the Albanian Party was that the novel, which proceeded in realistic fashion to describe the actual conditions on a working site, did not set out from "healthy ideological positions." Both publisher Brahimi and author Xhuvani were accused of having lacked class vigilance and of failing to examine the topic "from the political point of view." What Brahimi had, in fact, done was to expose to the world the true conditions of Albanian workers—an unforgivable sin.

One should not realistically expect that such a small country as Albania, which was eighty per cent illiterate before the war, could produce a meaningful contribution to world culture. Today, Albania's only fascination rests on its anomalous status as a negative cultural phenomenon. However, the Albanians view their own progress quite differently. "The path Albanian literature has beaten from liberation to this day," outlines one Tirana anthology, "has been one of uninterrupted progress, along which it attained considerable success." The Albanians proudly claim that, while before the war the number of people who engaged in the fine arts could be counted on one hand, "after the liberation the ranks of the gifted artists have been swollen and they have turned out works of

116

art characterized by lofty ideals." It is purported by Albanians that in their literature "social clashes are described in the bitterest terms," and that "truth is the other important motto of contemporary Albanian men of letters." Calluses, not truth, would appear to be the litmus test of contemporary Albanian culture. Most creative energies in Albania now seem to go into the composition of socialist-realist doggerel. One of the finer examples of this wretchedly servile composition is the following hymn:

PARTY MINE, O STAR, O LIGHT
Comrades, I propose a song.
To the country we belong,
For the changes it has made,
Changes that are well displayed.
All these twenty-five last years,
Years of freedom, years of cheers;
To the Party that was born
Twenty-five summers this morn.
What a blessing for our land
To be under the command
Of the Party that is guided
By Enver Hoxha, far-sighted!
Party mine, O star, O light,
All your foes you have defied,
You have never been afraid,
You have never been dismayed
By the traps they laid for you,
By the hardships you passed through.
I shall sing a song most hearty
To Enver and to the Party!

Appropriately, this song is always closed with cheers of *"Lavdi Hoxha!"* (Glory to Hoxha!) and, inevitably, *"Lavdi Marksismi Leninismit!"* Such is the course of culture in the *Alice-in-Wonderland* that is Albania today.

CHAPTER VII

Unsocialist Expressionism

Contemporary Polish painting can best be understood as escapism from the barren struggle for existence that marks socialist Poland in the mid-sixties. Walk down Warsaw's main boulevard, the Nowy Swiat, and the colors are ashen. The Warsavian workers are all bundled up in somber blue, black, gray, umber woolens with patches of lamb and fox here and there; the windows are covered with gray, grimy frost; the pavements, the houses, the cars, and the sky are only mutations of the dark, pastel shades of the winter garments. Then to enter one of the minor art galleries and see Kenneth Noland-like primary colors splashing, sparkling on clean white canvases is to break through the color barrier into a new world; the artist's aspiration to transpose himself to the brighter artistic and economic scene of New York or London truly jars. One intuitively senses that whoever the painter may be, he has become an expatriate in his native land. His canvases have the reality of a Disneyland—a grown artist's exercise in wish fulfillment. One feels the painter lives in a separate and isolated unit that is as tied to Western culture as the Polish Catholic Church is tied to the Vatican. However, despite the artist's faith in it, the West—where both financial stability and public recognition lie—hardly bothers to extend its blessings.

The Polish artist is alone with his dreams and his colors. Not that this predicament is so dramatically different from that of other painters all over the world. The Polish painter, like any other, must find a personal as well as a commercial identity. Some artists choose an intellectual approach to art, others an emotional approach, and by far the largest category of Poles seek the most remunerative path. Critics of Polish art are justifiably dismayed by the degree to which Polish painting, like Polish ham, represents an export item. This is because no paintings are sold to other communist states (most are even banned in the Soviet Union) and only a few Polish museums can afford to buy a representational selection of the works of leading artists. Wincenty Sliwinski (b. 1926) offers an extreme example, perhaps, of a Polish painter who opted for cash. After exhibiting his abstract works on the restored red-brick ramparts of the reconstructed Old Town of Warsaw for three successive summers, he decided he had had enough. The Western girls found him attractive as a man, but few capitalists paid any serious attention to his canvases. So he decided to mass-produce "new" works by Chagall, Utrillo, Renoir, Cézanne, and Modigliani. To add an air of authenticity to his efforts, he made a rubber stamp of the swastika and imperial German eagle inscribed with *"Geheime Staatspolizei."* Even Sliwinski was surprised to find how easy it was to convince gullible visitors from Texas, as well as more sophisticated ones from Switzerland, that his paintings had been stolen from French state museums during World War II. After an American tourist had been caught trying to smuggle a couple of phony Chagalls out of Poland, the police raided Sliwinski's studio and found one hundred and thirty new masterpieces, some five thousand dollars in cash, and a check for twenty-seven hundred dollars drawn on a Swiss bank. His trial, which ended with an eight months' sentence for the possession of foreign currency—a much more serious offense in Poland than the forgery of paintings—added some color to the other trials that have embarrassed the regime during the middle sixties. "After the milk, meat, herring, and leather scandals that have plagued us, this is a welcome change," commented one cynical Polish art critic.

Sliwinski was motivated not only by greed but also by sheer economic necessity. There is not a single private buyer in Poland who has a large collection of paintings. This means almost no painter in Poland lives from his oils alone. Some must teach, others are curators and restorers, while still others illustrate book or record jackets, design Christmas cards, work as decorators or industrial designers, and serve as artistic consultants for those state-operated enterprises concerned with their public image.* Some "progressive" state firms do buy figurative paintings to decorate offices and dining rooms, because the directors, many of whom are relatively uneducated, feel obliged to show their sympathy with culture.

However, conditions are such that even the leading artists seldom expect to sell anything in the few domestic art galleries. For their bread and butter they depend on a socialist state trading company, Desa, established some six years ago to export furniture, souvenirs, rugs, sculptures, and paintings to the West in return for hard currency. This curious enterprise, which suffers from most of the sins of bureaucratic state apparatuses, has a narrow, bourgeois attitude toward Polish art. Most of Desa's turnover, explained its heavy-set director, Leon Przywarski, comes from selling "rolled paintings" to Austrian and American firms. These paintings, depicting horses being whipped on in the snow while the troika is being chased by wolves, or undressed girls from the harem of an unsocialist *Thousand and One Nights,* are sold at bulk rates amounting to about ten dollars apiece. Przywarski explained that they are intended for those people in the West who "want to have a real oil painting in their home." On Fifth Avenue, these very oils, properly framed, sell for a hundred dollars and more in the not-so-fine stores. Przywarski, who had no paintings in his own office and confessed that he had little sympathy with what he sold, explained that prestige-class paintings are chosen by four "artistic consultants"

* The salaries here will average about five thousand zlotys per month or somewhere around twice the national average—this is a tricky sum to convert into a relevant figure because there are five different rates of exchange in Poland: The official world rate of exchange is a totally unrealistic four zlotys to the dollars. The tourist rate of exchange is twenty-four zlotys to the dollar, but, to encourage tourists to convert more dollars, they are given an additional fifteen zlotys to the dollar in scrip, in effect raising the rate to forty zlotys to the dollar. Then, Poles who receive money from their relatives abroad get seventy-two zlotys for their special dollars, while the shady characters who peddle zlotys in front of every ORBIS hotel offer anywhere up to a hundred zlotys to the dollar. These complications serve as a testimonial to the state of the Polish economy.

headed by art critic Ryszard Stanislawski. The commission chooses a few hundred works every year selected from the stock of leading artists. These paintings are then exported for exhibitions and ultimate sale. In 1966, exhibits of seventeen Polish painters were shown at the D'Arcy Galleries in New York, some twenty-six Polish artists were touring Germany, and thirty-five Polish artists were shown in a representative group exhibit in Israel. While Desa charges the painters no commission, the most a painter can get in dollars is half of the price fixed by Desa. The remainder the artist must take in zlotys so that the state can use the hard-earned dollars, D-marks, and francs to buy technical equipment, such as computers, from the West. Tadeusz Brzozowski, Tadeusz Kantor, and Kazimierz Mikulski, the top sellers, receive about four hundred dollars per painting. Considering that New York and Chicago galleries charge more than double the price asked by Desa, this is almost underselling. Asked why these prices were so low, Przywarski said, with a certain deviousness, "Our painters are not really on the same international level as those of Italy, France, and England—so we cannot charge the same prices." When pressed on the question of relative values in the art world, Przywarski backed out, saying he left such matters to his consultants. As far as he was concerned, he thought Polish painters produced far too little—at best only one or two paintings per month—and that many painters, such as Kantor, were unwilling to give their works to Desa at the prevailing prices. This is particularly unfortunate, as there is no legal way for Polish painters to sell their works abroad except through Desa.

What Przywarski inadvertently failed to mention was that in establishing the prices of paintings Desa cannot exceed a certain multiple of the figures set in a book called *Prawo Autorskie* (*The Rights of an Author*), 1965 edition. This book states on page 238 that a simple oil portrait is to be valued at three thousand zlotys. A portrait with two people should cost thirty-six hundred zlotys, while a group portrait, as in the time of Rembrandt, costs forty-five hundred zlotys. The list price per square meter of a figure painting should be thirty-six hundred zlotys, a landscape twenty-four hundred zlotys, and a still life only twelve hundred zlotys. This book also itemized in detail the prices for frescoes, mosaics, lithographs, sculptures, photographs, and other works produced by Polish artists. Tadeusz Brzozowski (b. 1918), certainly one of the outstanding painters of his generation, and by far the most original, claimed that this book was not so ridiculous as it might initially appear to Western eyes. "When I am talking with some official from the Ministry of Culture who knows nothing about painting, this book serves as a most useful reference. The laws are there in black and white and can be readily understood. It makes all discussion of my paintings very simple." Brzozowski added that Desa was unhappy that he exhibited at the Galerie Lambert, an émigré gallery in Paris. Even though the Polish state is desperate for its dollars, it is unwilling to have its painters exploited by the émigré opposition.

In addition to the purely financial aspects, the painter's plight is aggravated by the fact that Poland is producing an overabundance of new artists. There are currently more than two thousand students in the fine arts institutes in Gdansk, Cracow, Katowice, Lodz, Poznan, Wroclaw, and Warsaw, and there are some five thousand active members of the Union of Artists, all struggling to gain public recognition. (By comparison, there were slightly more than two thousand painters in Holland in 1630—of whom an astonishing handful are revered today.) Such is the pressure that many artists feel compelled to earn their living abroad. During my most recent visit to Poland, Tadeusz Kantor was working on an exhibit in Paris, Izaak Celnikier was painting in Israel, Aleksander Kobzdej was working in Hamburg, while others—like Jan Lebenstein, winner of the first double prize at the 1959 Paris Biennale—maintained a permanent and unhappy exile in France.

For those experimentally inclined young painters like Bogdan Kostrzynski (b. 1937) who now want to show, the obstacles are many. First of all, exhibition space is scarce in Poland. In Warsaw only seven galleries show paintings on a full-time basis. Since each individual exhibit is limited to three weeks, critic Stanislawski estimates that there are about a hundred painters shown annually in Warsaw and about fifty in Cracow. And the state is not sympathetic. What limited funds are made available for the fine arts—the sum is calculated on the basis of a minuscule percentage of the equivalent of the Polish GNP—are not to be wasted on experiments. The aim of the Party is to popularize works that are valuable from the socialist point of view. Zenon Kliszko (b. 1908), the zealous Party ideologist, noted in 1965 that the Party's aim is to "enrich the consciousness and spiritual life of our people." What is produced on commission for the government must fulfill this command. Such patronage could, at best, be classified as "industrial art," glorifying the workers and factories of People's Poland. There are also a few socialist-realist survivors who insist on portraying the glory of Lenin addressing the workers or a farmer embracing his new tractor, but the "Stalin by moonlight" school is now restricted to exposition in military buildings, bureaucratic secretariats, and outhouses. Such canvases are seen and almost instantly forgotten. As the British critic John Berger poignantly observed, "The social content of the official art is framed before it is painted."

Abstract paintings are hung only very seldom in the state museums, and none permanently. What is acceptable to the state, aside from socialist realism, is the work of Jan Cybis (b. 1897), an antiquated postimpressionist colorist who produces standard, and, to my eyes, dull varieties of Bonnard landscapes. If this opinion seems harsh, it is necessary to state a few harsher historical facts. Poland has had no great tradition of painting. There has never been a Polish painter of world renown, despite the post-1956 upsurge in painting. Even the much-celebrated Veit Stoss (Wit Stwosz in Polish), who created such masterpieces in Cracow during the fifteenth century, was of German origin. There have been many acceptable painters in Polish history, such as the Cistercian monk Stanislaw Samostrzelnik in the sixteenth century, who created murals and miniatures, and Antoni Brodowski (1783–1832), a court classicist who painted mythological scenes in profusion. However, Poland has traditionally been a land of epigonists. The first symptoms of Polish impressionism, for example, punctually appeared in Warsaw in the early eighteen-nineties. By the nineteen-twenties there was a respectable group of nonobjective artists in Poland who were dedicated to experimenting with structuralism along the lines of the Russian painter Malevich. Known as the "Blok" group, these artists created their own school, which they

[handwritten marginal note: Jan Matejko, St. Wyspiański]

123

called "Unism." Beauty and truth were regarded by the Unists as products and functions of mathematics. Intuition was regarded as "the indulgence of individualists," because only the "useful" and the "measurable" were respected. Unism eliminated all illusions of emotion, as well as most references to the recognizable, and tried to achieve unity through color and form. Henryk Stazewski (b. 1894), who still continues to work in the tradition of the Unists today, was a founding member of this group. From 1939 to 1945 Polish art was forced underground—because Hitler denied the existence of a Polish nation, much less of a Polish culture. With the 1945 liberation, Polish artists soon found themselves subjected to the straitjacket of socialist realism. The worst hacks were glorified by the regime and given positions of power over those painters with talent.

When in 1956, after seventeen years of repression, Polish art was liberated from its artificial strictures, fresh styles, forms, and talent all burst through the surface like a newborn volcano. Many painters, among them Aleksander Kobzdej (b. 1920), hurled themselves into painting abstractions—just as they had flung themselves into creating socialist-realist caricatures. Now, more than a decade later, Polish artists are still experimenting with ways to exploit this artistic freedom. With few exceptions, the younger generation of artists sees itself removed from the mainstream of so-called "socialist progress." The Polish painter has no belief in the profound moral and social purpose of his work. Usually alienated from society, he has no confidence in the efficacy of his art in helping to transform Poland. What is being painted today consequently has little relationship to what is happening in other areas of Polish life. Some Polish painters have opted for a satiric, contrived form of avant-gardism. Benon Liberski (b. 1926), for example, paints Bernard Buffet-influenced sheriffs holding guns and large signs marked "Saloon" and "Western." Liberski would find a welcome audience in the Place du Tertre or in a Washington Square show. Such pseudo-Pop slang may represent a path toward artistic recognition, but it is neither indigenous nor honest. All it reflects is the lengths to which artists will go to develop a new pictorial syntax.

Any tourist can get a bird's-eye view of what is happening in Polish art at the new Dom Plastyka (House of Plastic Art), which opened in March 1966 and now serves as an artistic center in Warsaw. It is instantly apparent that the exhibitors enjoy a perfect freedom to paint whatever they like in any way they like. (There have been no Party attacks on Polish painting since July 1963, and the government has generally maintained a position of noninterference, which envious Russian painters find both surprising and hypocritical, because the Polish government does not include abstract works in its foreign exhibits. At a large show in Bucharest in 1966, nearly every Polish painting shown was socialist-realist. In fact, the few cubist and nonobjective works were so timid that the Rumanians were puzzled as to how the Poles had acquired such a reputation in the West.) Artists such as Roman Owidzki (b. 1912), Marian Bogusz (b. 1920), Zbigniew Gostomski (b. 1932), and Stefan Gierworski (b. 1925), to name but a few of an immense school, toy with geometric abstractions and try to establish a new "image" for themselves. These painters, heavily influenced by what is happening in London and New York, have guaranteed that Polish painting has an up-to-date, international reputation. However, they are contributing little that is original, and even less that is meritorious. The opening exhibit in the small cellar of the Dom Plastyka revealed some of the inopportune efforts now being made by the younger generation. The show, titled "Studio '66," consisted of Op Art patterns so primitive they would have embarrassed any highschool art student. Two roughly cut wire screens meshing against a red background were supposed to illustrate new trends in Polish Op Art. A slowly rotating spiral, which cast off uneven orange shadows, purportedly symbolized the new, daring spirit prevailing in Warsaw.

Jerzy Tchorzewski (b. 1928), a professor at the Academy of Fine Arts in Warsaw, says that "there are dangerous tendencies in the crowd here." Claiming that Polish Optical Art was moving toward Pop, the thin, gaunt Tchorzewski noted with sarcasm, "Regrettably, we are a little behind the times." Tchorzewski, who is still involved in action painting, admits there is a "definite tendency" to paint for export. "My paintings sell for fifteen thousand zlotys in Paris, which is half a year's salary for a worker here," he says. So if he can manage to sell three paintings abroad every year, he can live royally at home. To sell abroad, he must keep abreast of new techniques.

For Tchorzewski, painting has become a mixture of accident and invention. Like the Dubuffet of the mid-fifties (whose styles he closely observes), Tchorzewski laces his paintings with a network of fissures and leathery, corrugated crackles achieved by mixing oil and enamel. The result is effective as décor and dubious as painting. Tchorzewski shrugs his shoulders to the commentary produced by Polish critics and claims that the level of taste in his own country is not yet high enough to savor fully his figurative abstractions. Fashionably dressed, as are most Polish artists, in British tweeds and suède shoes, Tchorzewski apologized that "like the French Forced de Frappe, our Op and Pop are simply first-generation imitations." The true misfortune is that Polish artists have no concrete internal market for their works, he said. Moreover, Tchorzewski felt the dilemma of the painters is compounded by the fact that there are no intelligent, active collectors to give direction to Polish painting and that most of the critics are incompetent, old-fashioned, or bought out.

Critic Stanislawski agrees that there is no Polish painting *per se*. But he contends that there are identifiable Polish paintings. He considers the works of bearded Professor Jerzy Nowosielski (b. 1923), a teacher at the Cracow Academy of Fine Arts, as being heavily influenced by Polish iconography, even in their portrayal of modern life. Nowosielski's clearly defined shapes and the sharp colors of his subjects—such as two cars merging on a forked highway in between flat, green fields—combines the abstraction of early icons and the tones of the large school of Polish primitivists. Similarly, Stanislawski argues that Tadeusz Dominik (b. 1928), a professor at the Warsaw Academy of Fine Arts, is "very Polish," despite the fact that he came out of the school of Bonnard. Dominik specializes in making individual spots of color appear as lights forming coherent patterns. Dabs of white mixed with chrome green on a divided red-and-black background are used to portray a still life of grapes on a tablecloth. However, no painter is more Polish than Tadeusz Brzozowski, a gentle, comical soul whose looks are distinctly Neapolitan. Brzozowski, who lives with his wife and two sons in the skiing village of Zakopane high in the Tatra Mountains in southern Poland, paints large, abstract—sometimes ominous, sometimes comic—Bosch-inspired insectlike forms. He effectively combines deep purplish or greenish phosphorescent expanses with nets of thick black strokes evoking spiderwebs. There is great freedom in these semiabstract figurations, and it is obvious that he elaborates on the haphazard as it happens on the canvas. Frequently, Brzozowski starts with nothing more than a recherché Polish word for medieval armor or the Latin nomenclature for a plague rat, and works on from there. Afterward, when the painting is finished, he uses thick varnishes and glues to elaborate and unify his reactions. There is much that is mysterious in Brzozowski's work. But there is no pseudo mysticism.

Brzozowski studied in Cracow at the Academy of Fine Arts before the war and was much influenced by the impressionists. A 1939 self-portrait he did looked very much like a Cézanne—the round, balding foreheads of both artists enhancing the similarity. But after the war Brzozowski slowly moved toward socialist realism. "In the early nineteen-fifties I tried to paint for the masses. I did a portrait of Mao Tse-tung in Pop Art fashion back in 1951. Really," he said with a lemurlike grin, "it looked very much like a Palmolive advertisement. But then I really believed in what I was doing." Now, Brzozowski admits, "my painting is only for a very few people. However, I am told that sometimes even peasant women stop in front of my paintings to admire the color." Being a painter who understands color in an intuitive and emotional sense rather than in an intellectual one, he appeared to derive great satisfaction from the fact that peasant women appreciate his colors. As a devout Catholic, Brzozowski has a strong feeling of duty to his fellow men. "Art is not the contemplation of beauty," he says, "but the perception of all that is human." He teaches painting at Poznan University, some four hundred miles from Zakopane, every other week because he feels he owes this debt to society. "In France and in the United States," he said, "the best artists don't bother to teach—here in Poland we have a very different tradition."

Wladyslaw Hasior, thirty-six, a neighbor of Brzozowski's in Zakopane, is an entirely different type of creator. He is not really a painter. Perhaps he is closer to being a conjurer. He has transformed his home into a symbiosis between a Catholic chapel and a gallery of horrors. On entering his home, at any time of day or night, Hasior will begin an elaborate ritual of pouring alcohol into various receptacles attached to the walls (much as if preparing a Four Seasons flambée) and lighting them. He will turn on numerous electrified sculptures, light dozens of candles to illuminate his own shattered iconography, and play a hi-fi recording of Penderecki's *Suite for Hiroshima*. Art, it would seem, is not to be judged here on its own merits, but only as part of a contrived stage effect. Sitting on his couch drinking tea, Hasior asks calmly, meditatively, for the infinite time, "Wouldn't it be wonderful if I possessed black light?"

What does one see in Hasior's three-room apartment? Certainly not painting or sculpture, nor even a collage—it is closer to an avant-garde junk shop. Hasior would immediately rail at the link of the word "avant-garde" with his name, although, actually, he would be inwardly delighted with the association. The walls and floors of his apartment are scattered with such effects as a Mona Lisa with nails stuck in her heart and small lamps screwed into her eyes; a weather-beaten, eighteenth-century wooden lion that Hasior has desecrated by pounding full of nails and metal rods; a clothes wringer, painted silver, out of which flow the long brown tresses of one of his girl friends, topped (like a marshmallow sundae) by four silver-coated crucifixes and a toy ladder symbolically rising to heaven; a clipping of Ava Gardner stretched onto a canvas, together with some old feathers and a slice of broken mirror he has glued on at a forty-five-degree angle, so that both Ava and the viewer can exercise their narcissism. What one sees through "Golgotha" and other works with such witty, original titles as "Holy Crook" is Hasior's obviously metaphoric view of life, death, sorrow, injustice, religion. Just as the cubists enjoyed putting newspaper cuttings into their works, so Hasior derives pleasure from stabbing dummies with kitchen knives or any other sharp objects his Zakopane neighbors may have donated. This is not to say that none of Hasior's works creates an effect. There is, for example, one pseudo sculpture entitled "Monte Cassino," which is direct, powerful, expressive. A partially cracked plaster hand rises in the broken hold of a three-foot-diameter bottle; around the base of the hand, which is impaled by a knife, are spaced dozens of somber black crosses, representing those Poles, Americans, Britons, and other soldiers who died at Monte Cassino. Hasior's creations do have that international flavor which will readily find a built-in Maraschino-type of "camp" acceptability. In one memorial to the dead (and Hasior specializes in these), there is a baking pan containing a burning candle, surrounded by crucifixes and an alarm clock. The whole unit is sitting on top of a stuffed deer's head. When asked if the clock keeps time, Hasior answers in dead earnest, "That is no clock, that is the stag's conscience. Every creature has its own individual conscience."

The distance between the metaphors of Hasior and the intellectualism of Warsaw painter Zbigniew Makowski would initially appear to be immense. Makowski, the most intellectual of all Polish artists, will quote Giordano Bruno, Raymond Lully, St. John of the Cross, Tolstoy, Copernicus—to round out the selection with a Pole—during the first minutes of a conversation. Makowski (b. 1930), who lives in a ten-square-yard superminiapartment with his wife, Mary, was smoking a Cuban cigarette and listening to sentimental Jewish songs on his air-conditioner-shaped Polish gramophone when I entered. His apartment, which is in a restored part of the Old Town of Warsaw, is arranged with the utmost care; it has to be, because it also serves as Makowski's studio. A bed occupies one fourth of the floor space. A corner with an easel occupies another fourth. A library of some two thousand books—mostly on art, but also on religion, philosophy, and the occult sciences—occupies another quarter. The rest of the room is cluttered with one chair, two lamps, and lots of Hindu bric-a-brac. More than illustrating the chronic housing shortage, which is the bane of every newly married Polish couple, the teeny apartment reflects Makowski's peculiar microcosm. Makowski, although he looks crew-cut and healthy, suffers from tuberculosis and claims he does not like to leave his corner. "I want to achieve my freedom in art, not in space," he says. Although he can easily afford any trips abroad or vacations he might want, he splits his time between his books and his semantic paintings and drawings. He leaves everything else to his wife, who takes care of him on a full-time basis—almost like a servant. This is in accordance with his ideal of a "simple life."

Makowski's paintings are full of geometrical doodlings, carefully blacked-out letters, and repetitive words forming staircases, circles, blocks, waves, and labyrinths. Symbolic sticks, candles, matches, hourglasses, pyramids, and odds and ends of patterns and designs fill every cranny of the canvas. Examining his work, one cannot help but feel like a phrenologist. One must first look at the whole form, its color and its shape before feeling every little bump or cleft for deep, perhaps hidden, symbolic significance. "There is a tension building up for semantic art," explains Makowski. "The epoch of postimpressionism is ending." Makowski believes his carefully thought-out patterns are deeply "intellectual," while the main-stream of Polish painting today is anti-intellectual. But his intellec-tualism is of a curious nature. "I am a materialist," he shouts with exultation. "I am connected with psychoanalysis rather than with Tolstoy." Three sentences later Makowski says, "Artists possess a metaphysical feeling in an Aristotelian way. I am not sure of my way. Nobody who is a great artist is sure of his way." And, three sentences later, "I am really aggressive only in my work. I am not in a hurry. I do not want to make a career. A career means nothing after fifty years. I have no need to produce canvases. I teach little, but it doesn't matter. I have no urgent need for money."

Quoting Raymond Lully, Makowski also develops a stream of consciousness spun with a purpose: "The alphabet of art is sub-jected to various arrangements, enabling the artist to review all possible wholes composed of components, until he finally builds a machine of concentric wheels with autonomous movements." (This is very much like Makowski's designs.) Then Makowski elaborates: "We may relate this to art. But let us assume that the basic unit of components might be the whole world. All the constructions are artificial, infinitely odd and archiheterogenic—a Luna Park of all mythology; antique shops suspended above waters, underground birds, cloudlike minerals. Consequently, the Dada colleagues: a hybrid of a young lady with a sewing machine, Orpheus on runners. . . . Everything is permissible in the country of underground birds and cloudlike minerals. Yet there is a criterion of effectiveness (a minimum quality of well-used measures of expressionism). For example, a picture of a woman with a water jug at the well or of an

130

old man under a large tree is effective. Equally effective is a picture of a labyrinth as nostalgic geometry. . . . If once upon a time artists made a beautiful picture of the world, now the purpose is to change it. The siren, that swimming and singing metaphor, sweetens Ulysses' way with dangers." But Makowski's dream, as he expressed it, is to find his way to Tibet and undoubtedly toward a socialist form of LSD.

Polish art critic Andrzej Oseka, writing in *Kultura*, correctly observes that Makowski's "figures and designs, formerly treated seriously as symbolic conjurations, have been reduced to the role of dainty, coaxing ornamentations." Looking at Makowski, Oseka reasons, one is supposed to feel modern, up to date. But the critic contends that Makowski now caters to easily contrived, if unconventional, mysticism. He argues that the artist has, in fact, submitted to one of the consecutive new waves that wash across the world art scene.

Jacek Sempolinski—an unmarried Warsaw painter, far less known than Makowski—who receives comparatively high prices for his configurations, is perhaps more representative of the genuine searching and seeking for identity torturing Polish artists today. Sempolinski, who has a weak, nervous, twitching mouth to match his rapidly blinking, pale-blue eyes, feels that "technique is our illness today." When queried about the light-blue splotches of turpentine that covered many of his paintings, he said this was part of "the spontaneity of the process of creation." Despite the fact that he spends as much as six weeks on a canvas, he desperately tries to achieve spontaneity. Like painters the world over, Sempolinski maintains that he does not want to "liquidate accidents." The proliferation of turpentine streaks on paintings is supposed to demonstrate the process of creativity. Gravity does not concern Sempolinski. He did not even appear to see the streaks. Moreover, Sempolinski left certain corners of his canvases white and unfinished, "to show that I started with nothing, that I started with a blank canvas."

"A painting is not an object," said Sempolinski intently, "but a state in a process." When queried about the nervous, hesitant strokes that appeared to be the trademark of his artistry, the

131

twitching Sempolinski explained, "When I look at nature I see the nervosity of God who created nature—I feel obliged to catch that nervosity and to reproduce it." Continuing his line of reasoning with extraordinary torque, he said, "I feel something most strongly against harmony," and then, without even a pause, continued, "I want to create harmony from disorder." In one canvas, in which he attempted to capture the essence of sky, trees, and water, he explained that he wanted "to complicate space." Sempolinski felt very strongly that space, when seen through trees, is less deep than space as seen above a lake or the ocean. Pulling out a canvas that looked like a painting of reeds blowing in the wind, Sempolinski said, "The names of my paintings are very important. This one is called 'Trees on the Edge of the Lake' or 'The Lake at Night,' whichever you prefer." What Sempolinski's striving seemed to indicate, above all, was the universality of intellectual double-talk and confusion among painters of lesser rank. Of much greater significance are the serious, almost pathetic efforts of young artists like Ryszard Gieryszewski (b. 1936), who had his first one-man show in Warsaw at the Gallery of Debutants in the spring of 1966. Gieryszewski's eyes were bloodshot with fatigue as his show opened, his thin face was almost gray from the strain, and his hands were shaking. Two or three young girls sipping cocktails and dressed à la mode in black and white Op patterns passed inane critiques on his canvases. Gieryszewski, although a graduate of the Academy of Fine Arts in Warsaw, explained that until the exhibition he had been a decorator for a large firm. Apparently, when his boss heard that he was having a show, that he was a painter who would have reviews in the newspaper, he accused Gieryszewski of working as a decorator only to make a living. So Ryszard quit. "On the average I could paint only some two hours per day while working, so I was happy to be able to prepare for this exhibit." Ryszard had little money, and his first show cost him some two thousand zlotys. "No one is going to buy my paintings," he said without emotion. "As a matter of fact, I cannot sell any paintings before I have done some new ones." Gieryszewski anxiously said he had to keep his canvases as visiting cards. "You must understand that without my paintings—well, I am not a painter."

Gieryszewski asserted that not even the Academy of Fine Arts would buy his works (as is customary), for they could only accept flat canvases. Because one of his paintings had a typewriter and plastic legs attached to it and another had a broken doll glued against the frame, "the bureaucracy claimed it was incapable of transporting or storing them." Ryszard said he would be happy if painters in Poland had the same status as athletes. "My God, if we had their privileges!" he exclaimed with envy. Only "group painting" was receiving much support, he said, because "in our country we are very strong on collective mediocrity."

Asked why he had staged this exhibit, for which he had to pay one month's salary and in which he had no hope of selling any pictures, Gieryszewski replied, "All of us only paint for ourselves, our colleagues, and the critics. Me, I'm very happy if there is some mention of my work in the papers." When interrogated along this line, Ryszard confided that he thought the official critics dreadful; he could already recite what the reviews would say, because they always repeated the same thing. "Mr. X, who studied at such and such an academy, showed x number of paintings—which show promise. We hope to see more of his work in the future." Gieryszewski then went on to explain that someday, after his third or fourth exhibit at the age of forty, the more serious critics would begin to take notice. "We are in a very difficult situation because we are not in the first group of moderns, the 1956 group of painters like Kobzdej, who left socialist realism at the right time," he said. "We have not yet found a place for ourselves."

After Op and Pop what, indeed, is left to the Poles? The forced sense of style, self-consciousness, and lack of innocence have resulted in the development of what might be called "No" art. "No" art is exactly the opposite of what most Polish painters suppose their painting to be. It is also the antithesis of the Noh art of Japan, where everything is masked, for Polish painting is almost entirely on the surface. There is little that is currently seductive, in either style or image. After kinetic, environmental, and structural art, "No" is the logical end of the line. The progressions of style have worked their full circle. Polish art critic Oseka admits in *Kultura* that his compatriots paint "roseate red and green triangles instead of roseate nymphs playing in the foam," but that in a deeply aesthetic sense, even though the terms of reference are no longer the same, exceptionally little has changed. If a new aesthetic is, in fact, developing in Poland, it is a form of black-market aestheticism. Only in trying to copy or adapt something that is smuggled in from the West can an artist achieve public acceptability.

Modern Polish painting evokes little emotion, nor does there appear to be passionate enjoyment in the act of painting; the work, like the intended effects, is calculated, premeditated, studied to the point of desiccation. Only occasionally does the sense of frustration lead to aggression on canvas—but even this aggression seems self-conscious. Perhaps, after the horrors of World War II and the convolutions that followed under Stalinism, innocence is no longer possible. Regrettably, most of what is being expressed in the mid-sixties is pedestrian. The disappearance of stags roaring at rutting time might have been marked by the emergence of paintings reflecting contemporary aesthetic values, but, as critic Oseka notes with a trace of sadness, "Banality seems to be immortal."

Contemporary society demands that the painter must of necessity "adapt himself to the ever changing rules of the game," remarks Oseka. The Polish public, for example, wants to be among the initiates of the latest fashion in art, just as the Polish girls must dance the "monkey" in glittering silver stockings and golden mini-skirts. Tadeusz Kantor (b. 1915), the most fashion-conscious of all Polish painters, has made it a habit to bring back a new idiom after each of his many trips abroad. Kantor developed his own form of *tachisme* after a trip to Paris in 1955, and, as the former director of an avant-garde Cracow theater, he "introduced" artistic happenings to Poland in the mid-sixties. Then, after another trip, rags, old clothes, shopping bags, and umbrellas began to be incorporated in his work. Kantor saw artistic possibilities in the fact that products that had once served useful lives could be resuscitated on canvas. With a little glue and a lot of thick oils, he combines the media until a canvas may look like blue jeans floating on whipped cream. Kantor earnestly claims there is great poetry in creating beauty out of what others have discarded. As a result of these and parallel redundancies, the little true originality that occasionally surfaces fails to impress the Poles. Like many another so-called "sophisticated" public, it has become shockproof.

Where is Polish painting headed in the nineteen-seventies? Art pursues the market, and, since capital lies abroad, the outlook is unpromising. The indications are that art will closely pattern itself on the trends set in London, New York, and Paris. As an indigenous movement, Polish painting *per se* seems to have little future; only one or two talented creators, like Brzozowski, are likely to withstand the test of time. The same holds true for the rest of Eastern Europe, where the painters have had less freedom and fewer opportunities to follow their impulses than in Poland. If any lesson is to be derived from the Polish experience since 1956, it is that more is needed to produce great art than the state's aloof tolerance of individual styles. The Czech painters, for example, have been far more harassed by narrow-minded Party ideologists, but because they are economically and psychologically less dependent upon developments in the West, their work also presents greater hope for the next decade. The attraction of the Czechs is that they are not so much concerned with what is happening in New York and London as they are with what is happening within themselves. If what they find appears to be melancholy introspection, it is at least genuine. The experience of Czech painting partially seems to repeat that of the cinema, where the Poles led off with a new wave and the Czechs followed in their tracks. Prague, with such promising young artists as painter Rudolf Nemec (b. 1936) and etcher Oldrich Kulhanek (b. 1940), is just beginning to capture the international spotlight. The remarkable technical skill, control, and patience of these young Czechs should place them favorably in the "cool," automated seventies, whereas the prospect for Polish painters would appear to be stygian.

CHAPTER VIII

Straight Circles

Hungarians are the only artists who successfully manage to combine love and politics in their poetry. There is, perhaps, something inherently sexual about storming a barricade, if only in a Freudian sense, but for a non-Hungarian it is far more difficult to fathom the political or revolutionary nature of making love to a woman. The Magyar hunger-in-satiety frustration experienced in love parallels the despair of attaining fulfillment in freedom. Freedom has become a passionate woman whose promise is infinite, but whose favor is but fleeting. What is left for the Hungarian poet is an afterglow of melancholy and pathos. And what is presented to foreign readers is but an unintelligible regurgitation of patriotism, politics, and love.

Poet Mihaly Vaci (b. 1924), who is also the editor of the leading literary monthly *Uj Iras* (New Writing), says, "Every nation wants to be great in one respect. . . . Hungarians want to be great in two, through our love and through our poetry." Vaci explained that Balint Balassa (1551–1594) was the first poet to write a whole cycle of Hungarian lyrical love verses to his "Beatrice" and "Laura," Anna Losonczi, while also evoking the joys and tribulations of his encounter with the Turks. Like so many Hungarian poets, he died on the battlefield. Sandor Petofi (1823–1849), the leading Hungarian poet of the nineteenth century, whose tragedy it is to remain virtually unknown outside the Magyar-speaking world, died a hero's death on the barricades of the 1848–1849 revolution. Petofi combined great sensuality with extreme idealism. His political ideals were so far ahead of his epoch that the literary circles of Budapest regarded him as half-mad during his own lifetime. However, the succeeding generations of poets took to heart his superb challenge: "When the people shall rule in poetry, they shall be close to ruling in politics as well." Petofi is admired today not only for his exceptional lyricism, which was popular even among the illiterate peasantry of his day, but also because his poems represent the incarnation of Hungary's social and political aspirations.

Endre Ady (1877–1919), the outstanding Hungarian lyricist of the twentieth century, continued the tradition of blending the professions of patriot (devout in his anticlericalism and his republicanism) and poet of sensual love. No one shocked and rocked Budapest society more than did Ady with his unusual declarations of love. Jozsef Attila (1905–1937), the meteor of modern Hungarian poetry, also embodied this romantic tradition. Now regarded as a socialist lyricist by the communists, Attila's life work is viewed as a struggle for understanding, as a challenge against social injustice. To Attila, alienation meant not only painful rejection by several women, but also rejection by society and excommunication from the Hungarian Communist Party. For him, to live meant to have living contact with one's yearnings. But this contact was broken through a tragic love affair. A manic depressive, he committed suicide, after leaving a mental hospital, by hurling himself in front of a freight train. Poverty-stricken, Attila was buried almost unnoticed. Even at his funeral he was spurned by his comrades in the communist underground, who had denounced him as a "fascist" for his heretical efforts to combine Marxism with psychoanalytic forms. Attila said Marx had to be corrected with Freud in order to save the people from their inhibitions and their revolt against the superego. A generation after his death, Attila plays a larger role in the life of every Hungarian than an American could imagine. Streets, homes, hospitals, and riverboats—everything but salami— are now being named after him. He is as revered as Lincoln in America or Garibaldi in Italy.

Poetry has been the strongest side of Hungarian writing ever since the sixteenth century, and Hungarian poets have become the exponents of national expectations. Like the authors of the Bible, Hungarian poets are prophets among their people. The Hungarians believe poetry has the force, the vigor, to shape reality. Gyula Illyes (b. 1902), regarded as the Hungarian poet-laureate, or the closest an artist can come today to being a national poet, says, "Poets are respected in our country because of their role in history, because only the poets were right in the past." While British or American aesthetes oppose the notion that poetry can be integrated with politics (because this defiles an otherwise "pure art"), Hungarians have never had such inhibitions.

Illyes, even though he agrees that national romanticism—the expression of political ideas in poetical form—is on the wane, remains committed to sociopoetry. According to Illyes, "Poetry is the incarnation of liberty and responsibility." He says it is the duty of the poet to examine such themes as power and morality. Moreover, Illyes considers it crucial for poets to be "anti," to be in the opposition, because poets are and should be more courageous than journalists. To Hungarians the armed protest of LeRoi Jones is completely understandable; this is the type of defiance the muses appreciate. Consequently, in Hungary, "there is a tendency for people, even for intellectuals, to wait and see what position certain poets will take on an issue," says poet Istvan Simon (b. 1926). A member of Parliament and editor of the literary monthly *Kortars*, Simon thinks poets and writers were to a large degree responsible for the bloody 1956 revolution in Budapest. The poets, after all, helped "awaken the self-consciousness of the people."

Like Aeschylus, Vergil, and Dante, the Hungarian poets are not afraid to tackle political realities. They attempt to grasp and interpret the present. The British and the Americans do not look to their poets for illuminations about society; in fact, poets are regarded by the population as upper-class aesthetes. Whereas in Hungary political poets command authority, in the Anglo-Saxon world political poetry is suspect because of its emotionalism, because it does not deal with immediate, personal experience but with events usually known from hearsay. The poet's feeling may be compelling, but it does not share the respect given to the observations of a journalist who has witnessed the scene at first hand.

While there is nothing intrinsically wrong about injecting politics into poetry, the danger, as C. M. Bowra points out in his *Poetry and Politics, 1900–1960,* is that, by being overemotional or simplifying facts beyond the point of truth, the poet undermines his authority with the rational, legalistic Anglo-Saxons. In the United States, for example, poets such as Robert Lowell or Gregory Corso are unsuccessful in arousing the national consciousness on Vietnam. But not all Hungarians are in agreement with this exalted status of verse. Agnes Nemes-Nagy (b. 1922) believes "the role of the poet is to be a guide of the people." However, she feels this inevitably degrades poetry into forced rhetoricism. "We are adults," she says, "consequently, we must not be pedagogic . . . we should not explain from A to Z." This seems an inevitable reaction in a country where the best verses still read like editorials.

The readiness with which Hungarian poets have accepted involvement—both romantic and political—certainly is one of the explanations for their phenomenal popularity. Over five hundred new volumes of poetry a year were published in the mid-sixties, and in the better Budapest bookstores one can usually choose from the works of at least a hundred different poets. In an overheated Pest bookshop, an obese salesgirl patiently explained to me that "every mood in Hungary has its own poet." To commemorate the birth of Attila (April 11), Poetry Day has been stretched into Poetry Week, and the salesgirl, whose overwhelming passion obviously was poets and their verse, said that, while the last volume of Attila's poems, published shortly before his suicide in 1937, sold only twenty of the three hundred volumes printed, more than one million volumes of his poems have been sold in the past few years. "If only our poetry could be understood as readily as Hungarian music," she said, her eyes glistening, "Hungarian poets of this century would be more famous than Bartók, Kodály, or even Liszt."

It is in lyric verse that one continues to encounter the best, most original voices, the freshest and most startling initiatives in Hungary today. Laszlo Benjamin (b. 1915), one of the leading poet-fighters of the 1956 revolution, says, "I feel the skill of the young writers has increased incredibly over the past generation. . . . They are showing a prodigious gift for form." Himself a reader for

139

a literary review, Benjamin explained that not only are poets such as Illyes, Uhasz, and Weores producing first-rate works, but also talented new poets are making their debuts in the literary periodicals almost every month. (The eight Hungarian literary magazines publish an average of about twelve hundred poems a year.) Quips Benjamin: "In Hungary, we have some ten million inhabitants, almost as many poets, and no unemployed." The popularity of poetry and the esteem associated with being a poet are so great that Mihaly Vaci, poet-editor of *Uj Iras,* says he receives eight to ten packets of new poems every day. This is far more than he and his associate editors can read and digest, so Vaci says, "The reason why Hungary is so full of unhappy people is that there are just not enough editors to read and publish all that is written!" And this despite the fact that Hungarian television features a special poetry reading once a week, the radio announces the publication of new volumes of poetry every day, and several poems are read over the airwaves by professional actors during breakfast and lunchtime.* In addition to all this public promotion of poetry, hundreds of poems are published every week in the daily press.

Vaci, a communist deputy in the Hungarian Parliament, says his monthly is raising an entire new generation of poets.† Vaci appeared sincere when he said, "I publish anything: right wing, mystic, folk art, Catholic poems, or communist poems—as long as they are worthy from the artistic viewpoint." And, he added, "from very young poets I will accept any good poetry that is honest." However, several young poets in search of a publisher complained to me that *Uj Iras* screens its authors most carefully ever since its format was changed in 1964. Then, as a result of new typography, new make-up, and graphic insertions, its literary section was considerably curtailed. Apparently this was intentional. Now *Uj Iras* includes

---

* I am told that these readings are actively listened to. In Hungary poets very rarely recite their own verse in public. Instead, professional actors read poetry on the more than a hundred "literary" stages throughout the country.

† *Uj Iras* has a paid circulation of only seventeen thousand copies a month, but the demand is so great that its black-market value is twenty times its modest newsstand price. As justification for the limited editions of literary periodicals and books, the government always cites the shortage of paper.

lengthy monthly features on subjects—such as industrial agriculture—that have nothing in common with the character of the periodical. As elsewhere in the socialist world, the Party is anxious to control the number of new voices that can be heard and seeks to limit the risk of new and possibly "alien and harmful opinions and ideals." Even Vaci, who is the recipient of the highest state literary prize, a communist in good standing, and a member of Parliament, is not exempt from surveillance. As an editor, Vaci knows exactly how far he can safely go, but in 1963 eyebrows were raised when he wrote a poem entitled "Siamese Twins," which described the bitter feelings of a Hungarian, always faithful to the Party line, who envies those who fled the country in 1956 and now enjoy material abundance. In tones of both mockery and disillusionment, Vaci narrates how the faithful twin who remains in Budapest has little hope of ever purchasing the small car and the other items he cherished; but at least he is not an exile.

Censorship in Hungary is limited to "comradely guidance" and to threats of prosecution for "instigation." The first, in the form of freely dispensed suggestions, is often offered. The concept of "instigation," however, is open to interpretation under the penal code. In this respect, the government is very clever. All bodies and institutions serving the objectives of socialism are protected by law against the threat of "instigation," providing the regime with sufficient elasticity to prosecute any writer while spreading enough uncertainty to force the poets to exercise self-censorship. Nevertheless, the Party attitude toward poetry could not be defined as restrictive. In fact, the regime takes such pride in some "progressive" poetry that it tolerates reasonable dissent.

As in the Soviet Union, the young people are the greatest fans and purchasers of poetry and are most anxious to know what individual poets are thinking and feeling. In Moscow and Leningrad thousands of students will congregate to hear "licensed nonconformist" Yevgeny Yevtushenko or "true nonconformist" Andrei Voznesensky express radical ideas in the context of poetry that might be too dangerous to expound in other forms. In Hungary the younger generation is especially attracted to Ferenc Baranyi (b. 1937), whose first volume of poetry, *Ballad of Lightning,* appeared

141

in 1962. In one of his poems, "Ballad on Pampered Youth," which he recites with all the bravado of a Yevtushenko, Baranyi brilliantly contrasted the promise of socialism with the actual state of affairs: less than eight square yards of floor space for the average Budapest resident and the near impossibility for a young married couple to lead a tolerable existence together. I consider Baranyi interesting as a political poet because of the melodramatic way in which he treats subjects alluring to the younger Hungarian generation, his generation. A good illustration of this is the following poem:

THE HEROES

Bloody Thursday, Red Friday.
They, the heroes of yesteryear,
who, flags in hand,
descended into the streets;
they fought well. A struggle
not harder, but more spectacular,
than ours. Fighting adorned by streams of blood
conquered by fire.

Ours is different. Ours is a fight
free of blood in a doubting world.
We fight, certainly, but when do we fight?
When do we not fight? And where hides the enemy?
Our struggle has nothing in common with a specific battle.
The attack does not occur on such a day,
at that place, under such circumstances.
The fire is on all fronts.
Hundreds of fronts are consolidated
In thousands of crossed wires,
which bind one parent,
which tie one friend.
We fight quietly, we fight prudently,
in covered words or in hard speech.
We fight for—we fight against
those who despise us,
although occasionally we also
show, even we, signs of fatigue.
But everything is struggle for us: the action that inflames

142

and the apparent relaxation.
To act or not to act.
What is the best course for every moment,
that's a problem of strategy.

Workers formerly shoved the cold bayonets against your chest.
Now, it is the cannon of traitors that stops us
and it is suspicion that kills us,
and that is not less terrible.
When you lost—you had excuses.
When we lose—we will have none.
To conquer, for you, was a matter of glory.
For us, it is but a matter of duty.*

Ivan Boldizsar, editor of the English-language *New Hungarian Quarterly*, a slick cultural-propaganda periodical (whose English translations are corrected by none other than the aging and ailing American deserter Noel Field), says Baranyi exerts a "fake revolutionism." Boldizsar, whose profession it is to make Hungary and its regime seem more palatable and palpable than they really are, considers Baranyi's verse the Pop Art of modern Hungarian poetry. As the father of a teen-age son, Boldizsar thinks this political poetry titillates Hungarian youth by occasionally bringing up forbidden or semiforbidden fruit. Boldizsar, in his capacity of self-styled *"commis voyageur"* of Hungarian literature, feels Baranyi's "free-verse thrills" are immature. And declamation does not make poetry, insists Boldizsar. Mihaly Vaci modifies this view. Vaci says, "A great many poets talk against Baranyi because of his popularity. I believe he has written many good poems, and, while some may exhibit a slightly superficial spontaneity, he is attractive because he speaks the idiom of youth." Whatever the criticisms of Baranyi, there is a definite meeting of minds between the young Hungarian generation, which feels the outlets for its energies are restricted, and the new group of poets who are trying to find an outlet for their pent-up tensions and their personal unrest. Asked to comment on the fact that Baranyi's latest volume of poetry sold fifteen thousand

* Translated by Barbara Frischmuth and Yorick Blumenfeld.

copies in a week, Boldizsar remarked caustically, "More children are reading than ever, but what they are reading is worse. If Baranyi is fifteenth-rate, it is because he repeats the conformist theme of alienation."

Baranyi's position in Hungary can be compared to John Lennon's in England. Similarly, the popular adulation of the older generation of poets is comparable to that granted Hollywood stars. The Hungarian poet is a public figure whose life is the subject of constant popular scrutiny and gossip. Not only that, but, on the more favorable side, a genuine exchange also exists between the poets and their readers—something very rare in world literature today. If Sandor Weores, regarded as Hungary's leading contemporary poet, writes a poem about his feelings during the sexual act, hundreds of letters will come flowing in from all over the country— written by critics who are outraged as well as by those who are moved by his description. When Gyula Illyes wrote a poem on nationalism, irate factory workers sent him letters asking him to elaborate its meaning, for they were anxious to know if he had not, in fact, been guilty of anti-Semitic innuendos. Illyes explained to me that he derived strength from the knowledge that his every poem was being dissected and analyzed not only in Budapest coffeehouses but also in remote Transdanubian villages.

The glory that accompanies publication naturally also produces contrapuntal despair. One rural insurance doctor who, after years of writing verse, finally succeeded in getting a volume published, immediately thought of himself as covered with laurels and stopped his medical practice. His wife subsequently paid five visits to Budapest to try to get the publishers to do something so her husband would go back to work and support his family, but to no avail. A divorce seemed imminent.

As soon as young people are published, they leave their jobs and even the university to write poetry. Gyorgy Somlyo (b. 1920), a poet and secretary of the poetry branch of the Hungarian Writers' Association, comments on the veritable poetry craze: "Here Sunday poets fill our local press and are paid a few forints. In America you hand out unemployment compensation and instead fill your local newspapers with advertisements!" Nevertheless, Somlyo thinks it is somewhat easier for Hungarian poets to earn their living than for their counterparts in France or the United States. A young Hungarian poet, without a family, who writes between forty and fifty poems a year could theoretically live from his verse alone. What is really astounding about this system is that a student of twenty, who has had about twenty poems printed in various newspapers and magazines, will have little trouble getting his first volume of poetry published and—no matter what the sales—be equitably paid for it.

In Hungary poets are paid by the line, not by the number of volumes sold, nor by the number of pages in the book, nor by the number of editions printed. Poet Istvan Vac (b. 1910) tried to explain the system by which poets are divided into categories. A first-category poet gets twelve forints (about fifty cents) per line while a fourth-category poet receives half that amount. "The system is really so complicated, I myself don't know exactly how it works, but I get about twenty forints per line," said Vac. Royalties are paid in advance for the first edition. However, the poet receives less for the second edition and almost nothing should there be a third edition of the same volume. This is because Party ideologists reason that poetry is a social function and that, beyond a certain minimal income, society does not owe the poet, whose intellectual development is formed by society, any additional reward. At this point, the heroic light in which Hungarian poets are viewed is regarded as ample recognition for their special talent.

Hungarian poets are still categorized by the Party as socialist, populist, and bourgeois humanist.* Gabor Garai (b. 1929) skillfully combines political careerism, as a member of the Central

---

* In this connection, it should be noted that the proletarian editors of the *1966 Hungarian Yearbook* opened their section on literature with the following sentence: "The development of Hungarian poetry began as early as in the ancient classless society, where songs and rhythm facilitated collective work." They then went on to write: "It is characteristic of present-day Hungarian lyrical poetry that among the bourgeois poets there is a certain growing *rapprochement* with social issues and the issues raised by the new order. Isolation and a sense of loneliness dissolve in the common anxiety of the fear of war, and a certain universal humanism prevails."

Committee of the Hungarian Communist Party (the equivalent of Cabinet rank in the West) and as the secretary of the Hungarian Writers' Association, with his career as a "committed" socialist poet dedicated to furthering the Party's ideals. Garai is a political poet not above writing doggerel on such subjects as cleanliness (*e.g.*, "Give Us Clean Austerity"). However, Garai says he is looked down upon by his "populist" colleagues because he is a city-bred intellectual. Long before they were divided into the categories of socialist, bourgeois, and populist, Hungarian poets were classified as urbanists and ruralists. And even now many critics feel it is an irreparable loss for any poet not to have shared the peasant's intimate communion with nature. For the communist critics, what counts is that Garai worked eight years as a clerk for the Hungarian railways; for the populists, what is held against him is that he doesn't understand the peasantry, the true keepers of the "Hungarian soul." Garai, whose thin, sensual fingers were quivering somewhat nervously, claims to be broad-minded. Although he declared that the new development in socialist literature is realism, Garai said, "It is of immense value and importance to us if a bourgeois or a Catholic can say something beautiful."

Garai explained that it was quite possible to be a "committed" poet without debasing one's verse to the level of an elegant editorial. He narrated how he struggled for weeks on end to write a poem about hunger as the world's greatest force. Finally, one morning, as he cut into his ham and eggs, he suddenly felt he "had it": how normal it seemed to eat every day, how we take the cutting of bread for granted. He said that the resulting poem was an immensely popular and widely quoted success. "Poetry is for most of us a mission assumed with sober devotion, and if we did not write poems, we would sew up hernias or drive locomotives," says Garai. Off the record, even Garai's socialist colleagues regard him as somewhat doctrinaire and didactic. Some critics are even more careful. Editor Ivan Boldizsar says tersely, "Garai is not a bad poet, he is a member of the Central Committee." As a "committed" poet, however, Garai manages to catch and balance the complex spirit of the straight circle that is Hungarian poetry, as evidenced in the following poem:

THE ACROBATS

Like living pincers, the man, upside down,
Somersaults on his trapeze,
Wagging the bit between his teeth
As if he had a magnetic mouth.

At the antipode dangles a woman.
She turns, she tightens her mouth!
What a kiss! Between them is naked space,
Silence, accidental death.

What a strange state—one dependent on the other
Floats under the sky, toward the roof.
What tenacious desire is being tested
To risk and save these two lives?

They turn, gripped in attention
And discipline, knowing they must fly
Together—if one makes a mistake,
Both of them will fall.

Ah! If we knew how to unite ourselves thus,
Like lovers to each other entrusted,
Always flying toward the heights
As if before the eternal fall!

Oh! If all those with common interests
Attached themselves thus, with such fatal trust
The one holding the other
By their nerves, with their teeth.

That we, who cling by the thousands, unite
With the faith with which they live
Up there, and that we make it each other's business
Concerns me with all my being. . . .

The woman turns and rotates between
His teeth—the music subsides.
Only the drum beats. Oh! Let the end be quick,
No matter what the conclusion!

147

And then? . . . The show comes to earth.
Above, a curtain of bravos already trembles,
Below, the two figures freeze,
The Statue of a single grotesque salute.*

Like the poetic acrobat that he himself is, Garai never tries to
grasp more than he can actually hold. "The Acrobats" has many
levels of meaning, some of them as contradictory or complementary
as its mixture of socialist realism and its desire for faith. Garai
combines a personal, physical note with universal human aspirations. He desires the socialist applause, but is uncertain about its
ultimate significance. One critic, who recalled Garai's long struggle
to overcome his reactionary family background (apparently his
uncle had served as an official in the fascist regime of Admiral
Horthy), wrote that Garai's "great experience is that socialism has
adopted him as its son. His loyalty is based on gratitude." The
questions of acceptance by society, of finding his place, appear
swiftly in the poem below:

AT HOME IN THE WORLD
How much you feel this world to be your own!
As you lie sunning in the grass of spring
in bathing suits, and let the sound of music
ooze to your hearts from small transistor sets;
and as you eat salami sandwiches,
and as you plunge with splashes into the pool,
with lazy bodies, muscles lax, untensed,
as if to cross the water back again
to mother-womb . . .
                         I walk among you here
watching my every gesture, every step,
setting my face lest you find out I am
naught but an awkward uninvited guest.
Whatever I experience I see
both from within and from without;
                                        I eat,
and see a man who's eating;
                              I look up

* Translated by Barbara Frischmuth and Yorick Blumenfeld.

skyward to see a man who's looking up—
Looked at, observed, unable to forget—
                                        And yet
I also crave for self-forgetting joy
no less than you, perhaps more hungrily;
you feel this world to be so much your own,
I am ordained to comprehend the world
and ceaselessly to study and dissect
its mysteries and, in them all, myself,
but nothing gave to me the joys of home
except the few short hours of making love
and making friends—all vanished with the years.
                    Look at me, you
who feel this world to be so much your own,
rolling upon the grass in bathing suits;
and do not say: "I've seen that fellow there
on television; he has all the luck!"
Nor should you pity me—
                        I live but once
as you, but I would like to make my life
as one of yours, content with little, you
who can forget yourselves in pain and joy,
who feel this world to be so much your own.
My life, as everyone's, can be endured,
for you it is who whet its quenchless thirst;
it never has enough of that delight
it takes from you:
                        you who will set me free,
make me at home with you until the day
the salts of earth, the worms within the earth
have laid the fever and the thirst in me.*

Garai's fever and thirst . . . It was evident that self-control (or
what he calls the "harsh law of my manhood") and the desire for
political power are uppermost in his consciousness. I asked him to
talk about this combination of poetry and politics, but he seemed
reluctant. "My poetry and my political career are in harmony

* Translated by L. T. Andras.

149

because my political life is no different from my writing," he said. When asked to explain what he actually did at Central Committee meetings, he said he was invited to attend in order to give his opinion on culture and the arts. "The Party leaders listen to me as a politician," he said, "because they know me as a poet."

Although many Hungarian poets feel that the national product contains an excessive amount of "foreign" or topical matter, and that the time has come for poets to abandon their editorial functions, Gyula Illyes disagrees. During a two-hour talk in his hillside villa in Buda, he sidetracked all discussion of poetry and launched into repeated nationalistic diatribes. Cursing the "rotten Czechs" and "those impossible barbarians—the Rumanians—who are torturing our poor peoples in Transylvania," Illyes insisted that "a poet must have the courage to talk because the politicians can't." If something doesn't click in Hungary, said Illyes, then the poets are certain to write about it. To him, the principal idea is that "when people can't express their ideas in a constitutional, legal way, they express them in literature." For Illyes, Hungarian poetry from Balassa to Attila is the poetry of agony and pessimism. (And this is a strong judgment for a poet for whom Beckett represents an optimistic literature, "a literature that proposes to better the world.") Hungarian poetry, Illyes maintains, began under the Turks to "express the agony of this suppressed people." Today, the Hungarians are not much happier, he insists, pointing out that they have the world's highest suicide rate (33 per 100,000), accompanied by the lowest birth rate. Illyes seemed veritably haunted by the fact that the Hungarians are a dying people. He twice repeated that in the fifteenth century there were as many Hungarians as Englishmen in the world—but today the Magyar nation is moribund.

"That a people sings its Constitution and its ways in verse and expresses its true laws in popular songs is undoubtedly a difficult thing to conceive in countries whose defense is principally assured by the sea," writes Illyes, "but it does not seem so for the sons of the people committed, during the course of a certain period of its history, to a movement of national resistance." Illyes sees Hungarian poetry, from its very inception, as a literature of resistance. And

*Painting of Czechs marching into a wall, by Eva Brydlova. The artist
specializes in paintings that illustrate the anonymity
of communist bureaucracy.*

Milos Forman, Czech film director, with his wife

Gyula Illyes, Hungary's national poet

Gabor Garai, Hungary's poet-politician

Jiri Trnka, the world's greatest puppeteer, in his Prague studio with one of the stars of his animated films

The new Belgrade Museum of Modern Art, exterior view

*Interior view of the Belgrade Museum of Modern Art, with marble nudes
by the prewar sculptor Ivan Mestrovic*

Polish sculptress Alina Szapocznikowa in her studio

Tadeusz Brzozowski, Poland's leading painter

Krzysztof Penderecki, Poland's foremost modern composer, correcting notations with a felt pen

Andrei Gulyashki, Bulgaria's "Ian Fleming"

during his entire life, writing poetry has been the way Illyes has expressed his personal resistance to the multitude of regimes, including the communist one, that have governed Hungary. Illyes spent his childhood on a large Transdanubian estate and finished his secondary schooling only at great financial sacrifice to his entire family. He joined the revolutionary army of the post–World War I Council Republic, but when it was overthrown in 1919 after a brief existence, he was forced to flee abroad. For six years he lived in Paris as an exile. In France he became a poet and, through his association with figures of the French literary avant-garde, he was able to combine French surrealism with his own parochial outlook. In a poem reminiscent of these youthful rebellious days, he wrote in the early sixties: "Paris, love, young workers' movement, farewell."

Returning to Budapest in 1926, he published his first book of poems, which coupled his peasant simplicity with Parisian sophistication and revolutionary social ideas. In the thirties, as economic conditions and the Horthy dictatorship tightened, he wrote a long descriptive sociological report, conceived almost as a prose poem, on the wretched life of the farmhands of his Transdanubian birthplace. *The People of the Puszta* portrays their misery through unimpassioned recitation of facts combined with Illyes's own recollections. Illyes depicts the life of these isolated peasants on their impoverished farmsteads as that of an autonomous moral community in which quite different and more humane moral norms prevailed than in the city. Above all, Illyes worked for a solution to the land question—that is, the breakup of the large estates—and hoped for a triumphal peasant revolution. He gauged socialism primarily by the elementary necessities—food, clothing, education, child welfare—that it could provide for the people, but was deluded as to its true political structure. That Hungarian socialism was born and triumphed in the cities, without a peasant revolution, was, for him, a tragedy.

Illyes, who looks like a Breton and who talks French like a Parisian, has structured an ethic out of being a Hungarian poet. The following is an example of the unadulterated patriotic schmaltz that professional nationalism has produced in him:

151

GOOD MOTHER

All-comprehending, good mother,
Finally, there can be no other.
She beckons to me and agrees
That right I am in all my pleas.

She takes me in her loving arms,
Dispensing justice, giving warmth.
As son she desires only me.
I alone will then Hungarian be.

The ever wandering youngest son,
I shall become her favorite one.
Her hand is resting on my face,
From me radiates the truth of race.*

To do him justice, which this poem does not, Illyes is an original, if somewhat antiquated, poet, who does not rest content with himself or his people. He is constantly seeking to "regenerate" the tongue of his tribe through poetry. "The uniqueness of the Hungarian language," he says, "is the force of its poetry."

Illyes bemoans the lack of manifest influence of Hungarian poetry on European poetry. In truth, it remains an exclusive Hungarian treasure. Hungarian socialist poetry remains largely unappreciated even by the obscurantist Polish poets and the more virile Soviet bards. The contemporary giants of Soviet poetry— Mayakovsky, Akhmatova, Pasternak, Voznesensky—have expressed more interest in Chilean or Turkish poetry than in Hungarian. Allen Ginsberg exerts a greater allure than Sandor Weores, who is incomparably more knowledgeable in his pantheism and far subtler in his versification. Agnes Nemes-Nagy, revealing a slightly wounded sense of pride, says, "We are always stupid in translation, but don't think we are so stupid in reality." Other poets similarly echoed their regret that so little of the essence of Hungarian poetry has passed into the European bloodstream, while European poetry has so profoundly influenced the Magyar.

Translations have exerted a powerful spell in Hungary, not only

* Translated by Barbara Frischmuth and Yorick Blumenfeld.

because the Hungarian language adapts itself so readily to nearly all metric forms, from Sophoclean choruses to Sanskrit strophes, but also because poets, not academic hacks, have done the translating. Mihaly Babits, editor of the most prestigious prewar literary review, when asked which was the most influential poem in the Hungarian language, replied: "Shelley's 'Ode to the West Wind,' as translated by Arpad Toth." Each of the more than two dozen poets I talked to in Hungary was involved in some kind of translation. Several maintained, in fact, that spiritual vogues in Hungarian poetry move in two-year cycles—usually following the translation of an important European poet. In 1957, for example, the early Rilke was very much in vogue; today it is the later Rilke, as well as Dylan Thomas. Apparently, the strongest influence is usually exerted by the most recent volume of translation. Although some Hungarian poetry is merely slavish imitation of foreign vogues, it seems less so now than in the prewar era, when the influence of French and German poets was at times overpowering. Modern Hungarian poetry, rebelling against the strictures of socialism, is becoming more personal and multiform. Techniques, images, and forms are being developed and re-examined by each poet in his own way. Sometimes, as in the case of Ferenc Juhasz (b. 1928), Hungarian poetry is becoming overcharged with metaphors. Juhasz, whose dark-brown eyes keep rolling in their whites as rapidly as the images in his verse, is among those who have reintroduced "folkloristics" into Hungarian poetry. Juhasz's early work was strongly influenced by the idiom of folk ballads. Then, in the late forties, he developed a complex style laced with an overabundant wealth of animal and vegetable imagery that served to illustrate his morbid preoccupation with the themes of death and decay, as in his poem "The Force of Flowers."

. . . You have heard the seething of a tremendous sea that never knew
    jellyfish, crab, or stingray,
And you have seen the towering jets of whales disporting in the bland
    moonlit bay,
and how the yellow-finned, pole-necked, mouse-toothed Plesiosaurians,
the swimming mammal lizards, kissed the purple sea anemones in the
    oceans.

You have seen the stranded rose-headed squids upon the sands drying out
  to glass,
how soft red bellies of the cactus-armored reptiles touch in gentle dal-
  liance,
back and forth swinging between shell-covered thighs, the soft-veined
  onion-clapper
in the blue furry nest, and glass-brittle melon balls in the lined sac move
  and quiver. . . .

Back in 1953 the Stalinist regime branded Juhasz a "biological
realist" for such verse, and the publication of his poems was held up
for a number of years. Since those days he has passed through
several phases and now enjoys great popularity. The obese salesgirl
in the poet's bookshop in Budapest told Juhasz one day, very shyly,
"I don't like your poetry." Somewhat taken back, he asked her why,
and she countered, "Because it goes too deep into my heart." Juhasz
feels he should talk about the world "according to his knowledge,
emotion, and impulse." He feels the poet should love life because
"life is lovable and lonesome." Even more strongly, he feels the poet
should never stop pointing out that the only meaning of human
existence is freedom and "nobody has the right to take this away
from the individual or from mankind." In one of his shorter poems,
entitled "My Years of Lethargy," he asks rhetorically:

> Have I talked too straight?
> Is silence my destiny?
> Sorcerer's heart, is it afraid?
> Is my throat blocked or free?

Laszlo Nagy (b. 1925) is another poet who, like Juhasz, came
from a poor rural family, was deeply influenced by folk music, and
has a penchant for sticking his neck out. The latter is one of the
reasons why he earns his living as a picture editor for a Budapest
weekly. In an interview published in the literary review *Elet es
Irodalom,* in the mid-sixties, Nagy said:

I was brought up among tales and ballads, under the compelling rhythm
of their enchantment, in the flood of folk song that filled our house, and
certain features of my poetry show it. As a translator I have had the
opportunity to get to know folklore pretty thoroughly . . . but I never

thought of imitating. . . . I think the whole business of adapting folk songs with an orchestra and God-knows-what is the work of bloody eunuchs. . . . Instead of to sweet and smooth clichés, I turned to folklore for stronger, more complex and dynamic rhythms in words and sound, for images that reached out to madness, to blasphemy, to an attitude of somber dependence.

Nagy, who is an unreformed moralist, believes that the poet has real power. "It is the *sine qua non* of his calling," he contends. "In primitive times the magician was also a poet. He had power over the community, and was, in fact, supposed to be able to exercise power over the forces of nature." Continues Nagy: "He assured the success of an undertaking because he strengthened and prepared the community for it. And if the hunt was a failure, he was rightly knocked on the head. Nowdays, we have the division of labor, and I, the magician of today, am happy if I have power over words and what I have to say. If I had political power—I'd give even more independence to those entitled to it. If I had power—I'd tear up all the official lists of 'establishment men,' but even if I had power, I would not and I could not attack genuine authority." Laszlo Nagy claims he doesn't long for the "freedom" of his Western colleagues. He says, as far as his own decisions as a man are concerned (and the fulfillment of his poetic aims), he is free—or, at least, has been until now.

Laszlo Benjamin (b. 1915), whose principal theme is the relation of man to society, was not permitted to publish between 1956 and 1961 because of his stand in the Hungarian Revolution. (A brief biography in the *New Hungarian Quarterly* stated that after 1956 Benjamin "went through a crucial phase in his development, from which he emerged in the late fifties with a broader vision and a deeper intellectual content to his poetry.") Surprisingly, although he doesn't believe in the school of socialist realism and says that he sees realism from the abstract viewpoint of a poet, Benjamin is considered a communist author by all his colleagues. Indeed, he is regarded as the most "committed" of all Hungarian poets. Benjamin is convinced that poetry concretely influences the Hungarian nation on the path of its development. It is up to the poet, therefore, to experience, to protest, in order to guide the course of his people. To be effective, he must live and suffer through both the agonies of self-examination and the day-to-day existence of the workers. Only in a moment of elation, in between the sweat and the agony, can the poet praise the promise of a better everyday life. When the vision begins to blur and the inspiration vanishes, the poet must then revert to his essential role as a contemporary moralist.

Mihaly Vaci also has a strong belief in the pedagogic value of his poems. Although his forms and imagery often evoke the wistfulness of Chagall and his style is frequently surrealistic, Vaci considers it the duty of the poet to serve in the public interest. Now a member of Parliament, Vaci explained he was a member of the Communist Party until 1956. "Now I want to be a real communist, not a Party functionary," he added. It was in this spirit that he wrote a poem entitled "It Is Not Enough . . ." which was highly esteemed by the younger generation. In this poem, Vaci teaches that a communist must never be satisfied, that he must always go further, and that party membership does not free him from the necessity of critical self-examination. Like Juhasz and so many of his contemporaries, Vaci believes poetry can overcome evil, that through verse and through hard work the world can be set right. Part of the reason for this optimistic vein is Vaci's own socialist success story. For years he was an elementary-school teacher in a poor farm district of the Great Hungarian Plain. He had his first poem published when he was twenty-nine and now ascribes his initial success to the fact that "people were moved by my description of illness, loneliness, and poverty." With no literary or intellectual background, Vaci was an outsider to the tight circle of Budapest poets. "My quiet and timid resistance against the pathos of the time," he says, won the sympathy of both editors and readers. But once he was published, his rise to the top was rapid and his outlook became increasingly optimistic.

Vaci is now less and less appreciated by a public tired of socialist optimism and revolutionary zeal. The Hungarian readers feel they have much more in common with those poets who really suffered and who share their loneliness, disillusionment, and brooding. The feeling of resignation, which is such a common Hungarian and East

European characteristic, is not dissolving (as the Party would have it) "in a certain universal humanism." Nor is the "cheerful and happy acceptance of the challenge of life" a common denominator of the new poetry—as some Party hacks maintain. "Party-minded public enthusiasm" does not evoke a "sing-along-with-Mitch" response. In fact, one group of writers, known as the "fire dancers" (who figured with Mihaly Vaci in an anthology published under the title *Fire Dance*), have earned popular disdain for their sectarian attitudes.

Far more appreciated is Zoltan Zelk (b. 1906), the son of a cantor, who was expelled from Hungary for illegal activities in 1928 and spent more than a year in jail for his active role in the 1956 uprising. His "Under Abstract Skies" gives the flavor of the mood that, to a large degree, still persists.

> The flood has ebbed. It's winter now.
> The cruel and cunning season.
> How stealthily the frost lays hands
> Upon this harmless garden!
> Dun-white and rumpled chaos come,
> The pits yawn in the ground,
> In the silence stifling every
> Rippling, humming, mottled sound.
> Winter glitters, too, I know,
> Flashing like a well-gripped knife.
> The snow turns into a squeaky shot
> In stray dogs' hearts and cast-off lives.
> Shreds of splintered sleet rip open
> Underbellies of scared deer,
> And under the skies, abstract, numb,
> Demonstrating birds march dumb
> The way to frozen death.*

Most of what Zelk has written has been carefully deposited in his desk drawers—but his instinct of self-censorship, so prevalent among socialist authors, does not restrict his verse.

Janos Pilinszky (b. 1921) is a Catholic poet of pessimism. His verses struggle with the existentialist dilemma of "being and noth-

---

* Translated by Andrew Feldmar.

ingness." He himself struggles whether to stay in Hungary or to choose exile. "I have always had a religious bondage, but I have not called myself a Catholic poet," he said in his tiny Budapest flat. If ever there was a "hole"—in the Dostoevskian use of the word— Pilinszky's quarters fit the description. I visited him at ten thirty on a bright Sunday morning but his quarters retained a nocturnal aura. All the blinds were tightly shut. Only one tiny lamp was burning in his book-crammed room, and Pilinszky had the pallor of a priest who spends all his time in a confessional booth. While talking, Pilinszky smoked incessantly and drank cup after cup of strong coffee he had prepared himself—for he lives alone, like a hermit. Pointing to a picture of Simone Weil on his wall, Pilinszky said that her faith had helped him remain alive.

Pilinszky regards the tragedy of European Jewry "the most universal scandal of our age." In his poetry he shows the inhuman loneliness of murderer and victim united in the depersonalized slaughters of the concentration camps. What he creates is painfully and meticulously thought out. Pilinszky explained how his own Catholicism grew through a series of ordeals and trials in a German prisoner-of-war camp, his contact with the concentration camps, and, afterward, with the terror under Rakosi. During the trials and persecution of the Hungarian Catholics of the late forties, he became increasingly involved with their fate and started to work on the religious monthly *Vigilia*. Pilinszky said he wrote very little verse and that during the decade from 1949 to 1959 he was not allowed to publish any poems. He himself was consequently pleasantly surprised when the one thousand volumes of his verse, published by the state publishing house at the end of 1959, sold out in one morning. He had believed everybody had forgotten him. But the audience for his forceful, subtle religious thoughts could not easily be reduced. The following poem is a typical example of Pilinszky's questioning:

COMPLAINT

Lively beings under the stars,
Buried in the morass of night,
Do you hear my silent coming?
Like a brace of birds in flight.

So I call you wordlessly:
From where eternal stillness lies,
Will you ever rescue me
In your foreign skies?

Are you listening to my appeal?
Am I beseeching you in vain?
All around me are glistening
The sandbanks of fear and pain.

Can I count on you, God?
I long for your being,
For the love of all love
I am ever more fearing!

Bury me in your arms,
Do not leave me in the cold,
Even when I am out of breath,
My calls shall not grow old.

Like a leaf to a tree,
Be the joy of my trepidation:
Give me names, wonderful names,
As a cushion against annihilation.*

At the opposite end of the poetical spectrum from the terse poems of Pilinszky are the visionary, all encompassing works of Sandor Weores (b. 1913), who has found his inspiration in a Jungian form of existentialism. His obsession with symbols and myths and their bearing on ethics has placed him completely beyond all political engagement, and he has been allowed to work unmolested through the Horthy, Rakosi, and Kadar governments—a tour de force in itself. Weores is a poetic phenomenon. He began what one critic called his "disreputable belief in art for art's sake" at the age of fourteen, and at seventeen he was deeply influenced by Lao-Tzu. He traveled to India on a fellowship before World War II and immersed himself in Hindu mythology. Slowly, influenced by Lao-

* Translated by Barbara Frischmuth and Yorick Blumenfeld.

Tzu's *Tao Teh King,* the works of Jaspers and Jung, the upani-
shads, the *Bhagavad-Gita,* the Babylonian epic of Gilgamesh, the
Polynesian Hainuvele cycle of myths, and numerous other sources,
Weores began to create his own cosmos. It was an unsettling
experience for me to visit Weores in his Buda home, because within
a few minutes we found each other talking on entirely different
planes. In a sense, it was like communicating with an opium
smoker. In answer to a question about the direction in which
Hungarian poetry was moving, Weores began to talk about the
sattva, about the empty sphere (of intuition), about rajas and
tamas. It was impossible to make any sense out of his answers—except by picking up random fragments of his sentences: "I am
eclectic, I am an island. . . . In the technical, materialistic world
of today . . . man has a third or fourth sphere filled with peace.
. . . There are always conflicts between groups, parties, and countries. . . . A poet must retain his roots in archetypal material."
Some critics have compared him to Michaux, but, although there
are similarities, the comparison does not do him justice, as this
excerpt from the long cycle *Internus* makes clear:

OUT OF THE INNER INFINITY

From inward infinities I still look out
now and again, seeing through my face
clouds or the winking lights of stars in space.
My eyesight fails, that leaves me like the rest,
the outside world has shut my gates, I'm left
where there is no earth, but only sky;
and no event, no grace and no surprise,
no surface, nothing seen, no nebulae,
only reality at peace and luminous,
boundless and measureless and nameless,
a love that's still desireless and still changeless.
The panic world is baffled at my gate:
"Madman! Egotist! Traitor!" its words beat.
But wait: I have a bakehouse in my head,
you'll feed someday on this still uncooled bread.*

* Translated by Edwin Morgan.

Critics agree that Weores's poetry is more versatile than any other being composed in Hungary today. His poetry defies imitation and loses infinitely in translation. His imagery is effortless and brilliant, like the movement of an Olympic champion leaping across a puddle. His mastery of techniques is such that he is as confident writing Ovidian distichs or iambic trimeters as he is writing ballads or surrealist verse. And the true scope of his talent is revealed, it seems to me, in his superb nursery rhymes, which truly animate nature. Like much work of true genius, it is equally popular with adults and small children.

Weores's lack of poetical involvement in contemporary reality separates him from his contemporaries. Weores is an idealist. His principal challenge is the alienated ego—that is, the enigma of the loneliness of the individual. Because he sees the world as irrational, he feels that man's efforts to make it rational are no more than pathetic folly. Weores deeply senses the inadequacy of the human brain. His characters consequently turn their backs to the world. Weores is resigned to the promise of a nirvana as compensation for the painful endurance of earthly reality, as shown in the following poem:

THE MUDDY DRINK IS GOING DOWN AND THE BOTTOM OF THE GLASS SHOWS THROUGH

After death shall I still exist?
No handcuffs, then, upon my wrist.
I have dissolved identity.
Why wish it in eternity?
Being or nonbeing: nakedness
suits undying presences.

I never thought it could be so:
my body gasps for its last breath,
yet still and easy is my soul.
My life is wantless and unwanted,
a beggar going on undaunted,
even by my death unhaunted,
with losses and with gains untainted.

161

Fate is too kind! I had best not
die this way, like a dying god,
a smiling victory well flaunted;
I should be pulled up by the root
with a cowardly last shout
and get the real end of a man,
not judged for what I solely am.*

Weores says, "When either religion, or philosophy, or poetry faces
the ultimate questions, it somehow becomes, in a sense, misty,
barren, obscure, dark. It is so difficult to cross the thresholds beyond
the limits of everyday practical life." Weores long ago made the
leap of accepting daily life as mere semblance. He regards his ego's
relations to everyday problems as strictly superfluous to meaning.
That may be one of the reasons why he rises in the late afternoon,
works all night, and sleeps through the day in order to escape the
deadly, humdrum concerns of his colleagues.

For Weores, the sexual act is the surest way toward terrestial
nirvana. He believes in the supremacy of love. In the preface to his
latest volume, *Tuzhkut,* he writes: "I wish to X-ray you, to rouse
you so that you may transform yourself from your closed, finite ego,
into an open, social, cosmic ego." On occasion, his love poems have
aroused storms of controversy, pornography being almost as offensive to a communist as Voice of America propaganda. However,
some readers and critics regard Part VI of *Fairy Spring* among the
most beautiful lines that he has written.

As one being killed, her body fell back, legs writhing,
Her rounded bosom crushed under my bony chest.
My beautiful playmate, the girl with the heavenly blue eyes,
Fresh, with the boyish figure, virgin with girlish blond tresses,
Now she was frightened: "What do you want, fool? I was only joking.
    Stop!"

She, the arsonist, was now afraid to scream, in the fire.
If someone should come now and catch the bold coquette
Just as a bull's weight is lowered onto her frothy shivering—

* Translated by Edwin Morgan.

She preferred to scratch and bite, and I covered with kisses
Her opened lips and shimmering teeth.
The whiteness of shoulders, roundness of breasts, and slimness of hips,
Slipping between her prancing knees, I searched for the cleft,
Shooting the liquid of my lust on her tights and crumpled petticoat.

I was ashamed and therefore cross with her.
She motherly cuddled my head: "You wicked one! Was it good?
Now you feel better. Stop, little jackass! Stop that nonsense!"
She stroked me gently and with slight mocking: "My lord, are you
    satisfied?"
I crushed the girl in my arms. "I shall devour this mockingbird."
Her face became flushed; she gasped: "You are tearing me to pieces. Wait,
    my sweet,
My dress is all crumpled, don't ruin it. Let me take it off!"
She opens a hook, and the skirt drops onto a chair,
A few slight pushes and down come her silken panties,
And what convention and virtue kept hidden under bright garments
Is now laid bare in secret to the companion.
As in a fever I embraced her, she threw her legs apart,
Wrapped them around my back and fell back on the bed.
So melted, in the air of a fiery thunderstorm, boy and girl
Into one body, form a primeval figure with two heads.
The bright clay figurines of the girl's room were ashamed.
They dared not look at their beautiful, naïve mistress;
She miaowed like a cat and writhed like a dying swan
And, quaking, her little bed groaned under the rain and the storm.
My beautiful playmate, whom I had often embraced while dancing,
Whom I had carried, barefooted, across the brook in my arms.
I knew her moods, the tiny kisses, and the fleeting face:
Here she is one with me and still far away, new, and strange.
Her radiant, fresh look is now veiled like a cow's eye.
She became feminine, yielding, an impassioned lover.
Finally, the lady turned her back to me crying, rolling over
Into entangled pillows and sobbing: "Is it better for you like this,
    scoundrel?"
I begged her, whispering: "Forgive me!" Then she threw back her head,
And her blue eyes sparkled at me, laughing like an accomplice.*

* Translated by Barbara Frischmuth, Hilde Bennett, and Yorick Blumenfeld.

Weores is thus involved in a love-religion. In the love-making process, as his intellect plunges deeper and deeper into the unconscious, the conscious mind also loses itself in the sexual act and alters itself as it enters another person. What is ultimately left, as he writes in *Internus,* is that "each cell and seed he has would in its fervor go on fucking and gorging forever." Weores's belief in the power of sex to transform the human being and the human intellect link him to D. H. Lawrence. However, Weores's form of sexual other-worldliness is restricted to the few who think they understand him, and even Weores does not seem to make his escape good. Weores looks tired, tortured, and unhappy as a human being. It would seem to me that whether a Hungarian poet chooses love or politics, or whether he combines them, he cannot avoid alienation from the socialist society encircling him. Poetry alone—and in Hungary *"tout finit par un poème"*—is not sufficient.

CHAPTER IX

Red in Black and White

The questions raised by television in Rumania, where the airwaves belong to the people, would rattle American sensibilities. What American would dream of asking such Rumanian posers as:

Why can't we see more of those commercials?

When will the state stop rigging news programs?

Is boredom really in the public interest?

Must the man in the street always prove his literacy by reading his so-called "spontaneous" reactions?

But since there is no Federal Communications Commission in Bucharest to look after the interests of the two existing networks, the Party steps in and obligingly spells out the tenets of the TV Manifesto. The gist of this ukase is that if the people are not being bored, they are not being enlightened. And there is always some Communist Party official with an authoritative quotation from Marx or Lenin on his lips to corroborate that the Rumanian concept of magazine programing is, in fact, the only scientifically correct approach.

Communists believe that the object of American programing, or of capitalist programing in general, is to make people apathetic, to drug and to distract them from serious thought to the point where they are incapable of protest. By way of contrast, Rumanian officials emphasize that their programing concentrates on education, information, and the general "upgrading" of the admittedly low cultural level of the people. As one Rumanian news director, who had spent some time in the United States, saw it: "American television causes the fragmentation of society. It sets one class against the other; it breeds nihilism and violence. Our Rumanian television, on the other hand, inspires a deep-seated optimism and a profound faith in socialism."

Georg Ivascu, an ebullient Rumanian literary editor, professor, and sometime television lecturer, initiated a luncheon conversation on the subject of Rumanian television by asking me why an intelligent man, who has only so many minutes a day for reading the paper, perusing a book, or watching television, should be forced to view idiotic propaganda for soap, mouthwash, shaving cream, detergents, toothpaste, dandruff, or deodorants? "We are not out to profit from the viewers," said Ivascu, "or to inspire them to buy more than they need. We want to develop their intelligence, not to insult them. Maybe we don't succeed, but we try." While I was tempted to reply that the entire Rumanian TV schedule is basically nothing more than one long commercial for the state, I pointed out that TV commercials were on the increase throughout the socialist states and that the public seemed to like them. Foreign commercials for Pepsi-Cola, Martini & Rossi, and Remy Martin, for example, can now be seen in Bucharest every evening between six fifty-five and seven, along with a few slogans to the effect that margarine tastes better than butter or prompting Rumanian Pioneers to show more enthusiasm for their work brigades.

While Rumanian officials view the commercialization of television with trepidation, Mircea Crisan, the Rumanian Jackie Gleason, adopts quite a different approach. On one television program satirizing Rumanian razor blades, Crisan portrayed a prisoner being cross-examined somewhat brusquely by the state militia. The officers threaten him and warn, "If you don't tell us everything, we'll use the water treatment on you." Crisan is unimpressed and keeps mum. The police escalate their threats. "We'll use the fingernail method," menaces an officer. Still Crisan remains imperturbable. Finally, as a last resort, the interrogators say, "Okay, then we will shave you with a Bucharest Razor Blade." This prospect is overwhelming even for Crisan, and he agrees to confess everything. On another show, Crisan gave a talk about the famous

Rumanian apples. "We grow many varieties," says Crisan, "but the only ones for sale are the kind with worms." (The rest are exported to the West for hard currency.)

Crisan (b. 1926) is a small, fat Jewish comedian with boundless energy, lively dark eyes, and a gift for exceptionally swift repartee. As a television "personality" in a country where, aside from Ceausescu, there are no personalities on the screen, Crisan is the first to admit that "it is not really possible to create works of art for Rumanian television." Instead, Crisan tries to lighten the fare. "On New Year's Eve, Rumanian television presented eight continuous hours of the best in song, dance, acting, and comedy that the country could provide—but still the public was not satisfied," said Crisan. "Most viewers complained last year's show was better." As a consequence, even Crisan, who is the only Rumanian performer to have what might be called "international class," tries to avoid overexposure on the Red tube. "Television is a knife with two edges," says Crisan, who writes all his own scripts, "because while a comedian may reach a much larger audience in this medium, his appeal can evaporate faster than boiling water."

As an Artist Emerit (an honor granted by the state) Crisan enjoys certain privileges not granted other Rumanians. Not only is he entitled to forty-five days of vacation a year (instead of the usual thirty), an extra room, and a fifty per cent reduction of his taxes (Crisan is reputed to be the richest man in Rumania), but he is also permitted to speak his mind a little more freely. On one television program, Crisan appeared dressed like a hunter with a rifle slung across his shoulder. A friend approached in the woods, bragging about how many deer he had killed, or almost killed. Replied Crisan, "Yes, and I almost saw a spiritual and enlightened program on television."

There is no great tradition of satire in Rumania, but even though "satire for satire's sake is not popular with us," says Crisan, this hardly stops the comedian. While the rest of the world has been introducing birth control, Rumania passed legislation in 1966 prohibiting abortions, and Ceausescu, for reasons of national aggrandizement, embarked on a reckless campaign to promote live births (reckless, because there was not enough space in the hos-

167

pitals to accommodate the tidal wave of new babies, and domestic industry was completely unprepared to meet the sudden demand for diapers, baby foods, and baby carriages). When I asked Crisan, who is well known as a *"coureur"* in Bucharest, what he thought of the campaign for more numerous families, he replied he had given serious attention to it. (His own motto, a Latin maxim, is: "One can't have all the women in the world, but one should keep on trying.) In a recent television skit Crisan was shown sitting on a park bench while an attractive Rumanian girl with long tresses walked by in the most provocative fashion. The comedian didn't even look up. Another buxom young creature strolled by and even winked, but Crisan retained his dead pan. Suddenly a woman with gray hair, well in her fifties (and thus perfectly safe), passed. Crisan abruptly looked up, adjusted his tie, and prepared his pursuit. Obviously, for some Rumanians there will always be a way to dodge governmental decrees.

While Rumanian television may not represent the ultimate in cultural attainment, it does occupy a central place in the Party's cultural strategy. Rumanian opinion polls have shown that the seventeen-inch tube has a suggestive power five times more potent than the radio. The public revealed the same changes in its views, habits, and speech patterns after half a year of watching television as after about four years of radio listening. This, quite obviously, makes television the ideal medium for the dissemination of propaganda. Indicative of the importance attached to television is the Rumanian military guard, submachine gun in hand, who stiffly patrols the marble lobby of the Bucharest TV center. He is not there to protect the programing staff of some eight hundred people, but to ward off any dissatisfied counterrevolutionary viewers. Television, then, is seen as an ideal tool with which to ladle daily doses of government pap directly into the home. It presents no dangers, as does the short-wave radio set, which can be used to tune in to perfidious stations like Radio Free Europe, the BBC, or the Voice of America. Consequently, the communist governments throughout Eastern Europe subsidize the cost of television sets more than any other type of durable consumer goods except washing machines. By 1968, there were about seven hundred and fifty thousand TV sets in operation in Rumania, and about thirteen million sets in the rest of Eastern Europe—excluding Russia. By the time color television will be introduced in 1970, it is estimated that the Rumanian market will be saturated with two million receivers. The Rumanian State TV Committee introduced a second channel in 1968. However, this did not really offer viewers a greater variety of programing. Rumanian TV producers are well aware that the people want entertainment—not enlightenment—and so they try to follow the Soviet pattern. In Moscow, if there is an educational lecture on one channel, the TV directors make certain there will be a round-table discussion or an "uplifting" program on the other channel. In other words, the viewer cannot escape having his mind "upgraded."*

Until the fall of 1967, Rumania had no television programs on Monday. Despite the massive allocations for TV programing, Rumania just could not afford the luxury of round-the-clock shows. Time is not money on Rumanian TV, but the costs of programing are such that the state is forced to adopt a more casual pace. One channel broadcasts from 6:00 P.M. to 11:30 P.M. five days a week and from 8:30 A.M. to 11:30 P.M. on Sunday; the other, from 8:00 P.M. to 11:00 P.M. every weekday evening. Despite the night-owlish habits of the Rumanian people, they are not provided with late shows. This, it is thought, would cause absenteeism. Programing is fixed at the beginning of each season according to a paternalistic magazine concept that encourages viewers to know exactly what is being shown each week throughout the year. This schedule, which permits people to allocate their time rationally, is decided upon by a "college" of television executives and Party members. Every Tuesday, Wednesday, and Thursday the channel opens at six with a half-hour program on economic news. This is followed by a half-hour program for youth and by another half hour on either science or literature. From seven thirty to eight there is a news broadcast, succeeded by a movie. The broadcasting day closes with a

* The Russians have recently completed the tallest TV tower in the world, and at the fiftieth anniversary of the Bolshevik revolution there were an estimated twenty-five million sets operating in the Soviet Union. In Moscow, there are now three channels—including an educational channel—providing a total of about thirty viewing hours per day.

news summary. On Tuesdays, there is always one play broadcast "live" from the Bucharest stage (usually presented after it has run a couple of months and public attendance has begun to sag). Every Wednesday night, from eight thirty to nine, there is a program entitled "Youth Club," which, appropriately, emphasizes rock-and-roll. On Fridays, there is a program on tourism, telling Rumanians about the ways to welcome visiting capitalists. On Saturdays the programing is more complex: It includes a transmission on homemaking, a prominent feature, of special interest to women; a projection of "Tele-encyclopedia," which dramatizes the in-depth examination of one word (Doric, gold, motor, elephant), using film clips, scholarly commentary, and even round-table discussion; and, finally, a British mystery series, "The Saint," shown after the kids have gone to bed. Sunday mornings open with calisthenics, followed by an hour and a half of children's programing and an hour and a half of information for the backward peasantry. At noon a live concert is broadcast, followed by the soccer or basketball "game of the week." Sunday evening is quiz time, and this draws between four and five million viewers. Different schools compete to answer a variety of specialized questions. The top prize on this show is equivalent to a thousand dollars. The most popular of all Rumanian programs are competitive folklore and folk-dance contests between teams from different regions of the country. Apparently, the programers cannot satisfy the demand for more and still more local folk dancing and music. It is not that the Ceausescu regime, which has been waging an aggressive campaign to promote nationalism over the past few years, would not like to build up pride in Rumania's national traditions; it's just that Rumania's television budget cannot be stretched any further.

Tudor Vornicu (b. 1926), the fast-speaking, humorless editor-in-chief of news of Rumanian television, explained that news broadcasting is necessarily a sensitive and difficult operation. "We present no material on the China-Russia dispute," he said, "because the minute we were to show this . . . well, you understand." Similarly, the Rumanians make it a policy not to mention difficulties in the internal affairs of other nations—so there has been no hint, to date, of the cultural revolution in China. On major communist conferences (such as the summit conference in the spring of 1967 at Karlovy Vary, Czechoslovakia) the only comment by Channel 1 Bucharest often is that the Rumanians are not attending. One of the anomalies of socialist news broadcasts in general is that radio and television must usually wait until the full commentary has appeared in the daily press. Sometimes the newscasters read their text verbatim from the official Party organ, *Scantea*, but a good portion of the blame for the inferior quality of the news reporting must be attributed to the timidity of the producers. "The main principles of our socialist journalism are truthfulness, seriousness, and objectivity," explained one of Vornicu's assistants. Therefore, the Rumanian telecaster must always check on news reports and wait for confirmation from other sources before broadcasting any item. "This means we are sometimes late—even two or three days late—but our listeners would not appreciate news reports that would have to be denied after an hour," maintained this pudgy bureaucrat quite straight-facedly.

Rumanian television newscasters are almost exclusively rather plump, unattractive, middle-aged mothers. Asked why he chooses such homely creatures to report the news, Vornicu replied, "I prefer intelligent to beautiful women to feed me the news. For one thing, I think they are far more believable than speakerines." In a television world where the "star" system is unknown, there is no appeal in glamour for its own sake. Perhaps Vornicu's logic is not so wrong, because plausibility does seem to be a primary concern of socialist broadcasters. The public places as little faith in the newscasts as it does in the shifty and usually evasive weather predictions. By and large, I had the impression Bucharest viewers are extremely discontented with the news coverage. "I see nothing of life in other countries," said one housewife. "I don't know how the average Czech or Russian lives," she went on to complain. "All I get is a series of pictures of flowers, celebrations, toasts, and send-offs." She frankly admitted that protocol just didn't interest her, but that's about the only film footage presented on the news programs. There rarely are any film clips or taped reports from Rumanian foreign correspondents. Although these glaring inadequacies are overlooked, there is dissatisfaction in official circles over other "defi-

171

ciencies." A Rumanian foreign ministry official lectured me one afternoon to the effect that socialist television does not place enough stress on the weak sides of capitalism. "Bolivia, Portugal, and even Turkey are also part of the capitalist system," he said. "Rumanians think America represents capitalism," he maintained, "but they forget those other capitalist countries where there is little glitter—only dehumanized, impoverishing exploitation."

Rumanians are not the only Eastern Europeans to be dissatisfied with the news broadcasts. Wlodzimierz Sokorski, Chairman for Radio and Television in Poland, confesses: "It is hard to deny that informative and economic programs are burdened on the one hand with weaknesses of a technical nature, and on the other hand with insufficient professional and even political qualifications." This is a roundabout, Middle-European way of saying he is unhappy with the competition from Radio Free Europe, located in Munich, which is usually faster to spread information about events occurring in Poland than either Polish radio or TV. One Polish viewer, writing a letter of protest to the daily *Zycie Warszawy,* said that he had recently been watching a newscast, waiting for information for news about Vietnam and the Middle East. "Yet before the foreign news came on, I was cold-bloodedly treated to two reports on local town meetings in X and Y." This impatient viewer continued: "To save my life, I could not tell what was the informational, political, or emotional value of the picture representing the unchanging ritual of dignitaries of varying caliber, sitting dumbly behind a table, speaking like fish, without a sound. At such meetings, the most vital questions in Poland are sometimes analyzed, and there are violent and serious discussions. But all we hear are the most banal statements of the off-screen commentator." The viewer then questioned rhetorically, "What has this to do with a newscast? About as much as the 365th showing of steel ingots being rolled," he concluded. This protest could have come equally well from Budapest, Sofia, or Bucharest.

The total absence of spontaneity on socialist television makes for a stultifying dullness. Whatever is unrehearsed, whatever cannot be controlled, is viewed with suspicion. Participants on "discussion" programs on Bucharest television almost always rehearse their script several times. The unofficial explanation for such preparations is that the program directors are instructed not to air conflicting or contradictory viewpoints. There are ample soporifics about Rumania's economic development, about the increasing output of butterfat on collective farms—but when it comes to real criticism, it is as if a gloved hand were standing by, ready to muffle any screams. One popular Rumanian public affairs program, "The Reflector," does criticize social and economic mismanagement, but in a carefully guarded fashion. For instance, a factory manager will publicly explain that the new plant he has been appointed to direct is already out of date—although it has not even been completed—and that there actually is no need for such a factory in Rumania. The MC of "The Reflector" then calls the ministry responsible for the establishment of the factory to explain how this is possible. As often as not, some subaltern in the Ministry for Light Industry will respond, in writing, with an evasive reply some three weeks later. By then, most of the viewers have forgotten what the storm was all about, but they retain a vague feeling that criticism of mismanagement does come out into the open. However, no television commentator would ever dream of criticizing the conduct of foreign affairs, the behavior of Foreign Minister Corneliu Manescu, the operation of the organs of state, or the performance of Ceausescu's minions.

Another Rumanian discussion program, "Face to Face," features panel analyses of such various topics as marriage and divorce, children's complaints about schoolwork, training of soccer players, and employment of graduate students. One program featured a discussion at a motorcycle plant about the effect of the new (seven to five) working day in the factory. "Characters" with a good sense of humor or an odd approach do occasionally animate such discussions, but these talks generate none of the controversy or "heat" we are accustomed to on Western television screens.

Just before the general relaxation of censorship on Czech TV in early 1968, Jiri Pelikan, director-general of Czech TV, said that in the "Open Forum" series he had tried to confront the "views of the man in the street with the standpoint of responsible authorities" on universal issues such as the new wage policy. Although Pelikan claimed that the Czech viewers found the public explanations attractive, the wretched Bohemian or Moravian worker, when confronted with the written declarations of some unseen minister, found himself stuttering and sputtering. Occasionally, when participants did speak their minds, such round-table programs ran into heavy fire. After one discussion, dedicated to questions on attitude toward work (a sensitive point in an economy where absenteeism, drinking during working hours, and carelessness are rampant), the Party reprimanded the MC of the show for "superficial preparation, poor selection of participants, and faulty direction," which led to "wholesale, distortive criticism."

The goal of television, as seen by the Central Committee of the Czechoslovakian Communist Party in 1967 was "systematically and purposefully to assist in the ideological education of the working class, to deepen the socialist attitude of the listeners, and openly and actively to combat incorrect ideas in the field of ideology, culture, and the national economy." Of course, such an edict from the top crippled spontaneity in public affairs programing, but the Czechs were far more ingenious in cutting corners than the Rumanians. For example, a program called "Crime Archive" administered a moderate dose of detective stories, for which there was a great demand among the older generation. While there was no pandering to sensationalism or sadism and the accent was placed on detection, not on the crime, the Czechs were offered the usual titillations of melodrama. The directors of "Crime Archive" got away with this only by placing stress on the motives of criminality and on the social and psychological background of the criminals.

Programs dealing with social problems have gained increasing prominence in Czechoslovakia. Although a few years ago such topics were ignored, the communist leaders felt something had to be done to stimulate the social conscience of the young and halt the rising crime and delinquency rates. It still strikes the Western viewer as odd that "human values" seem to receive far more stress on Bucharest or Budapest TV than in real life. Motherhood, family togetherness, respect for the individual are treated in sanctimonious fashion on the screen, but concern for the dignity of man seems to shrink considerably in the controlled and semiregimented aspects of daily life. Conversely, in the United States the popular TV series are detached from reality in their pandering to brutality, their disregard for conventions, and their stress on the abnormal.

A Czech series called "Civil Proceedings" investigated the universal problem of juvenile delinquency before the 1968 revolution. Using real court cases, a psychologist, a sociologist, a lawyer, and a reform school worker discussed the aspects of each crime and gave the offenders a hearing. The sound track and the over-all scenes were authentic, but the close-ups were acted and identities protected. Programs dealt with the social causes of venereal disease among teenage girls, drinking among university students, and teen-age theft in the Prague streets. Before the ouster of Novotny in 1968, the very ambivalent views of the Czech Communist Party toward the younger generation was revealed in this type of programing. On the one hand, the top leaders felt themselves bitterly criticized by the younger generation—whom they did not understand—and, on the other, they were aware that all hopes for the future rested with this age group. Condemning TV programs and plays that accentuated the "worship of youth as a generation of 'clean hands' unsullied by the mistakes of the past, but having the right to criticize the acts of their fathers," the regime attacked the "immature taste" of directors offering such presentations. As in every socialist state, television was forced to express the viewpoint of the Party and assist in the realization of its program.

Dubcek's liberal outlook and his rapport with the intellectual community immediately resulted in a far more adventurous programing policy. For the first time in any communist state, television became a powerful instrument for effecting political change. Even the outwardly phlegmatic Czech viewers were astounded to see Premier Josef Lenart confess to his mistakes, or to observe a bumbling defense minister evade questions on the home screen. Where television had previously been off limits to such sensitive domestic issues as the abuse of power by the police and the Ministry of the Interior, suddenly no holds were barred. TV cameras were permitted to record the proceedings of a Central Committee meeting. The widow of Rudolf Slansky (the ex-Foreign Minister who was framed and executed in the early fifties) related in an interview

175

how the state prosecutor had even refused to hand over her husband's ashes. Czech television was no longer restricted to expressing the Party viewpoint or to propagandize the social and economic goals of the communists. Instead, the television reporters went out into the streets, the homes, the farms, and the church to get the viewpoints of the people. In one interview a village cleric spoke forthrightly on the suppression of the Catholic Church since 1948 and asked for full religious freedom. The cleric then went on to compare Dubcek's program of liberalization to Pope John XXIII's spiritual reform of the Church. Such a statement, in itself, had been completely unthinkable a few months earlier. On another program, Eugene Loebl, director of the state bank and a leading Slovak economist, went on the air to suggest a mixed economy for Czechoslovakia—"with two hundred thousand to three hundred thousand small, privately owned enterprises." Again there were gasps from student groups watching the program. When a deputy defense minister committed suicide, a sick joke made the rounds in Prague that he had really feared being sentenced to half an hour of cross-examination on Czech TV. The sudden appearance of free speech made Czech television radically different from the neighboring, state-controlled monopolies. However, no one could predict how long such freedom would last or whether it would spread to Poland or Hungary.

While the seesaw might temporarily tip the other way again, even in Czechoslovakia, it would seem unlikely that the other communist parties would find it advantageous to continue the distribution of low-calorie programing on a long-term basis. Poland's TV boss, Sokorski, admitted that an investigation conducted by his organization forced him to agree with "many complaints" from viewers who felt the programs were "too verbose, tiring, and sometimes completely lacking in entertainment." And yet, one out of every three Polish programs is light entertainment (ranging from quizzes to musicals), and Polish television annually presents one hundred and forty theatrical premières, not including musicals or vaudeville-type shows. Numerically, this statistic might be envied by the three major American television networks; qualitatively, Polish TV drama is vapid.

Slick serial adventures were the most widely viewed Polish programs in 1967. "Doctor Kildare" was running neck and neck with "Bonanza" and "The Saint" for the most popular Polish TV series. When students in a Wroclaw high school were directed to write essays on the heroic figure of their dreams, the greatest number chose to write not on Gomulka, Marx, or Lenin, but on Doctor Kildare. (What is wrong with Polish TV is, in a sense, a reflection of what is wrong with Poland itself, a mistress whose soul yearns for the West and whose body is tied to the Soviet Union.)

Because Western TV serials not only cost foreign exchange but glamorize capitalist decadence, Sokorski says, "Our leading task is the production of our own, ideologically committed films in search of a positive hero." One of these new heroes is Lieutenant Sowa (Owl), a plain-clothes officer who chases criminals, thieves, and smugglers—but never political criminals. Sowa is blond, good-looking, well-dressed, and—like any soap opera hero—never loses. He is typical of the real Polish flatfoot. Sowa even has "inner struggles" about a smoking habit he never succeeds in giving up. Another positive hero indigenous to Polish serials is a World War II relic, Captain Klos—an undercover officer of the Polish military intelligence—who wears the uniform of the Nazi *"Abwehr."* The double role of Klos is the source of endless thrills. And perhaps because he boldly sports a German uniform, he is idolized by the youngsters. In the mid-sixties, the ordeal of grinding out World War II episodes every week proved such a trial to the scriptwriters that the Klos series was stopped. But the TV viewers demanded further adventures, and the tired writers were forced to resuscitate this hero of sterling integrity and unexampled courage.

The Party committee in charge of the Hungarian radio and TV network also admitted, in a study conducted in the mid-sixties, that "Frequently in our daily material, we do not speak about matters in which people are interested. . . . We prefer to stick to what we ourselves wish to report, irrespective of whether it interests people or not." But while most viewers may be fed up with the abundant lectures about safety in the factory and the perseverance of lecturing on Marxism, there are also those dogmatists who feel the Party

177

is not doing its share. "Why does the Party tolerate this flood of detective stories on our television screens?" questioned one irate Magyar militant. The rebuttal given by the press was that "the Party is not responsible for everything." But the press went along with the dissenter by advising him that all this was only chewing gum for the eyes, and that "one day we shall get fed up with these programs and that will be the end of that." Usually, however, the response is far more combative. One poll of listener complaints sounded by the Hungarian TV network greatly upset Party officials because many of the factory workers and peasants took issue with TV's portrayal of the working man. "More than once, in cabaret programs, the worker is ridiculed, while in political programs he is a dry, statistical entry," they said, implying that TV directors lacked sympathy and understanding for the working class. As in every other socialist state, the Party pleaded for production personnel to show more "positive worker and peasant heroes" on television. Then, focusing on specifics, the Party committee analyzed a television play entitled "The Red-Stemmed Reed," which depicted a communist co-operative leader who was engaged in continual arguments with his collectivized shepherds, but who was powerless to correct their lackadaisical methods. The Hungarian TV committee cautioned, "We cannot arouse the impression in the public that we only talk and criticize and mention mistakes in vain." Of course, the same could be said for television itself. One of the Hungarian TV directors wonders why the public makes such baffling appraisals" (*i.e.*, negative criticism) of TV programing when it is given such generous doses of opera, theater, detective stories, news, education, music, and entertainment. Nothing, he seemed to suggest, would satisfy the new Hungarian proletariat.

Bulgaria faced much the same dilemma as its Balkan neighbors: a rather puritanical-minded regime was trying to impose its morality on a fun-loving and easygoing population. Illustrative of the anxiety aroused by the twenty-one-inch tube was a letter sent in April 1968 by strong man Todor Zhivkov to the Director of Bulgarian TV, the Chairman of the Committee for Art and Culture, and other high-ranking officials:

Comrades:

An ever-growing number of people have recently expressed to me in letters, by telephone, and in conversation their indignation and alarm that artists, dressed in a showy and extravagant manner, who appear on television and variety shows, are imitating in apparel and bearing rather dubious images from Western variety and television shows.

Recently I watched a TV program for secondary school students. You will agree with me that the long hair of the boys made it difficult to distinguish them from the girls, and that the unaesthetically short skirts of the latter have hardly anything in common with the sound feelings of the Bulgarians for what is beautiful. . . .

Of course, young people, and all the people in Bulgaria, have the right to dress according to their taste and to behave in a manner befitting their education and culture, provided this does not infringe upon the public code of ethics and standards of behavior. But ought the television and the variety shows, in their role of serious socialist institutions, entrusted by the state and the public with the task of working for the education of the new generations, to compromise their taste and convictions by popularizing, endorsing, and propagating with the force of their impact, such sad, alien, and pitiable phenomena as models to be imitated, and as a standard of behavior to be followed in Bulgaria? . . .

Truly yours,
Todor Zhivkov

It is to be believed that the Party Secretary's letter was not merely relegated to the "out" box of the letters department.

Bucharest TV, like all socialist television stations, is highly sensitive to viewer critique. Every month between five thousand and six thousand letters are received in response to specific programs—and the majority of these letters are negative. To Westerners not familiar with the practice of self-criticism in communist states, such a flow of signed letters may come as a surprise. General complaints by the viewers are that there is "too much talk," that the variety programs are no good, and that there are not enough shows devoted to popular music and jazz. In addition to these letters, the Rumanian TV committee conducts in-depth polls. Three broad polling samples are taken every year, but teams are sent to study specific sections of the population all the time. Asked how Rumanian TV responds to viewer preferences, news director Vornicu replied, "We

179

change a program if the viewers demand it; we will even kill it, if necessary." Vornicu explained how the directors had stopped a sagging variety show because there just did not seem to be enough talent to fill the weekly slot. A poll quickly revealed that the viewers were most unhappy with this decision, and the program was reinstated—despite the lack of talent.

Although, for some Rumanians, the television set has become a status symbol—an essential accessory to their living room, which they seldom bother to switch on*—in general, the black-and-white screen is opening up the cultural horizon of the viewers. Not only can Rumanians watch "The Saint" every Saturday night, or "The Incorruptibles," but even collective farmers from Slobozia can get an occasional glimpse of Sammy Davis, Jr., "Bonanza," and a few special NBC documentaries. Somehow the Rumanians have the notion that American TV is filled with crime and striptease, but in time they will be disappointed to discover they are only half right. Eurovision, too, has given them the chance to broaden their perspective. It has brought them such events as Kennedy's funeral, the Olympic games, and Beatrix's wedding. Intervision, on the other hand, has linked all the countries of Eastern Europe for the coverage of sports events. Culturally, television remains a distant promise, yet even in Rumania it is fast overtaking the newspapers, the theater, the movies, and the soccer field as the prime time-consumer of the population. When asked to comment on the changing status of Rumanian TV, Bucharest playwright Alexander Mirodan replied: "Culturally, it lags behind poetry, prose, criticism, and the theater. In fact, it is at the very bottom of the heap. Perhaps that is why people spend so much time watching it."

* Conversely, I visited homes in Bucharest where the set was never turned off, but no one bothered to watch it.

CHAPTER X

"Counter Bond"

Bulgarian literature should not be relegated to the stacks of central depositories. True, Bulgaria has not produced any Promethean literary figures, but then, there have been no Balzacs anywhere in Eastern Europe. Today, only Andrei Gulyashki, the author of a mystery series that pitted a Bulgarian counterintelligence agent against a resurrected James Bond, could evoke a vague recognition among Western *cognoscenti*. But despite its relative obscurity, Bulgaria does have a noteworthy literary tradition and an active, complex literary scene: That some twenty-two different state publishing houses printed close to four thousand different Bulgarian titles in 1967 indicates the scope of the literary bustle.* During the past few years, Bulgarian literature, which before the war had concentrated on the swordplay of Bulgaria's nineteenth-century struggle for liberation, has been experiencing turbulent change—mirroring the general transition of this small Balkan nation from an agricultural state to a semi-industrialized society, from a Stalinist dictatorship to a communist regime with a more pragmatic approach toward the arts.

Like writers in every communist country, the Bulgarian writers have been struggling for far more than their own literary advancement. In their poems, novels, and short stories they have been fur-

* Granted, many of these books were translations. For example, the mid-sixties saw the appearance in Bulgarian of Sartre's *Les Mots,* Camus's *La Peste,* and Kafka's *The Trial.*

181

thering the most liberal ideals of the Bulgarian intelligentsia. Their art permits them to comment on a variety of political and semi-political subjects, including the relationship between man and society, socialist legality, the significance of religion, the abuses of bureaucracy, and the like. One Bulgarian writer, defending the pro-Western proclivities of teen-age jazz enthusiasts, cautioned a concerned Bulgarian Communist Party leadership that "the trumpets of the Beatles are not the trumpets of Jericho that will cause the walls of socialism to come tumbling down." Another writer protested what he considered to be the foolish action of those Bulgarian militiamen who were taking Bulgarian beatniks into the district police stations and shearing their long hair. The critic, Damnyan Obreshkov, suggested that, rather than take administrative measures against hairdos or Western publications, communists would be far wiser to inculcate sound aesthetic tastes and criteria. "We don't need haircuts, but minds, clear and lofty minds!" he wrote. Obreshkov wondered whether by shaving beards and cutting hair the Party was not trimming its own influence.

As in all communist states, the cultural, social, and political ferment in Bulgaria has had rattling reverberations in the Bulgarian Union of Writers, which controls the national literary output. This literary unit, which contains some two hundred and ninety-seven writers, is patterned closely upon the Soviet model. As such, it represents far more than the administrative arm of the Party; it is the *sine qua non* for every Bulgarian man of letters. A young Bulgarian who wants to earn his livelihood by writing can ignore the Union's promptings to "develop nationalism" in his prose, but if he boycotts the Union, he has about as much chance of publishing his works as a nonunion bricklayer in New York has of working on a housing project. Of course, there are a few rebels who continue to write for the drawer year after year. Those young authors who eventually join the union inevitably find there is a progressive divergence between their views and those of the older, more conservative members. And this is where the house of the Union of Writers starts to shake. Bulgarian literature was slow to emerge from Stalinism. The ideological confusion that prevailed regarding socialist writing made it possible for the old dogmatists to fight a solid rear-guard action. Although in a minority, the dog-matists were unwilling to deviate from the path of socialist realism: They did not want any extension of freedom that would permit artists and writers to experiment with new genres; they were afraid of losing their privileged status in Bulgarian society. These dog-matists considered criticism of the "cult of personality" unpatriotic. They felt it detracted from the revolutionary progress of Bulgarian communism, which had patterned itself so closely on the Russian model.*

The conservative faction continues to receive considerable sup-port from the ideological commission of the Party, which, if not exactly staffed with literary experts, still makes all the ground rules for literature on the basis of political considerations. The conserva-tives are opposed by the liberal and "advanced" liberal wings in the Union. These liberals are dedicated to a candid description of society as it is. They urge the relaxation of censorship and seek the extensions of such personal liberties as freedom to travel to the West. The small group of "advanced" liberals, on the other hand, goes one step further. The aim of these progressives is to create a link between Bulgarian writing and the West. They want to put themselves on the map. Being mostly in their twenties and early thirties, they want to infuse Bulgarian literature with their own vitality, with a genuine idealism.

The Party has tried to keep the peace between these two major conflicting groups, each contending for the advancement of its own views, with only a moderate degree of success. Georgi Dzhagarov (b.

---

* One Bulgarian author, Anton Polikarov, complained that "with an enviable self-assurance, which merits a better fate, some writers seem almost to think that they have a monopoly on absolute truth." Frequently attacked with what he termed "shattering force" in the so-called "scientific debates" at the Union of Writers, Polikarov said that, to the dogmatists, "discussion is a monologue, not a dialogue." The outcome of all such discussions is decided well in advance by the dogmatists and consequently assumes the nature of a farce. As "no open problems exist," and as there are no debatable principles, what remains is the "destruction of obvious misconceptions." In this camp, the maligned author contended, one only hears the speeches for the prosecution. With heavy sarcasm, Polikarov concluded that "One must bow down before the shattering logic of these Marx-ists who have decided: 'Marxism—that is I!'"

1925), the poet-playwright President of the Union, dances the tightrope between his own rather progressive inclinations and the "go slow" instructions from the Party. Stressing the official line in 1966, Dzhagarov said, "We, the writers-communists, once more declare that, for us, there is nothing more sacred and more dear than the cause of the Party, and that the meaning and the content of our lives is to serve our people and increase their artistic heritage. As always up to now, and from now on, too, we shall stand with the Party in life and in death." This was not mere theatrical bluster. Writers should align themselves solidly with the Party, Dzhagarov said, because it taught them where to stand on class positions. Only the Party could guide them in the relentless struggle against bourgeois ideology. Only the Party could help them preserve unity in the ranks. Bogumil Raynov, the editor-in-chief of *Literaturen Front* (the major organ of the Bulgarian Union of Writers), said in 1967: "We have arrived at the point where we must renounce unity if we want discussions. If we want unity, we must give up any thought of discussions." That Dzhagarov and Zhivkov were not interested in discussions was clearly indicated by the 1968 Writers' Congress, at which there was unanimity on all major issues.

The writers are not moved by such appeals for unity; they are pacified by the very considerable material benefits the Party showers on them. When Dzhagarov boasts that the "conditions for creative work among our writers have never been better," he is quite right. The salaries of the members of the Union of Writers are said to be the highest of any professional group in Bulgaria. Of the close to three hundred full-time members, half have their own cars. Their average income, according to Dzhagarov, is now over two hundred and fifty dollars per month. The Union maintains a retreat in the mountains where writers can stay at state expense, and it keeps another villa on the Black Sea where they can entertain foreign guests. In Sofia itself, the Union runs one of the best and most heavily subsidized restaurants in all of Bulgaria. Moreover, many of the authors travel abroad as often as their royalties permit and are privy to special contacts with the West. For example, the Union publishes a monthly bulletin, limited to some three hundred numbered copies, which assays a realistic assessment of literary and cultural developments in the West. This bulletin reproduces excerpts of articles from *Encounter*, the *New York Review of Books*, the *Cahiers du Cinéma*, and numerous other publications not generally accessible to the Bulgarian intelligentsia. The Communist Party of Bulgaria, whose leaders retain an ingrained anti-intellectualism, acts on the principle that the greater the privileges accorded to the writers, the easier it will be to keep their work within tolerable ideological confines. If such outright bribery has prevented serious negative abuses, it has also failed to produce positive literary results. The younger Bulgarian writers consider these privileges degrading. "It should be the mission of our Union to shield those writers who have the capacity to rouse the sleeping dogs in our country," said one member, sipping *pliska* (cognac) in the comfort of his leather-upholstered chair in the Union of Writers headquarters. "But no," he continued, "as soon as one of us holds office, he seems to become a bureaucrat. The title of the office goes to our heads. We are glad to hold cushy jobs and to be freed from the necessity to think. Those at the top only listen to the advice given to them by the Party as to what is best." When one of the officials of the Union was confronted with this judgment, he snapped back, with some justice, "As a rule, those who piss against the wind conform most readily at the critical juncture."

"What, exactly, is wrong?" demanded Party Secretary Todor Zhivkov somewhat rhetorically of his writers and poets not so long ago. Then, answering his own question, this modern coryphaeus of the arts declared: "Some of the younger Bulgarian poets write and publish decadent, pessimistic poetry, poetry expressing hopelessnes; they extol loneliness, despondency, and look for some abstract truth they can never find. They are ready to drive their lyrical hero to suicide. Some end by slashing their veins, throwing themselves to the sea, and God knows how else. What a 'novel' vision! What a 'novel' destiny for modern man, the builder of socialism."

Zhivkov's pronouncements provide a good illustration of the continuation of the "cult of personality" on the Bulgarian scene. While Zhivkov is on much shakier ideological ground than his mentor, Nikita Sergeyevich Khrushchev, was when he uttered his famous off-the-cuff declarations in Moscow's Menagerie in 1963, Zhivkov, in his decrees on prose and poetry, painting and sculpture, opera and jazz, remains supreme. It is not without considerable embarrassment that Bulgarian writers must listen to his dictum that such huge and unprofitable projects as the metallurgical complex of Kremikovtsi provide "an ideal theme for creative artists." Zhivkov, who seems to believe there is an organic link between socialism and talent, still warns his writers that their works will ultimately be judged by the degree to which they have helped mold a new society.

The man Zhivkov placed in charge of purging the pessimism of Bulgarian writers, Georgi Dzhagarov, views the three hundred new works of fiction published annually in Bulgaria with considerable alarm. Such an output, in a country of fewer than ten million people, places an awesome burden on the committees of publishers who must carefully examine each work for style, content, and ideological purity. In addition, the state subsidies, which bring the cost of a two-hundred-page book down to the price of a package of cigarettes, make such a volume highly unprofitable. Dzhagarov has favored greater editorial selectivity as one method of keeping the dissident writers under control. Imprisoned before the communist takeover for his revolutionary activity, Dzhagarov received his training at the Maxim Gorki Institute for Literature in Moscow. He won recognition as a poet in the early nineteen-fifties, and between 1959 and 1965 he wrote plays, some of them on such highly controversial subjects as socialist legality during the Stalin era. These caused such an uproar that Zhivkov told him in 1963: "Listen to the Party, and you will succeed and will be useful to your people." Dzhagarov listened. He was duly "elected" chairman of the Union of Writers in 1965. In his maiden speech, Dzhagarov used typical socialist lingo in describing the "turgid rivers across which more bridges of confidence and tolerance must be built." Dzhagarov faced up to the fact that he would not be able to eliminate the ferment in the ranks; instead, he concentrated on submerging the struggle between the "dogmatic sectarians," who believed that they alone had remained faithful to the Party since Stalin's death, and the "subjectivists," who demanded that the Party stop interfering with literature, for the sake of genuinely democratizing literary life. Simultaneously, Dzhagarov tried to stimulate those who were so disillusioned by the injustices and shortcomings of the past that they abstained from controversy altogether. However, a change in Dzhagarov's position soon revealed itself in his gratuitous attack on Daniel and Sinyavsky, whom he called "two traitors against freedom, two hypocrites, who committed a criminal act when they calumniated the Soviet order and transformed themselves into illegal tools of imperialism." Dzhagarov said his "position in their case can be none other than the position of truth, the position of Soviet justice."

Like any hack politician, Dzhagarov declared that the Bulgarian Union of Writers could follow only one possible path: the middle-of-the-road course following socialist realism. As the conformist pressures from the Party mounted in the mid-sixties, Dzhagarov found himself forced into an alliance with the conservative elements within the Union. Emil Manov, the liberal deputy chairman of the Writers' Union, best known abroad for his novels *The Unauthentic Case* (1957) and *The Mistake of Abel* (1964), was relieved of his job in the summer of 1967 for "reasons of health." (Actually, the Party denunciation of his manner of "painting over with a black brush the white surface of socialist construction" in his novels would seem to have been reason enough.) Manov had maintained at the Writers' Congress in 1966 that the "process of democratization and a free creative atmosphere had not yet been secured in Bulgaria." Such, in fact, were the tensions within the Union that when Dzhagarov went to Moscow to address the Fourth Congress of Soviet Writers in the summer of 1967, he made a spectacle of himself by warning his Russian colleagues that they were going overboard in their denunciations of the cult of personality. A Bulgarian had gone to Moscow to warn against liberalization!

Because of the close linguistic, cultural, and political ties between the two countries, it is quite natural that the Bulgarian Union of Writers should be heavily dependent on instructions coming from the much larger and more influential Soviet Union of Writers. Although the Bulgarians have not always toed the line set down by their Russian brethren, there have been few disagreements between them—even during the days of Khrushchev's mercurial ideological oscillations. The concept of creating a union of writers that would serve as the administrative arm of the government, instead of an organization dedicated to protecting the rights of authors, was adopted after the war by Sofia. Stalin had seen to that, just as he had seen to it in 1932 that all existing literary and artistic groups in Russia were welded into a single Union of Soviet Artists. The incontrovertible standard of this union became "socialist realism," which poet Vladimir Mayakovsky even then denounced as "the depths of hideous banality." A quarter of a century later, at a thrice-postponed Soviet Congress of Writers, the members reaffirmed the orthodox pieties that, in turn, set the tune for all the other unions in the communist states: "We regard our literature as part and parcel of the Communist Party cause. . . . We do not have nor can we have other interests besides those expressed by our Party. . . . Soviet literature is essentially optimistic. It is permeated with the theme of building communism," and so forth.

To a far greater degree than in Bulgaria, literature is the single field of activity in the Soviet Union where the hidden tensions, latent in the entire society, bubble to the surface and are distilled into a strong, spirited protest. Writing is the one medium in Russia that has historically rejected the strait jacket into which both czars and commissars have tried to bind it. Reading Herzen's *My Past and Thoughts,* one is struck by how little has changed in the position of Russian writers and dissidents since the reign of Nicholas I. As Pasternak noted so bitterly, "They only ask you to praise what you hate most and grovel before what makes you most unhappy." While some five hundred yes-men convened to rubber-stamp the views of the Party at the 1967 Congress, off the record many of the authors spoke with open contempt against censorship, the bought-out critics, and the entire corrupt structure. The protest of the Soviet nonconformists was far more vehement than that of their Bulgarian counterparts. Poet Andrei Voznesensky, in an angry letter protesting the cat-and-mouse tactics of the Union in refusing to grant him a visa to visit the United States, wrote, "Clearly the leadership of the Union does not regard writers as human beings." He continued, "this lying, prevarication, and knocking people's heads together is standard practice." What has, in fact, happened is that most of the young writers in Russia today are in "opposition"—that is, they are not active participants in the Writers' Union. Whereas, in 1934, seventy-one per cent of the delegates to the Congress were under forty years of age, in 1967 only twelve per cent were under forty—a clear indication that the older generation, which has been bought off with special-status and monetary rewards, now has a vested interest not to sell short. During the thirty-five years of its existence the Writers' Union has not stood up once for the rights of a single persecuted or maligned author—even though the statutes provide that it should arrange legal aid for writers and undertake the "necessary measures" in their defense.

Aleksandr Solzhenitsyn (b. 1918), author of *One Day in the Life of Ivan Denisovich*, who did not have access to the tribune of the Writers' Congress, wrote an open letter, which he circulated among the delegates and copies of which he sent to the West, thereby directly challenging the members. "The Soviet Constitution does not provide for censorship, which is therefore illegal and is never mentioned in public," wrote Solzhenitsyn, "but under the obscure name of Glavlit,* it weighs upon our literature, subjecting writers to the arbitrary will of unlettered officials." In one of the most daring and direct attacks on censorship ever made by a Soviet writer, Solzhenitsyn went on to characterize the system as "a medieval anachronism" that has been perpetuated "almost to the twenty-first century, and arrogates to itself the right to separate acceptable books from those it deems unacceptable." He claimed that Soviet censorship used such vague labels as "ideologically harmful," "vicious," and "incorrect," in rejecting novels, plays, short stories, poems, and essays. Solzhenitsyn then gamely proposed that "the Congress should demand and obtain the abolition of all censorship—open or concealed —of artistic works, that it should free the publishing houses of their obligation to obtain permission from the authorities before publishing any work." The editor of *Pravda*, Mikhail V. Simyanin, in refusing to print Solzhenitsyn's letter, asked why sordid topics of

---

* Glavlit, the Central Administration for Literary Affairs and Publishing, was established by decree in 1922. Actually, Glavrepertkom, "the Central Administration for the Protection of Military and State Secrets in the Press," is now the chief organ for censorship in the Soviet Union.

189

this kind should be disseminated for public airing. Solzhenitsyn is "a psychologically unbalanced person, a schizophrenic," he wrote. Simyanin claimed he saw nothing positive in Solzhenitsyn's description of Soviet society. "The only topic he is able to write about is life in a concentration camp," Simyanin noted, adding that "in the old days people were even put into prison for works of this kind."

While it was a sign of the times that Solzhenitsyn did not go to jail, the Soviet Union continued to pass through a painful transition period. The Russian police became convinced in 1967 that coercion had to be applied if the intelligentsia was to be silenced. Yevgeny Vagin, the editor of a multivolume edition of Dostoevsky's works, was sentenced to thirteen years' imprisonment; Vladimir Bukovsky was given three years for having organized a demonstration protesting the arrest of dissident writers; while Yuri Galanskov (b. 1939), who claimed that "in today's Russia only dishonest literature can develop in the open daylight," was sentenced to seven years behind barbed wire in 1968. Vsevolod Kochetov (b. 1912), the ultraconservative editor of the literary monthly *Oktyabr,* urged that literature be kept under tight control. Khrushchev's 1956 denunciation of Stalinism "almost threw out the baby with the bath water," he said. Kochetov believes that great art can be created on command and cites Raphael's Sistine Madonna (commissioned by the Vatican) as well as the Mona Lisa, the Colosseum, and the Pyramids as proof. Literature, he warned, "has prepared the way to revolution," but it could also prepare "the way to counterrevolution." His remarks did not go unheeded. Communist Party Secretary Leonid Brezhnev warned the dissident writers and intellectuals that "renegades cannot expect immunity." Although he is the leader of a country of three hundred million people, Brezhnev felt obliged to say that "Our enemies in the camp of imperialism clutch with tenacity at any manifestations of ideological immaturity and hesitations among individual representatives of the intellectuals."

The hostility of the Russian writers to the Party's demands for ideological conformity was clearly becoming more difficult to suppress. "The times spat at me," wrote Voznesensky, "I spit back at the times." Solzhenitsyn claimed that there was no hint of any "recognition of the right of our writers to state publicly their opinions about the moral life of men and of society," and asserted that the losers were both Russia and world literature.

The Bulgarians listened intently to the warning words of Brezhnev, and the conservative faction in Sofia took up his cudgels. Old-guard novelist Angel Todorov (b. 1905), who visited Moscow early in 1968, vigorously defended the sentences against Galanskov and Bukovsky, whom he called "criminals, hirelings of an anti-Soviet organization . . . lovers of foreign currency." But if the older generation of writers was applauding the hard line in Moscow, the liberals were scratching their heads at Todor Zhivkov's commandment that "writers should stick to socialist realism as their creative method of work." What exactly did Zhivkov mean when he said that "socialist realism inherits and develops all that is of aesthetic value in literature and the arts"? If every Bulgarian writer I talked to is for "socialist realism" today, it is because each can define it according to his wishes. It is one of those special terms that every communist uses to pigeonhole his ideas. During the course of an exhausting six-hour session with Dzhagarov and a group of Bulgarian writers, I made no progress in arriving at a meaningful definition. The take-off point of this open-ended discussion was a statement by one of the writers that "socialist realism stands alone, absolutely irreplaceable by any other philosophical, aesthetic, and humanist conception coming from the decadent bourgeois trends of the West." Sitting in their plush leather chairs, smoking American cigarettes, and drinking Black Label Johnny Walker whisky and soda water, these Bulgarian writers desperately tried to steer the conversation onto a different track. The definitions they did come up with were usually pleonasms. One believed it was "an artistic method that developed the socialist view of the reader." Another saw it as "literature of the truth of life, of real conflicts—enriched by the understanding and imagination of the writer." Finally, Dzhagarov, joined by some colleagues, tried to adopt a diluted version of Zhdanov's thesis. He rejected the "realism without limits" proposed by French communist Roger Garaudy, and tried to define it as an ideological "concept that develops in the reader a socialist spirit, a desire to fight, an optimism, a faith in man." *Ergo*, a communist halo.

Subsequent discussions about the positive hero turned out to be equally negative. The more conservative voices of the Union seemed to agree that their heroes could live or die according to the purpose of the writer, but that a hero could not have a ridiculous or meaningless end. Similarly, such a hero could be complex, but could not be complexed. "Complexity is the pitiful and hideous fruit of the extreme decay of the soul," suggested one writer, adding, "It is undoubtedly brought about by the living conditions of the petite bourgeoisie." Apparently, the modern socialist hero enjoys daydreaming because such dreams sometimes are transformed into reality, but he has no illusions. "He does not dream for himself, but for the collective; thus his dream turns into the image of the future," said novelist Todor Manov. A philosopher from the Department of Aesthetics of the Bulgarian Academy of Sciences (called in to assist the beleaguered writers) suggested that Western techniques of "psychologism" had nothing to offer the development of the positive hero. This aesthetician claimed that, while its theoretical basis was Freudianism, "contemporary psychologism corrupts the senses in order to isolate the individual from the epoch and to vilify not only man but what is human." Throughout this discussion, one man, who was chain-smoking cigarettes, remained silent. He was Andrei Gulyashki (b. 1914), the plump, balding Conan Doyle of the Balkans, creator of Bulgaria's most popular literary hero. He was obviously tired by all this talk.

Gulyashki, who modestly characterizes himself as the "Sherlock Holmes of the Atomic Age," lives rather more in the style of a socialist Ian Fleming. He has a small town house in Sofia and keeps a country villa in the nearby mountains. While he may not drive an Aston-Martin, he does quite well in a new Opel and a custom-built Land-Rover (to tackle the poor Bulgarian roads). And, when not engaged in his literary activities, he is expanding his collection of firearms and antique knives. Gulyashki's rise to the literary top has come entirely in the nineteen-sixties. He joined the prewar underground Communist Youth Organization at the age of nineteen because "communist ideology, with its emphasis on a better world, convinced me I had to join the Party," he says. Gulyashki worked his way up in the Writers' Union to become secretary of the Party

Bureau of the Union, but in novels like *The Golden Fleece* he protested obliquely against the contradiction between the "socialist-realist" ideal and practice. Eyebrows were raised within the Party because Gulyashki's hero, who showed an excessive concern for the misery of the peasants during the early years of forced collectivization, mysteriously committed suicide at the end of the book. However, in 1959, Gulyashki turned to writing a detective series because he sought a wider audience. "I wanted to develop adventure novels with the philosophical basis of humanism," said the author. Since then, six novels featuring his hero, Avakoum Zahov, have sold more than a million copies in the socialist bloc—besides appearing in translation in more than a dozen Western countries.

Gulyashki's most renowned book, although not his best literary work, is his *Avakoum Zahov Contra 07*. Because of a complex copyright dispute with the Fleming estate and United Artists, Bond's name had to be slightly altered in the Bulgarian, but his character is still readily recognizable. "I do not take Fleming's hero in my book as he is; I make him into a more real, a more plausible character," says Gulyashki. "My Bond thinks more, analyzes more, is more fully a master of his work," he said, his hands nervously fidgeting with an endless chain of Bulgarotobac cigarettes. Gulyashki's attitude toward Bond, which is indicative of the simultaneous attraction and repulsion of all communists for this magnetic Western figure, provides a fascinating insight into the reactions of communists toward Western literature in general. Gulyashki makes no effort to conceal his contempt, not to say repugnance, for Fleming's agent. This is in general agreement with the socialist line, which has banned both the Bond films and the Bond books. Soviet critic Yuri Zhukov, writing in *Pravda* in 1966, called Bond an "unthinking murderer and rapist" who defends the interests of the bourgeois ruling classes. "Frankly," says Gulyashki, "and I have read almost all the Bond novels, 007 is an elementary character lacking in psychological development." Gulyashki condemns Bond as emotionally and intellectually "poverty-stricken." To a Bulgarian communist, Bond embodies all the capitalist and bourgeois vices, including immorality, love of luxury, racism, and, above all, "hatred of communism and the Soviet Union." Bond's

love of luxury, for example, is seen as a defect of a "petit bourgeois." Gulyashki considers Bond's taste and outlook as distinctly
lower-class British.

Outlining his objections to Fleming's agent at great length,
Gulyashki felt obliged to explain that the fantasy world of Bond
was ridiculous. He said that Fleming arouses the primitive instincts
of his readers and vicariously induces an escapism otherwise un-
obtainable for the majority of the Western proletariat. As opium
for the masses, Fleming's books ultimately lead to man's enslavement by his baser instincts. By consciously diverting the attention of
his readers away from reality and by distorting public consciousness
toward the instinctual and pathological, Fleming has exercised a
negative influence on the development of society. "I insist on comparing Bond to a certain type of Nazi," said Gulyashki, "because
the Nazis created an atmosphere of recklessness toward life; they
had a total lack of sentiment toward man." What particularly upset
Gulyashki, who retains much of his youthful idealism, is that Bond
was not an agent seeking beauty. Gulyashki said that, to him, the
search for beauty is the only significant pursuit in life, and that an
intelligence agent's search for the truth should be beautiful in and
of itself. Bond he sees as a "pithecanthropus who, having finished
his secondary schooling and having graduated from the school of
savoir vivre, engages himself in the secret service." Showing no appreciation of the satiric commentary of Fleming's pen or of the dehumanized hero, Gulyashki seriously described Bond as a snob
without faith or principles. Bond's victories are not due to any
superior intelligence, so essential in the depiction of any socialist
hero, but to his luck and to his pistol. "Experience shows," explained Gulyashki, "that NATO's secret service is fighting socialism
with much more dangerous, shrewder, and cleverer agents than
007." Explaining that in his own portrayal of 007 he had been
forced to give Bond an intellectual booster shot, Gulyashki quipped,
"Allen Dulles would have given him a double zero for his activities."

The sexual life of 07 is the first to suffer. "My Bond has no carnal
adventures; he does not possess women at his usual rate," claims
Gulyashki, who has incorporated only such discreet allusions to sex

as are absolutely necessary for Bond's "strong personality." To up-
hold the reputation of socialist Bulgaria's black-eyed virgins, o7 is
given little opportunity to chase the sun-tanned beauties who dot
the Black Sea resorts in their bikinis. Only once, while relaxing on
the coast, did o7's mind begin to wander.

Two chambermaids, their full breasts like southern amber grapes, were
already smiling at him invitingly. He hadn't made up his mind yet which
one of the two he would take up with first. With such lovely golden grapes
hanging from the vine, it would be a sin not to stretch out his hand and
pick them. The two chambermaids were like two thirsty does peeping
through the chinks of the thicket . . . imploring him: "Please taste me,
and see how tender my meat is! You'll swear by your hunter's honor that
you have never before had such a juicy steak."

So much for Agent o7's sex obsessions. What is at stake between
Bond and Gulyashki's Bulgarian hero, Zahov, is a super death ray
that would "finally insure the peace-loving socialist countries
against attack by imperialism." (To their credit, the NATO agents
correctly evaluate such a weapon as an attempt to bring the West to
its knees.) Agent o7 is sent to Bulgaria to kidnap a certain Soviet
professor, Konstantin Troffimov, the brain behind the ray, who is
about to attend an international scientific symposium on the Black
Sea. When Bond, pretending to be a Russian, calls the professor's
dedicated and curvaceous assistant "darling" on their second meeting, she protests in no uncertain terms. "Don't worry," replies Agent
o7 reassuringly, "I call all women from fifteen to forty 'darling.'
Surely you must know, Natasha, that the West has its own style.
Unfortunately, the West has been poisoning me for the last fifteen
years."

Gulyashki's own hero, counterintelligence agent Zahov, is supposed to carry the standard of "our ideal," explained Gulyashki,
"the ideal of all men of good will." Zahov is described on Bulgarian
book jackets as "a man of culture and learning who is guided in his
counterespionage by a love for his fellow man." He supposedly
exudes the essence of beauty while sleuthing in Bulgaria's Valley of
the Roses. However, like his plump and unprepossessing creator,
Zahov could in no way be described as attractive. Gulyashki de-

scribes Zahov as "an old boy in the style of Maupassant, who, after a brilliant success at an early age, slips irresistibly toward decline." Perhaps that is understating the basic nature of this thin, graying counterintelligence agent who delights in eating noodles with cabbage and lots of red pepper in Sofia's better restaurants. Zahov, who, Gulyashki insists, is much more of a Bulgarian hero than Bond is a British hero, usually wears a dark suit and a starched white shirt. Only his custom-made gold cuff links, inset with large jasper stones, keep him from being totally pedestrian. Writes Gulyashki: "Avakoum hates everything that is loud, vulgar, and that so attracts our Bulgarian youth." Indeed, the conformist cut of his clothes, his dowdy vest, and the silk dressing gown he wears in his rented, two-room flat in Sofia hardly fit the description of the dress of the "new socialist man." Zahov, like his creator, remains at heart a bourgeois of the prewar generation.

"Avakoum is an intellectual, an archaeologist who is a member of the Bulgarian Institute of Sciences," said Gulyashki, his chubby right hand gesticulating upward—as if to emphasize the importance of that erstwhile Balkan institute. "Avakoum assembles his scraps of evidence and pieces them together much as he assembles his archaeological potsherds," said Gulyashki. Narrowing down the focus of his dark-brown eyes, the Bulgarian author began to detail his hero's interests. Zahov likes music and is a balletomane. He reads historical literature and, when not whiling his time away with Plutarch, will occasionally stoop to Chekhov and Anatole France. He enjoys Bulgarian painting, but "greets with a smiling irony the new abstract 'attempts' without accepting the immobile realism that ignores new forms and the colored expression of reality." (It still remains every Bulgarian writer's duty to denigrate abstract art.) Basically, Avakoum Zahov is a bore. He talks far too much and is always telling his associates in a Sherlock Holmes tone the whys and wherefores of deductive reasoning. Given the pompousness of his Bulgarian demeanor, most Western readers will find him somewhat offensive. What, for example, does the top socialist counterintelligence agent enjoy most in life? "To walk across his room when the evening has come, his pipe in his mouth, and, when it is cold, to watch the fire burn in the chimney." It would somehow appear as if Bond had been mismatched against a time-clock version of Sherlock Holmes. Perhaps most extraordinary in the Bondian era, Zahov is a gentleman of the old school, who respects fair play and recoils from violence. Like all communist detective writers, Gulyashki never permits his agent to use immoral or amoral means to achieve his ends. Gulyashki said that in real life "Bulgarian agents try not to be beasts." This, he said, is partly a result of their schooling and partly because, "as communists, they try to serve the cause of socialism." Gulyashki insists, moreover, that Western agents are painted in a much better light by communist authors than communist agents are depicted in the capitalist West.

Pouring some powerful Bulgarian five-star *pliska* into a glass, Gulyashki proudly retold how his creature Zahov successfully stops Bond from capturing the super death ray. It is the symbolic defeat of a decadent Westerner, whose only happiness could come from serving his own passion and egoism, by "the convinced fighter for the preservation and consolidation of a more just social system." To Gulyashki, Bond only represents "the executor of the orders of his superiors in the defense of a social system to which he, in fact, is indifferent." Gulyashki pointed out, by way of contrast, that no gap could exist between society and Avakoum Zahov, who "puts all his energies at the service of the people." Money, women, fast cars (although he has a rank of captain in the Bulgarian counterintelligence, Zahov does not even rate a secondhand car), nothing would tempt Zahov away from socialism. His total attachment to Bulgaria makes him, in the literary sense, a weak character. Avakoum Zahov is never even challenged by the possibility of temptation. Agent 07, on the other hand, is challenged not only by a new aesthetic *raison d'être* (the pursuit of beauty), by more serious work habits, and by the stress of being forced to adopt deductive reasoning, but also by a far more idealistically motivated ideological order.

Only occasionally in the *Avakoum Zahov Contra 07* adventure is there any realistic reference to the contemporary intelligence scene. At the end of the novel, Agent 07 and Avakoum find themselves improbably alone on an antarctic ice floe, philosophizing.

"What you're doing is all useless!" o7 smiled coldly.

"It is?" Avakoum said. "How?"

"Simple!" o7 said. "You've lost this second round, too. You've lost it hopelessly! In fact, Zahov, you've been losing out all along lately—Penkovsky, Abel, that Assen of yours . . . Sad, eh? Knockouts all around. . . ."

"You will die a bitter man!" Avakoum said. "Bitter man!" he repeated. "Because the victories you sing are just pickings! Mere pickings, no more! Because for a very long time, both Penkovsky and Assen played our line and led you by the nose, before we unmasked them! And Rudolph pulled the biggest trick on you there ever was and kept it up for years and years!"

Party Secretary Todor Zhivkov could hardly accuse Gulyashki of being antisocialist in pitting Zahov against Bond. It is a patriotic match. But Zhivkov could—and did—protest that this detective novel, like so much of Bulgarian literature in the mid-sixties, fails to agitate the revolutionary workers and peasants. It is a remarkable achievement in the annals of Bulgarian communist literature that Zahov places as little stress on Marxism-Leninism as James Bond places on the ideology of free enterprise. This may go a long way to explain Zahov's extraordinary popularity among the mass of readers, because Gulyashki's narration borders on the turgid.

In all fairness to Zhivkov, it must be pointed out that the Party leader was not so wrong in publicly damning one of Gulyashki's other detective novels, *Counterintelligence,* for being "a work of nebulous ideology, standing on shaky positions, which treats justice and truth in general, and in which the author keeps mum about communism and the Party." Quickly after this reproach, Gulyashki recanted by condemning the "reactionary trends and tendencies of bourgeois art, such as surrealism and Hermetism in poetry, abstractionism, and the vulgar naturalism in prose." Antiaction and alogism, sadism and sexual perversion, symbolism, and the "philosophical concept of the absolute insignificance of man" were also publicly rejected by Gulyashki from the "aesthetic arsenal" of socialism. Gulyashki was also forced to condemn all forms of "modernism" as aspects of "parvenu snobbism." This recantation has created the greatest difficulties for Gulyashki when he now attempts to use impressionistic techniques in his descriptive writing. While he was still editor* of the influential Bulgarian literary monthly *Plamuk* (*The Flame*), Gulyashki wrote that, as "a creative method for the realization and reproduction of life, impressionism will not and cannot have anything in common with socialist realism." What, then, should the writer do? His words of wisdom were that he should continue to search and to introduce innovations in order not to "lag behind life."

Gulyashki's novels are indicative of a new trend on the Bulgarian literary scene. That his hero is permitted to tackle the corrupt and decadent 07 is already a "great leap forward." Avakoum Zahov is symbolic of the birth of a new, not very socialist, hero: He is not a shock-worker breaking records in the coal mines or at a collective pig-breeding station, but a nineteenth-century humanist with an appreciation for beauty, a longing for truth, and an active conscience. Despite his all too obvious weaknesses, Zahov fills a void. In the tricky political climate of Sofia, Gulyashki has walked a literary tightrope in fashioning a popular and politically acceptable hero. Gulyashki is, however, a writer of the older generation and represents only the surfaced peak of the iceberg. The newer talents, such as Slav Karaslavov and Lada Galina, are developing humanist heroes with a far greater measure of unsocialist doubt and universal sensitivity. What assures their ascendancy is that, as long as it remains impossible to debate controversial issues openly in Sofia, books and periodicals will continue to be viewed as political dynamite. The very awareness of the power of the written word is inspiring the young writers to strive for a provocative, controversial literature.

---

* In 1966, Gulyashki was placed in charge of a new international literary magazine, *Contact*, and in 1967 he was unexpectedly appointed dramaturge of a Sofia playhouse.

CHAPTER XI

Concerto for Hammer and Saw

As the shimmering, platinum-blue curtain rose above the gaping forty-five-yard stage of Warsaw's Teatr Wielki, I thought I had been transported, in Jules Verne fashion, back into the mid-nineteenth century. To be sure, the obscure opera *The Haunted Manor,* by Stanislaw Moniuszko (1819–1872), had not been taken out of the skeleton closet of musical history for my benefit. Together with Moniuszko's *Halka,* it forms the backbone of the permanent repertoire of Polish opera, the *pièce de résistance* of Polish romanticism. Called a comic opera, *The Haunted Manor* actually seems closer to a parody of the chivalrous, knighted nationalism of old Polonia. The music is homey, the theme distinctly provincial. And what more fitting way to toast old times than to open the opera with a chorus of fifty Polish warriors raising their glasses to toast the annihilation of some national enemy. Fortunately, the directors of the Teatr Wielki had long ago decided to compensate, through the generous deployment of crowds, for what individual singers might lack in talent. And to make certain no one could discern what the rabble was singing, conductor Witold Rowicki hectically egged on his brass-laden orchestra. Meanwhile, to the satisfaction of the nationality-conscious audience, the red-and-white colors of Poland were waving high above the Pop Art candy-striped tents in which the knights were feasting. Mistimed cannonades followed. Scene after scene unfolded with ever more talent crammed on stage singing "Dobrze, Dobrze" ("Fine, Fine"). Finally, in the weird carnival scene that concluded the epic, I counted a chorus of about two hundred dancers, singers, and stagehands dressed in everything from miniskirts to shimmering medieval robes. The production had been so garish that the mediocrity of Moniuszko's middling melodies almost escaped notice.

The Haunted Manor had been described to me as the epitome of "Polishness" in music. Consequently, the trauma of this memorable night at the opera for a long time obscured the fact that music is the most developed and vital of the Polish arts in the sixties. In fact, Polish music is more radical and avant-garde than any other art form in the socialist world. It, alone, is completely emancipated. "I think the Polish *'musica nova'* is the strongest such group in the world today," boasts Polish composer Krzysztof Penderecki (b. 1934), who himself is regarded by many critics as the most impressive of Europe's new "concretists." As a consequence of Poland's bold musical experimentation, Western music lovers and performers are traveling in ever increasing numbers to Poland each fall to attend the Warsaw Fall Festival. There the most abstract aural collages, the finest in high-frequency buzz saws, and the most profound pools of silence are presented to a musically attuned public.

The acclaim being given Polish composers, conductors, and ensembles has generated the greatest Western interest in Polish music since the days of Chopin. However, the rather widespread notion that Polish music started with Frédéric Chopin and has since included three or four minor composers is so erroneous that it is necessary to recapitulate briefly the glories of Poland's sonorous past. Poland already possessed a flourishing musical history between the eleventh and fifteenth centuries when, for example, the Cracow Diocese had a three-year music school that specialized in its own style of Gregorian—that is, Cracovian—chant. Under the patronage of the famous Jagiellonian King Zygmunt I (1467–1548), Polish music entered its "golden age." Zygmunt married a Sforza from Milan, who was not only an accomplished player herself, but who also insisted on importing entire orchestras from Italy. Few of the Polish compositions of this period are extant; only the glorious memories remain. Although the vitality of Polish music declined with the transfer of the Polish court from Cracow to Warsaw in the late sixteenth century, Polish music, especially its dances, maintained its renown. Bach, Handel, and Telemann were among the score of composers who wrote "polonaises" during the eighteenth century.

No Polish composer or virtuoso became as famous as Chopin (1810–1849), whose name has since become identified with Polish nationalism. But Chopin was not a genius who blossomed in a musical desert. His work grew out of the spirit of European romanticism that flourished in the Warsaw of his time.* Chopin's proud polonaises, the great pianoforte poems, his mazurkas, nocturnes, and preludes are colored by that tinge of melancholy that even to his contemporaries presented the essence of the Polish national style. Chopin was succeeded by Karol Szymanowski (1883–1937), who climaxed the era of Polish romanticism and paved the way for the entry of modern music into Poland. With such famous works as his polytonal *First String Quartet,* Szymanowski laid the foundation for the European, rather than the specifically Polish, character of today's avant-gardists. As a teacher to an entire generation of composers, Szymanowski must get the credit for pulling down the walls of Poland's musical provincialism.

Witold Lutoslawski (b. 1913) is now generally regarded as the leader of the so-called school of *"musica nova."* Not only is Lutoslawski the most powerful musical personality of the composers writing since World War II, but his compositions also reveal the tortuous path followed by Polish music in his own lifetime. When Lutoslawski graduated from the Warsaw Conservatory in 1937, the tonal system was fast crumbling as a fashionable medium in Poland. However, Lutoslawski wished to continue in the school of Stravinsky and Bartók. In retrospect, Lutoslawski now says, "In the music of the twentieth century, I see altogether two fruitful traditions: One is the Vienna school [of Webern and Berg] with all of its flowing consequences; the second, everything one can find in common with Debussy, Stravinsky, Bartók, and Varèse, if I may be

---

* Some of his lesser contemporaries were Jozef Elsner (1769–1854), founder of the first Warsaw Conservatory, Karol Kurpinski (1785–1857), composer of some two dozen operas, Karol Lipinski (1790–1861), a virtuoso of Paganini's stature, and Stanislaw Moniuszko.

permitted to make such a simplification. Of these two, the tradition of the Vienna school is distant and foreign to me." During the early years of the German occupation, Lutoslawski began to sense the necessity of some ordering musical principle, "a means that would help me to move more easily within the confines of the twelve notes." And to clarify his search, he wrote thirty short polyphonic pieces for brass—merely as an exercise in discipline. Then, just before the official sanctions against musical formalism began to be enforced, Lutoslawski finished his monumental *Symphony* (1947), which demonstrated he had mastered the modern musical language. His symphony was, in a sense, an intense, personal confrontation with his own musical past, with all that had happened in Polish music thus far.

When the official ground rules for realist music were laid down by Zhdanov in Moscow, the backwash soon flowed into Poland. Wlodzimierz Sokorski, who later was to become Minister of Culture and then czar of Polish radio and TV, adopted the ground rules in 1949 against any imitation of the detested capitalist-inspired "formalism." Although nobody could exactly define what this terrifying word meant, Prokofiev said it was "the name given to music not understood on first hearing." In any case, the word "formalism" was typical of the paranoid jargon of the day. What was wanted was a "realistic form of artistic expression," which really meant a rehash of old nationalist tunes. "Realism" was the vogue, and the commandment was, "Music must be national"—that is, "connected with folklore." The musical hierarchy of Poland, forced to follow Stalin's demands for tunes he could whistle or to which he could tap his feet, only accepted the most superficial neoclassical idiom. (And for all that effort, Stalin, who was hard of hearing, paid no visits to Poland to savor this international debasement of culture.) In this black era, when music was made of ideas instead of notes, the works of Debussy, Ravel, Stravinsky, and Szymanowski were all banned as examples of the "antihumanist, abstract formalist music of imperialism." The directive to which even Lutoslawski was forced to bend was to fight "atonal, unharmonic" trends and to create songs for the millions of workers. The people's folk opera was filled with the so-called "humanistic tones" of socialism, but, in effect, from

1949 to 1954 most Polish composers wrote only for themselves. Polish composers of the period were subjected to the weird Soviet theory of musical intonations. This had been formulated by the composer-critic Boris Asafiev, who had developed the idea that intonations are a function of social consciousness. Asafiev related the means of musical expression to basic aspects of speech intonations. He wrote that the inflections of the human voice, as revealed by fluctuations of tempo, pitch, timbre, and so forth, denote character, emotion, intensity. Asafiev said that, because the process of musical intoning is interwoven with human thinking, composers should write music based on those intoned meanings that carry the uplifting message of communism. According to this theory, Asafiev contended that each historical epoch possessed its own grammar, its own "dictionary of intonations." In fact, he said, music was subject to "intonational crises" that reflect the social conditions of the era. Twelve-tone music was therefore regarded as a mirror of the spiritual chaos of the capitalist states. Music became an art of intoned meaning, of sound images that should reflect socialist reality. And the problem for Soviet composers then simply became one of mastering the positive "intonations" of the social environment.

According to Soviet aestheticians, Beethoven's *Appassionata Sonata* (Op. 57) reveals the intonations of nature in their cosmic aspect. Beethoven's inner conflict, his griefs and joys, his meditations and lyrical monologues are part of the vast "intonational cosmos" he bequeathed to mankind. The Soviets see Beethoven as the grand master of thematic development in music. More than in the music of any other composer, they hear how the revolutionary idealism of his time influenced his work. What tantalized the Soviets was that if Beethoven could create intonations evoking Hegelian dialectics, if he could compose works of social significance, why couldn't modern-day Soviet composers capture the dynamism, as well as the so-called "peaceful" character, of socialist reality, for the benefit of the entire world? But even if the Russians could not achieve this supreme goal, they saw no reason why they should not impose this theory on the composers of Eastern Europe.

After Stalin's death, Lutoslawski's *Concerto for Orchestra* (1954) was one of the first works to break the realist spell. With the October 1956 revolution in Poland came the musical thaw. The First International Festival of Contemporary Music took place in Warsaw that same autumn, and Gomulka proclaimed that music was unsuitable as an instrument of propaganda. Consequently, composers suddenly obtained complete freedom of action. After a decade of controls, limitations, and even kibitzing about the kind of music that ought and ought not to be written, the permissiveness that followed the October revolution was like a gift of the gods. Polish composers, who had been completely isolated from the West since 1939, found the most "poisonous" and experimental fruits of the decadent capitalist composers absolutely irresistible. Lutoslawski says, "The major impetus for this turn to the avant-garde came during the years 1956–1959, when the influence of such composers as Pierre Boulez, Karlheinz Stockhausen, and John Cage became widespread in Poland." How completely the new ideas were assimilated can best be judged from the manner in which they affected the neoclassic, neoromantic compositions of Boleslaw Szabelski (b. 1896), who, at the age of sixty, suddenly abandoned his old style and threw himself into the arms of the atonal muse.

While in the Soviet Union (where musical development is suppressed even as of this writing by Tikhon Khrennikov, Secretary-General of the Union of Composers since 1948) formalism was still being denounced, the Polish Communist Party, encouraged by the prizes and foreign recognition their musicians were amassing, decided to support these musical endeavors. The Ministry of Culture began to propagate avant-garde scores as part of Polish messianism. The International Festival of Contemporary Music soon became an important musical information center for all of Eastern Europe and was immediately seen as a corrupting influence by the East German, Russian, and Bulgarian unions of composers. Dmitri Shostakovich, for example, was forced in 1959 to denounce the Fall Festival on behalf of the Soviet Ministry of Culture. Shostakovich said, after his visit to Warsaw, that he was "greatly alarmed that some Polish composers, and especially young ones, are clinging to music of the type composed by Schoenberg." He thought they were mistaken to see in their "blind experiments" the future of musical art. "I should like to warn them sincerely away from this tendency and advise

205

them to study more deeply and attentively the national traditions of Polish music," said the Soviet Union's leading composer. Shostakovich feigned great perturbation over the "Western experiments" performed at the 1959 Warsaw Festival, which made it appear as if the works of "progressive composers" in the Soviet Union were intentionally slighted. Shostakovich pretended that what the Poles were creating was against human nature and against the art of music. It seems tragic to recollect that a talented creator of Shostakovich's stature should have been compelled to make the following parting statement: "My desire is that the next Warsaw Festival will present symphonies, songs, and cantatas and works of other types that would reflect the thoughts and feelings of millions of ordinary people who live a creative and peaceful life, who strive for friendship and mutual co-operation." Shostakovich, who has led such a long and unhappy career at the hands of Soviet Russia's musical censors, pointed out to the Poles that composers like Prokofiev, Khachaturian, and Sviridov "do not need to experiment in atonal music because they have virgin lands of folk music." The modern creations of Schoenberg, Shostakovich said, convey a "narrow dogmatism" and "limit the creative art of composers and eliminate their individuality." The most the Polish composers could hope to express with their atonalism would be "a condition of depression, prostration, or horror—moods that are not characteristic of a normal man." This type of music, Shostakovich insisted, was "invented by people who are afraid of the present and do not believe in the future." Unlike Russian composers, the followers of Schoenberg "do not see great and bright perspectives." Needless to say, the Poles did not heed Shostakovich's advice. Quite to the contrary, the Polish public became the first mass audience in the world to become familiar with the new idiom of electronic music and the Polish State Radio, as well as such groups as Ensemble MW2, played a leading role in expanding the musical vocabulary of a whole nation.

Lutoslawski's *Funeral Music* for strings, dedicated to the memory of Béla Bartók, was the first major postwar composition in the twelve-tone scheme. His idea was to repeat a series, with variations, within a set arrangement of intervals. Lutoslawski described the work more specifically: "The basic unit is the twelve-tone row, or a vertical aggregation of all the notes of the scale—natural harmonic phenomena. Of course, unlimited possibilities exist, in practice, for creating countless other twelve-tone rows. In my technique, I use, above all, those rows which, for me, possess a specific expressive and coloristic physiognomy and, along with it, a characteristic structure. Between the individual twelve-note rows there frequently exist sharp contrasts. The interplay of these contrasts is one of the basic principles of my technique." Lutoslawski believes this has little in common with the dodecaphony of serialism, although it does include a "total chromaticism." However, Lutoslawski says serialism is a method "that leads to effects completely alien to me," and he therefore finds it difficult "to imagine myself approaching it."

The next great influence in Lutoslawski's work was the aleatoric element. Lutoslawski heard and saw John Cage and his chance music at Darmstadt in 1961. "The experience provided a spark that ignited a powder keg in me," he says. "I was a mature composer with many things to say, but in less than half an hour I had an insight into new possibilities open to me by incorporating Cage's ideas into my music." *Jeux Vénitiens* (1961) was the result. In this work he stressed what he calls "harmonic phenomena," which he feels were very important in establishing an anti-Webern trend in his music. The application of the chance technique gave him a feeling of release from restraints "that had hampered a serious development of my musical thought." Lutoslawski had found a way in which to use sound combinations that had interested him for a long time. "The dissolution of the time connections between sounds does not appear a great novelty," he said, "yet its results may be of vast importance for a composer's technique." Lutoslawski wanted the music to change suddenly from one event to another, "like pictures from a slide projector," without stopping too long at the end of each slide. Although the composer remained the directing force in *Jeux Vénitiens,* there was an "admission of a free, complete performance of individual instruments within the orchestra."

Lutoslawski believes in the readily comprehensible logic of form, and in broad, sweeping—yet cohesive—musical designs. His compositions are marked by great clarity and precision in his musical thinking. His birdlike facial and hand movements, which reflect the rapid transition of emotions as he talks, give the impression that he is slightly scatterbrained, but this is misleading. His evolution in *Trois Poèmes d'Henri Michaux* (1963), *String Quartet* (1964), and *Woven Words* (1965) shows a distinct, linear progression. So much so, in fact, that Lutoslawski says, "I have come to regard my early works as passé." The calibre of his talent, the strength and passion with which he develops his own language, and the mastery with which he controls his musical sensibility have established him as Poland's leading contemporary composer. The question arises, of course, whether there is such a thing as a "Polish" composer in the era of chance music. Professor Zofia Lissa, Director of the Institute of Musicology at Warsaw University, claims, "Lutoslawski may use the newest methods, but I think they will always be in the Polish idiom." When I tried to elicit a definition of "the Polish idiom," she admitted there is no strict "school of modern Polish composition —but there are composers of different and recognizable stylistic tendencies, all of whom are interested in new techniques." Personally, I cannot detect nationalism in electronic composition. In fact, it would be quite impossible for me to identify as "Polish" the music of Tadeusz Baird, Kazimierz Serocki, Wlodzimierz Kotonski, Henryk Gorecki, or Krysztof Penderecki on first hearing.

Henryk Gorecki (b. 1933) is seeking the equivalent of a Heidegger style of existentialism in his music. Gorecki's compositions, such as his *Epitaphium,* are profoundly personal, intense convolutions. Despite their frequent redundancies, there is something eerie, lonely, chthonian about his screeching violins. His contemporary Penderecki regards Gorecki as a "brutal composer," but also admits that he is "perhaps the most talented of our generation." Works like his *Choros I* for violin (1964) build up such an emotional tension that one anxiously hopes for respite (just as in a subway I hope for the grating of the brakes to cease). Gorecki's *Refrain* is another composition that can arouse horripilation. It opens with sustained string-rasping, which gradually increases in density. Then there is an aleatoric passage in which the players can bang, scrape, and hit repeated notes as violently and orgiastically as they wish, and finally the work returns by degrees to the opening string tempo.

Tadeusz Baird (b. 1928), a snub-nosed, humorless man with a crew cut who even in his late thirties looks like an all-American boy, started his career writing imitations of Alban Berg's counterpoint mixed with medieval techniques. Critics everywhere have since been deeply divided over his compositions—although they admire his promotion of modern music in Poland. (He was one of the founders of the 1956 Fall Festival.) Vienna's Polish-born composer Haubenstock-Ramati thinks Baird's music is "Vaseline." Harold Schonberg, on the other hand, has written that Baird has a "good ear and feeling for orchestration," and that works like *Four Essays for Orchestra* (1958) showed delicate balance and "technical touches of real imagination." The fact is, Baird now inhabits a peculiarly serial world of fantasy, and his freak effects of scoring and his occasional introduction of jazz rhythms leave his public rather bewildered. His one-act opera, *Tomorrow* (1966), based on the novella by Joseph Conrad, received generally negative reviews at its première. The entire cast of *Tomorrow* consists of three singers, one actor, and an orchestra of seventy. Baird himself views it as a "classic" effort and rejects all contentions that it is "avant-gardist." One might say the characteristic trait of this work—like that of so many of his other compositions—is a strong, almost ecstatic, emotionalism not far removed from late-romantic symphonic monumentalism. This is especially true in his *Erotica* (1961) for soprano and orchestra, but then, Baird himself feels the Polish school of music is marked by a specific Slavonic touch, which he would define as "emotionality." Baird said he thought Polish composers, more than others, have been concentrating their attention on the new manner of conceiving musical time.

Krzysztof Penderecki (b. 1933) is perhaps the best known of the young Polish composers. His musical education was haphazard. At eighteen he was still concentrating on literature and philosophy, although he pursued the violin and cybernetics as hobbies. Penderecki leaped to world fame in 1959 when he entered three of his compositions anonymously in an impeccably honest Warsaw competition (sponsored by the Polish Composers' Association) and walked away with the first, second, and third prizes. One of the works he had entered in the competition was a composition for electronic music, which he entitled, according to its taped length, *Eight Minutes and Thirty-seven Seconds.* Only later was this threnody renamed *Suite for Hiroshima,* for Penderecki seemed to be expressing his contemporary engagement through tortured screams. Penderecki claims everybody was moved because, on the one hand, the "jungles of sound give an impression of compulsive chaos," while, on the other hand, "the score shows it is perfectly controlled." Penderecki says the aleatoric aspect of this work is limited, as "a number of elements of a fixed pattern have to be played as fast and as many times as possible within a given number of seconds." Somehow, these compositions seem to lack humor; they are too technological. For the *Suite for Hiroshima* (for fifty-two string instruments) and for his *Anaklasis* (1960), *The Dimensions of Time and Silence* (1961), and *Stabat Mater* (for three chapel choruses) (1962), Penderecki was forced to develop a new system of notation that has now become generally adopted in Poland. Among other signs, it has special marks for sawing, rubbing, and hammering. Most important, however, is his new way to note tone clusters—with a long black line. "Unfortunately, this is not something anyone can copyright," said the composer, explaining that he had been forced to find a new and abbreviated system of notation because he had no room to compose except on the crowded tabletops of his favorite smoke-filled Cracow café.

Penderecki, who was writing his notations in red, green, blue, and brown felt pens in his Essen (Germany) apartment while his actress wife, Elzbieta, was scoring special sheets with a ruler, said that, although he is now writing in a more classic idiom, he has not basically changed his style since he wrote *Polymorphia* in 1961. Penderecki, who admits his debt to Pierre Boulez, said that, except for the ancient, sacred music, traditional forms of Polish composition have had little influence on him. "I was quite self-contained from the beginning, I believe," he said in a slightly arrogant tone. Penderecki's execution is distinctly his own. He freely includes any musical mode that comes to mind as he scores. This may include the pounding of a typewriter, the humming of a computer, alarm clocks ringing or ticking, and the rasping of musical handsaws. However, Penderecki does not avoid rhythmic or melodic repetitions. He himself defines his style as "medieval surrealism." He attempts to find common ground between new and old music, between plain chant and atonal music. In his *Passion According to St. Luke* (1965), he tried to combine the best of all worlds: East and West, electronic and Stradivarian, post-Webern and pre-Monteverdi.

Penderecki is very much of a Catholic believer, and his *Passion*, written with strong religious feeling, was first performed in 1966 in the Cathedral of Münster in the presence of bishops and the apostolic nuncio. The *Passion* ventures into a realm of religious music that has hardly been touched by composers since Baroque times. The simplicity of expression reflects the devotional nature of Penderecki's Catholic text. The solemn, sparse words overpower the conflicting elements of diatonic, quarter-tone, serial, and atonal techniques that are the *Passion*'s musical foundation. As proof of its ecclesiastical acceptance, Penderecki said, "The Church in Poland is very receptive to this writing and recognized the *Passion* as spiritual, Catholic music."

The *Passion* is a two-hour oratorio that admirably blends a Gregorian chorus with twelve-tone violin strains. It is a symbiosis of pre-Baroque Netherlandish polyphony and dodecaphony. The prologue begins with a scream. Then orchestral sounds combine in elaborate clusters with the tenor choir to produce what musicologists call "bichromatic sighs." The role of Christ himself is sung by a solo baritone; Judas and Pilate are sung by basses. The lyrical passages are treated as great soprano scenes. The New Testament spirit of the *Passion*, whose over-all form corresponds to that of Bach's *Passion*, is highly dramatic. The free choral movements are also close to Bach, but the rasping whispers, the abrasive laughter, the snakelike hissing of the voices are distinctly twentieth-century. Penderecki is particularly effective in the crowd scenes, in which four mixed choruses not only sing but also whistle, whisper, scream, mutter, babble, and groan in antiphony. The crass, chilling string effects border on contemporary noise, while the contours of the tone clusters seem to defy aural comprehension.

Penderecki explained that when his *Passion* (which, admittedly, is an unusual format in the electronic age) was first played in Poland at the Tenth Annual Warsaw Fall Festival the musical snobs raised a cry that he had betrayed the avant-garde. "Poland is the land of musical snobbery," said Penderecki uneasily in the self-imposed exile of his Essen apartment, "but you must remember that these snobs also chased out Chopin." "Despite all the criticism from the *soi-disant* avant-gardists, I don't believe my *Passion* was a step backward," he said. Indeed, Penderecki intends to go on composing religious music. He has written a very moving, partly solemn and partly horror-filled, *Dies Irae* (1967), which was dedicated to the "Memory of the Assassinated at Auschwitz," and he is working on an Orthodox Russian Mass (commissioned by the Koussevitzky Foundation), which he is basing on Old Church Slavonic texts he found while in Russia on a recent trip. Penderecki explained that "the Gregorian singing I heard as a child had a deep influence on me"; its atonalities continue to work in his imagination. In effect, compared with America's new computerized adventurists, Penderecki must now be regarded as a throwback to traditionalism.

Penderecki doesn't find life agreeable in Germany, but he must remain there until the end of the decade. "Sometimes I feel as if I were one of the damned in Dante's Hell," he said, as the bars from Franck's *Variations* were rising from the apartment below. Apparently there is a German pianist who starts her exercises punctually at ten every morning. "For me, it is sheer torture," he said while sipping some Polish *Soplica*. "I must try to rush through my work before then because as soon as she starts her Franck I can't think any more. There are moments I think she will drive me crazy. But usually, I only drink *Soplica*." What is keeping Penderecki in self-imposed exile is a commission to write a full-length opera, *The Devils*, to be premièred in Hamburg in 1969. *The Devils* is based on Huxley's *The Devils of Loudon*, but the text will be written by Polish author Jerzy Andrzejewski (who wrote *Ashes and Diamonds*). "*The Devils* will include as large an orchestra as I can squeeze into the pit and as large a chorus as the Hamburg stage will support," said Penderecki with great enthusiasm. (As in painting, the prevalent notion in music is that the larger the medium, the more provocative the message.) Ideally, Penderecki would like to alleviate the Polish unemployment problem by utilizing choruses of thousands, but here the gleam in his dark eyes takes on a satanic glaze.

The Polish radio, which often plays Penderecki, has spurred the veritable musical revolution that has occurred in Poland. By devoting entire broadcast series to leading representatives of modern music, such as Webern and John Cage, Polish radio has stimulated the appetite for the contemporary idiom. Serial music demands intelligent listening, and it has taken considerable courage to deprive the public of its usual diet of passive enjoyment. Polish youth (which is not, as reported, entirely obsessed by jazz) is gradually changing its attitude toward the time, the form, and even the expectations it has had of music. The Studio of Experimental Music, opened in Warsaw in 1957 without any experience, says director Jozef Patkowski (b. 1921), "and in our original electronic team of five there was no composer." Patkowski claims that "first of all, we were interested in the technology of sound, that is to say, musical acoustics and the problems of the perception of sound made by electroacoustic devices." Only later did the composer become the creator in the studio. "That the source of sound is not an acoustic instrument but an electric generator has no great importance to the composer creating a world of sound phenomena," said Patkowski.

Patkowski, who combined physics and musicology at the University of Warsaw, only gradually developed the Studio into the leading musical institution it is today. Not until January 1959 did his Studio perform the first major work, *Etiuda,* by Wlodzimierz Kotonski (b. 1925), who soon won the reputation of being the best Polish composer in the field of electronic music. Even Kotonski's most famous works, such as *Etiuda Konkret, Microstructures* (1963), and *Klangspiele* (1967), seem entirely faceless to me. *Klangspiele*—all of nine minutes long—is interpreted by four musicians playing various radioelectronic devices. During its performance in Warsaw, I kept on wondering what bonds were created in such a work between the composer and his public—the performer having been eliminated in electronic music. Unless the intent be one of alienation, there appears to be no emotional exchange whatsoever. However, it would seem that Kotonski's composition differs little from those being composed wherever electronic works are taped. Kotonski himself seemed evasive as to the originality of other electronic composers, but he ruled out the use of computers in Poland. "Some of us saw the center in Urbana, Illinois," he said, "but we were a bit skeptical of the possibilities of using computers in this way." Apparently, he felt that "this does not suit our national character." Kotonski seemed to indicate such instruments were fit for mathematicians, but, "as a composer, I do not plan to use a calculating machine in my work." There is still enough of a traditionalist in even the most avant-garde of the Poles for him to say, "I started with the piano, and I still love to play it."

There are indications that the "fad" for electronic freedom has passed its peak in Poland. When Andrzej Dobrowolski (b. 1921) performed his *Music for Tape Recorder and Oboe Solo* at the 1967 Warsaw Fall Festival, he received a rather cold reception from both public and critics. Similarly, Boguslaw Schaffer (b. 1929) also appears to be losing ground. Schaffer is Poland's leading musical phenomenologist (that is, he does not make use of any musical concept that he has not previously studied experimentally and whose theoretical musical validity he has not demonstrated to his own satisfaction). His works cannot easily be classified, described, or explained, because of their versatility; in many ways, they are as abstruse as the braying of an ass. Because Schaffer resorts to such tricks as a seven-hour performance of his work *Nonstop* (in conjunction with a "happening" by Poland's leading action painter Tadeusz Kantor), Penderecki labels his colleague Schaffer a "professional avant-gardist." Other critics, who are somewhat kinder, are at a loss to find any real development in Schaffer's more recent electronic experiments. There seems little that is satisfying or even intellectually challenging in his works. After five minutes of listening to his "arresting" sound patterns, one has the depressing feeling that forty-five minutes have passed—and afterward there is nothing left to remember. In spite of all the variations, it is always more of the same organ-grinding. It is too facile. "Music must remain in the hands of a composer and not in those of an engineer or a programmer," said Penderecki, who felt "the electric motor must lead to sterility."

But Polish music today is not headed for otiosity. On the contrary, it is the most potent of the arts in this country of thirty million people. Moreover, this musical activity is, and will continue to be, heavily endowed by the communist regime.* Liberated from the outworn slogans of the musical rear guard, there seems little doubt that music will not only continue to be the most emancipated of the arts in Poland, but will also move in this direction elsewhere in Eastern Europe in the decade ahead.

* Each ticket sold in Poland earns a three hundred per cent subsidy for the performing group. This makes it possible for Poles to go to a concert for half of what Americans pay for going to the movies. Each year some thirty-nine musical groups, including nine symphony orchestras and ten Philharmonic orchestras, attract about five million listeners.

πραξις

Eastern European communists look upon Yugoslav experimentation in the social and political sciences as heresy; at best, they regard it as "naïve" deviationism, at worst, as a "Trojan horse" within the world communist movement. The Yugoslavs, on the other hand, proudly assert that their horse has already infiltrated communist Troy and has changed the Marxist-Leninist outlook beyond recognition. Their achievements in the arts, as well as in politics, are indeed impressive: Specifically, Yugoslavia was the first socialist country to accept abstract expressionist painting, serial music, Western television shows, and pornographic literature. It was the first to decollectivize a collectivized agriculture (and in this it was followed by the Poles). It was the first to abandon centralized planning, in an effort to establish a socialist form of market economy (and in this it has been followed by every communist state except China and Albania). It was the leader in opening up the frontiers both to its own workers and to foreign tourists (and, ever since, the rest of the "bloc" has been vying with Yugoslavia for the tourist dollar). Spurred by Milovan Djilas in the early nineteen-fifties, Yugoslavia was foremost in abandoning the use of administrative measures to maintain political control and to dismantle the power of the secret police. The Yugoslavs were the first to develop workers' councils and workers' self-management (in which no one, to date, has dared follow them). Finally, they have been paving the way in upgrading the rump parliaments of Eastern Europe, in the separation of powers, and in promoting the "withering away" of the state. The results are so anarchic that even members of the League of Communists of Yugoslavia admit they are now entering a phase whose end results they themselves cannot anticipate.

In this heady political-philosophical turmoil, a widely diffused group of philosophers, sociologists, and historians have been pointing ideological laser beams at what, in their opinion, should or should not be. This society of emancipated intellectuals has demonstrated an ambition that borders on the pretentious. What, after all, ask their Russian philosophical colleagues, has been the place of Serbo-Croat philosophy in world history, not to mention the twentieth century? And yet, this small group, under the protective wing of Zagreb's Croatian Philosophical Society (*Hrvatsko filozofsko drustvo*) has, since 1964, been printing the most influential theoretical publication in the communist world: Πραξις. "Praxis," according to Marx, represents the essence of free being: the life of action—as opposed to theory. No other publication has been so unyielding in demanding that theory be carried out in practice and no other publication has succeeded in causing as much philosophical ferment as *Praxis*. No Soviet or Polish magazine would have had the nerve to follow the example of the *Praxis* editors in postulating straightforwardly: "The Communist Party first? All right, but for what end?" Because *Praxis* holds no subject sacred and is eager to criticize, its influence has been many hundredfold greater than its circulation—only three thousand copies, published on an irregular bimonthly basis—would lead one to believe.

In their first issue (1963), the founders of *Praxis* proclaimed they intended to publish a "philosophical magazine that is not strictly professional, a philosophical magazine that will deal not with philosophical material exclusively, but also with all current problems of Yugoslav socialism and of the modern world." Although *Praxis* could only exist as a consequence of the peculiar conditions of Yugoslav turbulence, its editors were soon swarming the Yugoslav horse like Nietzsche's "fairground flies." They pestered the regime by their attacks on the inadequate ideological training of the members of the League of Communists of Yugoslavia and the Stalinist form of its bureaucratic organization. They aroused the bureaucrats by calling for an immediate overhaul of Marxist thinking, a closer examination of the process of alienation, a scientific analysis of the concept of self-management—in brief, a thoroughgoing review of the entire socialist course of development. To communist officials, with their predetermined idea that Marxism equals truth, this was a bitter cathartic. Such officials, who could perhaps be compared to American post-office managers in their outlook, are content to be right, and are totally unconcerned about the methods with which the Marxist shibboleths were originally sanctified. Seeking the truth is not a quest that challenges the rank-and-file communist. He has never developed intellectual tools of doubt such as the Western habit of at least attempting to exclude prejudgments. The *Praxis* group, consisting initially of some two dozen contributors, wrote in the first issue that they were "not interested in conserving Marx, but, rather, in developing the live, revolutionary thought inspired by Marx." Describing themselves as "creative Marxists," they followed the bearded prophet's call for "radical and unscrupulous criticism of everything that exists." It was as if, armed with the Bible, they began to attack the Church.

Rudi Supek, coeditor-in-chief of *Praxis,* whose wartime experiences in Nazi concentration camps have certainly contributed to the magazine's challenging, nonacademic format, considers radical dissent as having a dual purpose: to attack "Stalinist positivism" and to work for the development of a technocratic humanism. Supek sees "Stalinist positivism" as "the most widespread Marxist concept in the socialist world today." Lunching leisurely over a Croatian-style *pot-au-feu,* Supek explained that "Stalinist positivism" is not a scientifically oriented philosophical approach, but that it is the view that a new society can be constructed on top of the present bureaucratic foundations. "One cannot expect from people who have moved up from peasant rags to limousines a grasp of the humanist problems of socialism," he maintains. Moreover, as one of the most influential members of the *Praxis* group, Supek considers it both "paradoxical and absurd" that throughout the communist world it is thought that the "people who were brought up as so-called 'Marxists' during the era of Stalinist positivism are the most suitable and reliable elements for the development of socialist humanism." When Supek makes such remarks there is no more bitterness in his voice than when he talks about the nature of Croatian beer. However, his message is cogent. Supek believes that the problem of alienation remains the central point in socialism; that Marxism has failed to "mitigate the alienation of the worker and to provide a system of values to replace the Christian ethic." Instead, Supek maintains, Marxism has created its own "myths and mystification," including the concept that the theory of alienation is a Hegelian remnant in Marxism and that alienation is, by definition, contradictory to socialism.

Supek believes that only people who have complete freedom of thought and expression can feel morally bound to work for the genuine establishment of socialism. "The cultural and human situation under socialism is becoming more and more critical," he says, "because as the people living under socialism get rich, the system must change." Writing in *Praxis*, Supek lamented: "Even today—fifty years after the October revolution—it is more than deplorable to observe the cultural balance sheet of socialism as a historical epoch that promised a 'new type of man' and 'more human relationships among individuals.' Instead of humanism and culture, political pragmatism prevails, so that the writers are given the task of studying problems concerned with the sowing of corn and the realization of the five-year plans, instead of studying the problems of the human personality." Supek reflects the commitment of the supporters of *Praxis,* as a group, to fight for that human being, that *"Mensch,"* who is free in asserting his rights, who is free in his choices, who keeps an open mind, but who is—in the end—committed to a truly humanist socialism.

The *Praxis* philosophers believe there should be a division of labor between politicians and philosophers. Stalin's primary sin, as they see it, was to have been both the philosopher and the dictator of Marxism-Leninism. Consequently, in their struggle against Stalinist positivism, they want to ensure that philosophy shall not be falsified for political ends, that theory shall not be distorted to serve as an instrument of suppression. "The task of philosophers is to be the conscience and consciousness of their time," says one of the editors. Nevertheless, most agree with Supek that philosophers cannot become politicians, because their involvement necessarily would mean the end of their spiritual mission. The prospects of such a division of labor are not particularly welcome among Tito's entourage. Tito, for example, attacked those "Praxitists" who held symposiums and talks (outside the League of Communists of Yugoslavia) on what communism should be like. The questions of communist organization, Tito said, were the exclusive domain of the members of the Party and should not be discussed by outsiders. In fact, many Yugoslavs considered the *Praxis* program of "radical and unreserved criticism of everything that exists" as too strong a platform for the rank and file of the League members to tolerate—even in a society in such a state of flux as is Yugoslavia.

Supek says that the Yugoslav "hierarchy is not interested to learn whether somebody thinks well or not, whether somebody makes a contribution to the advancement of scientific and social ideas or not; it is chiefly concerned with only one thing: Does this man think favorably of me or not?" Supek honestly admits it is a tragedy for socialism that such poorly educated people have come to power —not only in Yugoslavia, but also elsewhere in Eastern Europe.* There is a tendency for people to "believe in 'wise leaders' who, once in office, then use a kind of mental-hygiene censorship designed to decide for the masses what they may read and think," says Supek, whose caustic observations continue to inflame the Yugoslav hierarchy.

* The *Praxis* philosophers are fond of recalling Marx's words to the effect that bureaucracy is the rule of incompetence. Professor Mladen Caldarovic of Zagreb University, one of the most outspoken of the *Praxis* editors, says with Montenegrin explicitness that "the education of most of our leaders has been in the school of Stalinist bureaucracy." The East European bureaucrat, that archenemy of spontaneity in the arts, considers it more effective to have decision making carried on behind the scenes. This bureaucrat does not like to act openly. He prefers to work within a narrow circle of select people, preferably fellow communists, who recognize his authority and are used to obey. Basically, the bureaucrat who takes refuge in his past achievements (as an underground leader or a resistance hero) "lacks confidence in people," says Caldarovic. Democratic decision making seems an impractical, overly complex method for such an operator. In Yugoslavia, the Party bureaucracy avoided excesses only because it was not obsessed by that harsh, humorless preoccupation with power which the typical East European communist carries about like psychic epaulets.

The *Praxis* editors had become so bold by early 1966 as to challenge Tito's party with the proposition that Marxist theory was lagging behind Yugoslav practice. Developing the theme Djilas had outlined in his *New Class*, that the *status quo* was unacceptable, they argued: Either the Communists had to adjust theory to practice or they had to introduce practice that was in accord with Marxism-Leninism. However, the Yugoslav leadership was unwilling to accept either of these alternatives and seemed perfectly content to compromise theory whenever and wherever need be. Therefore, the *Praxis* philosophers had no choice but to protest even louder against the mounting ideological chaos and distorted practices. It followed quite naturally in the spring of 1966 that the Croatian Assembly began systematically to denounce *Praxis*, while the Croatian communist leadership unleashed what the editors termed a "decisive political condemnation" of their magazine. "Controversial discussion is very useful," said Mika Tripalo (b. 1916), one of the more promising stars on the post-Tito political horizon, "but we are not used to genuine controversy." Tripalo, who is the Zagreb Party Secretary, branded the *Praxis* philosophers as "an avant-garde intelligentsia" whose views are "diametrically opposed" to the Party line. "They believe in the leading role of philosophers," he explained, "but rarely in history were philosophers leaders, and when they were, they wrecked that society."

When I confronted some of the *Praxis* members with Tripalo's charge, they replied that they were not seeking office; that Tripalo, by imputing a thirst for power to them, was only revealing his own appetite. Thumbing their noses at the "lyric sopranos and bald bassos" in the Croatian League of Communists, they said no official in power ever sees oppositional ideas as anything but an attack on his own job. While the communists unfairly suspect the *Praxis* philosophers of trying to establish a new political program, it is true that, as a group, the members of *Praxis* tend to favor "elitism." For example, the editors question whether the Yugoslav working man, being insufficiently educated and inadequately prepared, is equal to the task of self-management. Supek believes that the emancipated peasants and relatively unskilled workers, who still suffer from illiteracy, cannot meet the challenge of developing creative Marxism.

221

Instead, he thinks the workers must be led by a select group within the Party. And it would be sheer evasion for the editors of *Praxis* to deny they would like to be the mentors of such a benevolent elite.

Because the Yugoslav leadership is in no hurry to realize a cultured elitism, the struggle *Praxis* has faced in trying to survive has been dramatic. "No other publication in Yugoslavia," claims Supek, "has encountered such continual resistance as *Praxis*." Supek's co-editor-in-chief, Professor Gajo Petrovic (b. 1927), who was finally expelled from the League of Communists in June 1968 for "having sharply advocated some extreme demagogic anarcho-liberalistic views," said that "from its first issue the magazine found itself facing exceptional difficulties." It was not only a question of assembling the editorial staff, but also of trying to obtain paper and a printing plant, to set up a distribution system, and so on. Ever since that first issue, which sold for about one hundred and fifty dinars (twenty cents) a copy, the magazine has been perpetually in debt— despite considerable initial subsidies from the Croatian Philosophical Society. (Yugoslav law does not permit *Praxis* to receive money from abroad, except in the form of payment for individual subscriptions. Otherwise, *Praxis* would probably have received a subsidy from some CIA-front organization long ago, and Supek would today have had the reputation of a Yugoslav Melvin J. Lasky!) Not only does *Praxis* pay its contributing authors, including Lucien Goldmann, Erich Fromm, and Herbert Marcuse, nothing for their essays, but *Praxis* is even printed on credit. "The workers at the Joza Rozankovic printing plant give us an advance of their labor and costs," said Supek, "and we give them the satisfaction of printing an intellectual magazine." Because its financial and political basis is so unstable, the editors have often been forced to print three issues of the international edition in one. During an eight-month pause (from the summer of 1966 to the spring of 1967) there was some question as to whether *Praxis* would reappear at all. By the summer of 1968, *Praxis* was in such extreme financial straits that doubts arose whether any further issues would appear. The magazine found itself in debt for about eight thousand dollars, it was no longer receiving a subsidy from the Croatian Republic, and other sources of financial support also seemed to be drying up.

Although assurances had been given that there would be no "administrative suppression against *Praxis*," in fact, the cut in subsidies amounted to a covert way to halt its "deviationism." Previously an attempt had been made to silence the magazine, and one of its then joint editors-in-chief, Professor Danilo Pejovic, succumbed to Party blackmail and turned Judas to the group, denouncing his fellow editors from the rostrum and undermining their efforts. Pejovic was ultimately voted out of his job, but this did not end the strife within the magazine, because some Belgrade contributors considered publishing their own Serbian philosophic quarterly. Surprisingly to any outsiders, but not to the nationality-conscious Serbs and Croats, the difference between the engaged philosophers of Belgrade and Zagreb is considerable: The members of the Belgrade group, led by Mihailo Markovic, are far more technocratically oriented than their Zagreb cousins. They believe a more scientific, analytic approach is necessary if any real progress is to be made in the development of Marxism. The *Praxis* editors, such as Supek and Petrovic, are inclined to promote a philosophy that is free—and especially free of technocracy. The Zagreb group does not basically believe that science can tell man what is essence— what should be, what might be, what is historically possible in the present, what is optimal, what will satisfy genuine human needs, what is culture. Rather than split into two contending factions, the *Praxis* editors decided it would be far wiser to submerge these differences by expanding the editorial board to an international group of some forty-eight members. Kostas Axelos, Alfred J. Ayer, Norman Birnbaum, Ernst Bloch, Erich Fromm, Lucien Goldmann, Leszek Kolakowski, Henri Lefebvre, Georgy Lukacs, Serge Mallet, Herbert Marcuse, Howard L. Parsons, David Riesman, Julius Strinka, and Kurt Wolff were named—along with a number of Yugoslav philosophers, historians, and sociologists—as associate editors. Such an expansion matched the belief of the editorial board that Marxists, non-Marxists, and even anti-Marxists should and could participate in a meaningful dialogue on the basic philosophic questions of our time. Elevating the dialogue to an international *niveau* not only secured the magazine protection at home (because the Yugoslav communists are more reluctant to interfere in the affairs of an international organization than they are in a regional one), but it also provided a new and useful standard of comparison: While many of the top Yugoslav philosophers are at the level of their Western counterparts, others were initially embarrassed to discover that they were only repeating many of the truths that noncommunists in the West had uttered for several decades—but that had appeared to them to be startling self-discoveries. The international edition of *Praxis,* published partially in French, German, and English, and incorporating the leading contributions from the regular Serbo-Croat issues, illustrated the great "philosophic leap forward" the Zagreb philosophers had taken in four years of publication.

The Croatian Philosophical Society's mounting preoccupation with culture was another indication of its developing maturity. The magazine's table of contents increasingly includes such essays as: "For What Purpose Art?," "Art in the Technological World," "Philosophy and Art," "Art and Aesthetics," and "Socialism and Mass Culture." Much of the ground for these articles had already been cleared a decade before by that remarkable Montenegran Milovan Djilas (b. 1911), who was expelled from the Party in 1954 and then jailed for demanding the "democratization" of the communist apparatus. Djilas wrote at length in the mid-fifties about the "clinical refinement" with which the communists practiced what he called "tyranny over the mind." His *New Class* was a devastating condemnation of the methods used to emasculate the intellect. "Communists are traditionalists in art," he wrote, "mostly because of the need to maintain their monopoly over the minds of the people, but also because of their ignorance and one-sidedness." He said that communists could not resolve the contradiction between the freedom of form they had promised and the compulsory control of ideas. Similarly, the "uncurbed monopolistic aspirations of the regime and the irresistible creative aspirations of the artists" made art and Soviet-style communism irreconcilable. Djilas described the intellectual atmosphere of the Stalinist era as a theater without an audience where "the actors play and go into raptures over themselves."

The *Praxis* philosophers admire Djilas and have enlarged upon his ideas. They reject the so-called "orthodox" Marxist theory, which regards culture merely as a reflection of the needs of the social structure. Professor Pedrag Vranicki, a leading member of the editorial board, has written: "We have reached the stage where we must show the world that, in the cultural field, socialism means open thinking and not dictation." Vranicki believes that "the creation of a free cultural atmosphere is our primary task [in Yugoslavia], and if it has not yet been fully realized, the blame cannot be placed on *Praxis.*"

Professor Miladin Zivotic (b. 1930), a dynamic Belgrade sociologist, has examined the relationship between society and culture under socialism at considerable length. Zivotic's take-off point is Ortega y Gasset's proposition that culture must be seen as a struggle between two principles: When culture is in the hands of an elite, it is authentic; when culture belongs to the masses, the result is vulgarity.* In his essay for *Praxis,* Professor Zivotic, while not directly equating mass culture with what is happening in the Soviet Union, leaves little doubt that Russia is not currently producing anything approximating authentic culture. "Mass culture alienates man from his personal experience of reality, from personal creativeness, alienates him from the need to have personal experience, from the need to have a personal taste." Mass culture, Zivotic proposes, stifles the need for "an authentic personal relationship with reality and thus destroys the basis on which humanism is generally possible."

Zivotic sees mass culture as production "for satisfying the petty, impersonal taste of the masses." Such culture seeks and forms stereotyped tastes "that destroy intellectual and other differences, that destroy the need for personal efforts in experiencing and adopting cultural values." What is mass culture? It is the "standardized, stereotyped reproduction of reality and the presentation of such reproductions as a form of value." In contrast, authentic culture is founded "on the basis of a personal, creative rising. . . . It is the creation of those values that demand a change of the world."

---

* Ortega y Gasset wrote in *The Revolt of the Masses:* "The characteristic of the hour is that the commonplace mind, knowing itself to be commonplace, has the assurance to proclaim the rights of the commonplace and to impose them wherever it will."

Zivotic has little patience with mass culture. He feels mass culture is produced to order; whether that order be bureaucratic or commercial is immaterial. What matters is that it is "a cliché-ridden echo of banality," that while it assumes to reproduce reality, it actually dehumanizes it. The glorification of given reality is, after all, nothing more than Stalinism. The Soviets posit the theory of "people's culture," Zivotic says, and are continuing to promote the myth of the "creativeness of the mass" (in such pristine forms as folk dancing and choral groups). While Russian philosophers continue to talk about the "decisive entrance of the people's mass into the development of culture," they seem unaware that they are courting disaster. If this entrance were indeed to be realized, it would mean no less than the death of art. Fortunately for the Soviets, a powerful nonofficial art has given rise to an underground culture that is not the work of a professional team, but the achievement of what Zivotic calls the "unrepeatable personality." The trouble with mass culture, according to the Belgrade professor, is that it chokes any other form of culture. And the Russians, in their anxiety to transform the masses into active cultural participants, have greatly diminished the opportunities for the individual. As the *Praxis* philosophers pointed out in their 1967 summer conference on "Creativity and Reification": as soon as the measurement of art becomes the number of people it satisfies, art ends.

Zivotic contends there are many reasons why modern art has become anathema in the Soviet Union, as well as in the other socialist states. "Avant-garde modern art is nonconformist; its subject is the contemporary drama of human alienation, which the apologetic, quasi art of socialist realism cannot accept." Because it is symbolic of alienation, because it reflects the irrational nature of the contemporary world, because it tries to impart a human message, modern art must be rejected and denounced by socialist officialdom. The mission of socialist realism, after all, is to conceal the existing state of affairs by what Zivotic calls "fictitious positive values." The avant-garde must be branded as "outcast" because it refuses to serve "those who want to transform art into the handmaiden of politics." What is especially dangerous, says Rudi Supek, is that the Soviets have attempted to bribe the elite into creating mass culture by the extension of special privileges, and that such a corrupted, pseudo elite is undermining the traditional intelligentsia that produced Imperial Russia's artistic giants. Supek's viewpoint is that, because the position of the thinking man in society is necessarily that of an outsider, American artists, writers, and composers are almost as cut off from the community as are their Russian counterparts. It is Supek's impression that the isolation of Soviet writers (even in enforced exile) is no greater than the self-exile of America's creative artists.

The relationship between the Yugoslav philosophers and their Soviet counterparts has been mutually suspicious but correct. A group of Russian philosophers came to Yugoslavia in November 1965, and the Yugoslavs, represented by Zivotic, Grlic, Kangrga, Pejovic, and Kresic, returned the visit in the spring of 1966. The Russians first wanted to determine whether the Yugoslavs were, in fact, bona-fide Marxists. In Russian eyes, the *Praxis* revisionists had gone so far astray that their Marxism was scarcely recognizable. The attitude of these Soviet Marxmen was one of paternalism mixed with patronizing understanding that, in time, the Yugoslavs would come to realize the error of their ways. Nevertheless, they were quite startled to find the *Praxis* philosophers almost indifferent to certain "incontestable truths" and fundamental "axioms" of Marxism. This, the Soviets thought, undoubtedly was the result of their contamination by the simplistic, primitive distortions of Marxism in the West.

The emphasis of *Praxis* on the individual's free choice was correctly interpreted by the Russians as a clear break with Marxist determinism. *Praxis* philosophers believe that history cannot be regarded as "collective existence" but must be viewed as the fulfillment of human destiny in the lives of individual personalities. None of the *Praxis* group believes, as the Russians still pretend to, that freedom can only be the awareness of the inevitable. In fact, in the corridors of the Department of Philosophy at Zagreb University, socialism is regarded as no more than a historical alternative that may or may not triumph, depending on the course of its own self-purification. The Yugoslavs, for their part, deny that "dialectical materialism," as it is known in Moscow today, has anything in common with the philosophy of Marx. Supek goes even further and says, "Leninism is entirely old-fashioned. Lenin was fundamentally

227

concerned with the exploited, impoverished workers and peasants; we are interested primarily in the intellectuals and the affluent society." The basic difference between Zagreb and Moscow philosophers is that the Yugoslavs, having reached a certain standard of well-being, are now looking ahead—while the Muscovites continue to interpret the past.

Praxis editor Danko Grlic rejects the Talmudic approach to Marx. "A faithful adherence to whatever has once been proclaimed true is nothing but a substitute for practical impotence," said Grlic. "This is why it is absurd to insist, in Marx's name, persistently and in detail on everything that Marx ever wrote or said." The question of supreme ideological authority, Grlic contends, is today an open issue facing all of Marxist philosophy. Among the editors of *Praxis* there is the conviction that the "three holy kings" of communism are, in the words of Grlic, "really antiquated." Not only are Marx, Engels, and Lenin passé, but Grlic also considers them to be frequently in contradiction. Professor Gajo Petrovic has shown that the dialectical materialism of Engels, Plekhanov, and Lenin is entirely incompatible with Marx's humanist anthropology. Petrovic says that Yugoslav philosophers have revived Marx's conception of philosophy as an independent creative activity, and he points out that there no longer is any point in pretending that Marx and Engels ever were exclusive owners of philosophic truth, especially in the field of aesthetics.

Professor Pedrag Vranicki has written that there are contemporary philosophers who are still searching in the classics of Marxism for ready-made recipes. "Lenin," writes Vranicki, "who spoke from a platform valid in his lifetime, could not have anticipated the present-day situation." What is needed is a realistic analysis of contemporary capitalist society, says Vranicki, not polemics about exploitation of the workers. "A noncreative attitude toward the Marxist heritage means the abandonment of revolutionary Marxist methodology in dealing with realities," concludes Vranicki, "which inevitably results in serious practical and political consequences."

Stimulated by the *Economic and Philosophic Manuscripts of 1844,* in which Marx criticized capitalism from a humanist, anthropological position, the *Praxis* philosophers believe they can find the beginnings of a philosophical system acceptable to both East and West. For the "early Marx," the release of man's spiritual energies for creative ends was the goal of the entire revolutionary effort. Marx, who knew much of Shakespeare by heart and reread the Greek tragedies once a year, actually aspired to the reintegration of art into the life of the individual and the community. Citing this utopian aspect of Marx's writings, Belgrade's Mihailo Markovic said he is exploring the basis of a future humanity comprising creative individuals who are more interested in "being" than in "having." Markovic insists "the deepest meaning of Marx's revolutionary thought lies in his rebellion against all the conditions of life that hamper the full development of human beings, that prevent human activity from being a full and free assertion of all the essential internal powers of each individual."

The *Praxis* group has shifted the emphasis away from what it calls the "vulgar economism" and toward psychology, sociology, and anthropology. "Kissing and loving, hoping and hating are as intimate a part of the concept of *Praxis* as economic productivity is to dialectical materialism," asserts one editor. The *Praxis* contributors, by and large, reject the notion that culture is a "superstructure" built on and determined by the economic infrastructure. By questioning the fundamental rule of dialectical materialism—namely, that material values dominate the spiritual—these intellectuals are calling into question the very concept of Marxist determinism. "If culture is merely the reflection of the 'infrastructure,' then what is the role assigned to us?" asks Supek. Perhaps this is one of the reasons Supek claims that "Riesman and Fromm have something to tell us, but Soviet Marxism has nothing to offer that we feel is relevant in the social sciences."

This dramatic shift of interest does not mean that the *Praxis* group is ignoring economics as a factor in culture. For example, the editors wrote in 1965 that "The affluent society of the West has . . . in the realm of culture thrown large quantities of products onto the market that can satisfy the needs of the alienated human soul." Professor Mladen Caldarovic takes rigorous exception to the position of his colleagues, however. "To what purpose the entire revolutionary experience, when German capitalists are exploiting our workers, Americans are building hotels, and the government runs gambling casinos for the tourists? No, this is really utter nonsense." Caldarovic (who was expelled from the Yugoslav Communist Party in 1937 because he opposed Stalin's purge of the Red Army) has been a lifelong rebel. "I am against the so-called 'free-market planning' we can observe in Yugoslavia," says Caldarovic, who sees great dangers in an economy managed in a dilettante, Titoist manner. "It makes me ill to see shoddy, made-in-Japan Eiffel Towers sold in Zagreb to the armies of German tourists," he said. In an extended exposition of his paternalistic economic approach, Caldarovic said he considered the commercialization of Yugoslav culture a spiritual disaster for the country. However, Caldarovic believes Yugoslavia must experience a generation of economic trial and error; that the exploration of the unknown always leads to a number of easily ridiculed follies. For even Caldarovic recognizes the Yugoslav way as offering some hope that socialism can advance on a different course from that taken by the Soviet Union in the nineteen-twenties.

The contributors to *Praxis* believe that the Stalinist concept of a new "socialist culture" was no more than a "soap bubble." The Soviet orthodox hold that human history began with Marxism, that the "prehistory" was an epoch of inhuman economic and social realities. Consequently, the culture of this "prehistory" was barbaric and now is only fit to be exhibited in museums as evidence of pre-Marxist man's ignorance. The *Praxis* editors wrote in the introduction to their Yugoslav culture series that such "a nihilistic attitude toward the cultural heritage of the past is essentially . . . an anticultural attitude." The Yugoslavs believe that "in what we have called 'commodity-ridden,' feudal, or 'bourgeois' culture, there is often more of the all-human, truly humane than in what is sometimes explicitly proclaimed to be socialist culture."

There is a natural gravitation on the part of some *Praxis* writers toward the technocratic socialism currently being espoused by George Lichtheim and Serge Mallet. This is evident in such articles as Markovic's "Man and Technology" (1966) and Supek's "Karl Marx in the Era of Automation" (1967), as well as in the discussions held in the "summer school" on the Isle of Korcula about such topics as "program planning and human liberty" and "technocracy and the human being." Supek believes social scientists must urgently undertake in-depth studies of the alienation of the modern industrial workers, so as to provide humanity the possibility of fighting off technocratic enslavement. I believe Supek would really like to develop a new syndicalism: one in which technicians and workers would strive together for the humanization of labor, and in which leisure and education would be incorporated into production. Curiously, like the other members of the *Praxis* group, Supek truly believes that the Yugoslav system of workers' self-management may provide some of the answers in surmounting the rising threat of industrial alienation. As yet, there is no empirical proof that this most ambitious of all modern socialist experiments can succeed. (My own encounters with a variety of workers' councils, ranging from that of the Skoplje steel mill in Macedonia to the Rade Koncar electrical trust in Zagreb, have left me confused as to whether the methods or the workers are at fault. As attractive as the idea appeared in principle, the whole system seemed a time-consuming burden in practice, and did not impress me as being particularly conducive to economic progress.)

The editors of *Praxis* are convinced philosophy is essential in the twentieth century—not desiccated, academic theorizing, but heuristic thinking that penetrates the vital problems of contemporary culture. "We still believe that creative philosophic thought is not to be isolated from scientific, artistic, and cultural activity, but can only be successfully developed in co-operation with all other forms of spiritual creativity," wrote the editors in 1967. Supek, Petrovic, and Zivotic agree that the ultimate development of culture is the *raison d'être* of socialism. Perhaps the *Praxis* group remains more important for its potentials, for what it represents, than for its actual philosophic achievements, but its members have proved themselves perspicacious, open-minded, and far-seeing in their efforts to assist man in his collective and individual advancement. Supek may only have been boasting when he said that his magazine "furthers the freest expression of true humanism in the world today," nevertheless that he could still say this after more than four years of publication spoke promisingly for the future of Yugoslav socialism.

231

CHAPTER XIII

Off Wenceslas

While the quality and the influence of the Western theater have generally been declining in the postwar era, in Eastern Europe, and particularly in Poland, Rumania, and Czechoslovakia, the theater has become more vital. This anomaly can be explained in part by the fact that drama has traditionally been a medium of national protest in these countries. The communist regimes, unsuccessfully attempting to subvert the theater for ideological ends, have heavily subsidized the dramatic arts—giving individual companies a financial independence unknown, for example, in America. But the reasons why the theater should flourish in Eastern Europe go much deeper: Drama is not debased as "show biz." (Capital gains are not relevant to a Czech revival of Eugene O'Neill.) Prague newspapers list theater under *"Kultura,"* not under entertainment or amusements, as in England or the United States.* The Czechs take their theater, as well as what is said on stage, most seriously. To them, it

* The standard Czech dictionary defines *"kultura"* as "a complex of material and spiritual values created by mankind in the course of its historical development. The material values, above all, the forces of productivity, the mutual relations of man in the creation of economic and social conditions, make up material culture. The social concepts of a people—material and idealistic as well as philosophical concepts—together with scientific discoveries, artistic and moral values, and the general level of education of the nation, make up its spiritual culture. Idealistic philosophy interprets the meaning of the word 'culture' as spiritual culture only, and does not recognize its dependence upon material culture."

represents not only a medium of protest, but also a genuine outlet for pent-up tensions and frustrations—an escape. The Czech theater is intimately bound to the life of the nation, to its social problems, to its aspirations; it is not a medium of frivolity or decadence. The prevalent Western homosexual ethos of the theater without responsibility does not seem relevant in the setting of the dictatorship of the proletariat. (Albee, for example, is generally misinterpreted and is admired in Budapest and Prague for his portrayal of capitalist alienation.) Unlike its New York counterpart, the Prague public does not seek the illusion of irresolute postponement, which is beginning to haunt the American stage. The Czech playwrights and their audiences, faced with an untenable domestic situation, do not grasp for ineffectual palliatives. In Eastern Europe, procrastination may be presented as a necessity, but it is not accepted as a resolution of a dramatic situation.

The very process of going to the theater arouses vastly dissimilar expectations in the American and the East European publics. Czechs do not regard going to a play as something out of the ordinary. There is none of the self-conscious banter or peacock-strutting that used to characterize Shubert Alley. New Yorkers, for the most part, go to Broadway as they go to synagogue or to church: high holidays and a couple of "hits" are *"de rigueur."* Once a month or so they dutifully sit in expensive seats, and then, as the final curtain falls, virtuously applaud the star and themselves. (After all, they deserve the applause; they managed to survive a protracted, if occasionally diverting, bore.) In Prague, there is no conspicuous elite that goes out to be "seen," nor is there a do-good minority engaged in a valiant struggle to keep the theater "alive." Both cities, of course, have their flops, but what Prague has and New York lacks is a cluster of brilliant and fanatical directors, stage designers, dramaturges, and actors who are completely dedicated to excellence and to the satisfactions that its pursuit may bring.

The stage has become something of a "cult" in Czechoslovakia. Prague, a capital of a million, offers a wider selection of plays to its citizens than London, Paris, or New York. Prague has some nineteen permanent repertory companies. These offer everything from Ionesco and Lorca to Marlowe and Tennessee Williams. Professor

Jan Kopecky, the leading Czech critic, claims "the current repertory includes virtually everything that commands interest in the world of drama." In order to compensate for its isolation, Czech theater "has within a short spell graduated from a course in modern Western drama," says Kopecky. On the other hand, the new theatrical productions justify the assessment of critic Kenneth Tynan that Prague now has a strong claim "as the theater capital of Europe." Perhaps its only weakness in this respect is that, like Broadway or the West End, Wenceslas (the main square in Prague, named after the Czech king of Christmas carol renown) is obsessed with presenting the avant-garde and in being regarded as "avant-gardist."

Foreign critics are astounded by the avidity with which all this theatrical *"kultura"* is consumed in Prague. It has been remarked that audiences, well acquainted with the plays, wait for a specific line and break out into aggressive applause even before the actor completes the phrase. The dialogue between the public and the author, which is the ideal every small theater seeks to achieve, is remarkably animated in Prague. This is because the authors and actors share an extraordinary realm of experience with their public. Like war veterans meeting in an American Legion hall, they all have sharp recollections of a common past. Moreover, both are concerned with discovering a viable solution to their present moral and social quagmire: namely, the dictatorship of the proletariat. The audience is therefore always ready to give a sympathetic hearing to any author with a new approach, with a new style, or—until the 1968 revolution—with a new attack on the regime. "Despite their considerable demands on the mind and on the emotions, the small theaters have developed a very eager audience for their new plays," says Jan Grossman, director of Prague's best ministage, the Theater on the Balustrade. Grossman says small theaters like the Balustrade are always full, and the National Theater is always only half full, because the public is now eager for theaters with daring, with personality (that is, with a familiar repertory group), who present playwrights of the younger generation. These playwrights are not didactic. They urge people to think by stating problems without offering any finished theses. Grossman says these playwrights "don't know what is best for the audience; instead, they ask probing questions." In the Czech theater, as in all the arts, slogans are being replaced by dialogue.

Alfred Radok, an emotional, unorthodox, dictatorial, and controversial director at the National Theater, agrees with what he considers Grossman's "intellectual" analyses. "It is important that the audience should know how the questions will be asked and what will be asked in this or at that theater." Radok, who has directed an intense, fiery version of Romain Rolland's *Play of Love and Death,* says that the theater cannot answer questions. "It can only incite us to ask more probing questions." To the audience absorbed in the revolutionary debate of Rolland's play unfolding before them, Robespierre and Danton seem to be posing extremely topical questions. The theme, that it is better to betray one's ideals than to sacrifice one's friends to them, is highly relevant to Czechoslovakia today. As is often the case in theater under socialism, classic drama is used as a vehicle for contemporary ideas. But the greatest interest and enthusiasm are not for the classics—even in modern setting— but for the questions and the ideas of the young generation of playwrights.

Josef Topol, Ivan Klima, and Vaclav Havel—all dramatists in their thirties—are regarded as men of action by the public. Indeed, these authors frequently assume many of the tasks held by political commentators in the West. They take their responsibilities seriously. For them, it is difficult to imagine a Tennessee Williams who occasionally denounces the entire Broadway system—from his refuge in Key West, to be sure—and threatens to open his next play in London. (As if anyone really cared!) These Czech dramatists were aware before the 1968 revolution that the theater and literature were the primary means through which the tensions, the conflicts, and the problems of society could be surfaced and given public exposure. Because they were looked upon as potential spokesmen for the public, they were regarded with suspicion by the Novotny clique. However, the Party was not the only group to protest the political preoccupation of these playwrights. A large segment of the intelligentsia felt these artists were limiting their creativity by exhausting their energy in fighting the regime. Whatever the dangers of mixing art and political agitation, the authors attacked the political realities like boxers, and it kept them fit. Czech authors are not overwhelmed by the eternal and insoluble dilemmas that seem to stifle the creativity of so many Western playwrights. While these Czech dramatists find harmony, order, common sense, and rational behavior difficult to accept as theatrical motifs, they do not reject them as platitudes of another era, nor do they disdain the articulate development of values. Like their public, they are fundamentally idealists who retain an almost nineteenth-century faith in the improvement of the human condition. These playwrights view the greatest happiness for the greatest number as a desirable goal, despite the disastrous results that accompanied the introduction of socialism to Czechoslovakia in 1948. And although almost no one trusted the promises of a better future as outlined by the Party, many Czechs continue to trust the optimism and youthful idealism of their authors.

Vaclav Havel (b. 1936) is a blond, engaging, plump rebel who has retained his naughty-schoolboy looks. Personally outspoken and craftily courageous, he is regarded as the leading dramatist in Prague today. The incisive nature of his satirical dialogue and the skill with which he indirectly heaped ridicule on the regime earned him immense popularity. Havel does not invent absurd situations. Rather, he injects a single absurd element into otherwise perfectly rational, almost banal, situations. And this is, by implication, what he feels the communists also do. His message, it has been said, could be condensed into: "I know you know they know we know." He combines absurdity with conspiratorial intimacy to come up with successful comedy. Havel's first full-length play, *The Garden Party* (1963), was a satire touching on de-Stalinization and political bureaucracy. The excitement this first play and *The Memorandum* (1965) aroused suggests the vitality and validity of his message.

According to Jan Grossman, Havel has shown his true dramatic ability by unfolding the public's own story. Havel's key concern is the mechanization of man. In both plays, the protagonist is the mechanism of the cliché. In *The Garden Party* man does not use the cliché, the cliché uses man. The cliché is the hero; it causes, advances, and complicates the plot, determines human action, and, deviating further and further from man's given reality, multiplies its own improbabilities. However, Havel's treatment of the cliché also exposes his limitations as a playwright. The characters he portrays are always as anonymous and unformed as the ideological smoke screen of socialism he is parodying. The cast seems incapable of grasping anything, as if the actors lived in a state of suspended animation (perhaps this is true of some Czechs). But Havel's speciality, which used to arouse the Prague public to a frenzy of applause, is the way in which he manages to ridicule communist jargon. For example, there is the following discussion about the liquidational training of the Inaugurating Service in *The Garden Party:*

HERO: The best would be if we organize both trainings at the same time: The inaugurators will be training the liquidation officers, while the liquidation officers will be training the inaugurators.

DIRECTOR: And will it then be inaugurated by a liquidation officer trained by an inaugurator, or by an inaugurator trained by a liquidation officer?

HERO: Another training will have to be organized: inaugurationally trained liquidation officers training liquidationally trained inaugurators, and liquidationally trained inaugurators training inaugurationally trained liquidation officers.

DIRECTOR: And will it then be inaugurated by a liquidationally trained inaugurator trained by an inaugurationally trained liquidation officer, or by an inaugurationally trained liquidation officer trained by a liquidationally trained inaugurator?*

It is true that clichés, as absurd as these are, can take on a meaning, indeed a world of their own. When variations of the word "liquidation" are repeated some ninety-two times in Act Three alone, even the most patient of Western publics would begin to yawn. Nevertheless, it would seem from their enthusiastic reaction that the Czechs couldn't get enough of such serial repetitions. They felt exhilarated by the mere use of a word that was taboo for such a long period. This released the tensions created by the commonly shared terror.

Havel admits that "Ionesco's plays taught me that you can talk

* Translated by Vera Blackwell.

nothing but nonsense on stage, and yet the play may still seem like a slice of life." He carried this dictum out in *The Memorandum,* which deals with the Orwellian distortions of a bureaucratic language and all the havoc it creates for society. In the play, Havel has a rather nebulous "superior authority" order the introduction of an artificial language into a bureaucratic institution. Because its promoters declare the new language to be the touchstone of institutional loyalty, it naturally provokes considerable confusion as well as a complete changeover in the power structure. As this new and almost impenetrable language is institutionalized, a fresh order from above exposes it as nonsensical and demands that a new, "better and more advanced" language be adopted. Here the audience roars with laughter and breaks out into applause. *The Memorandum* skillfully satirizes the different ways in which man adapts himself to the "system," and Havel has had ample opportunity to study how the Czechs denounce the Party as evil or ridiculous, but serve it willingly, or in principle, or accept it with indifference. "The best allies of the system," he said, "are those who submit to it without respecting it."

Running his thick, pudgy fingers through his long, blond hair, Havel himself talks like the characters in his plays. One interview he gave *Svobodne Slovo* in early 1967 ran something like this:

> Q. Do you travel abroad?
> A. I used to.
> Q. Do you miss it?
> A. Not particularly.
> Q. But you are writing a play?
> A. Yes.
> Q. What is the title?
> A. *Eduard,* at the moment.
> Q. Similar to your previous two plays?
> A. Similar, but slightly different.
> Q. Do you write during the day or at night?
> A. At night.
> Q. Fast?
> A. Slowly. I use up a lot of paper.
> Q. Do you have a favorite author?

A. A difficult question.
Q. Even so, who?
A. Kafka.
Q. Which do you like to read more, Kafka or *Lucky Jim?*
A. Kafka.

"Havel does not exhort us; he tempts us by his playfulness," says Grossman. Once, when I asked him whether he was pro or contra vivisection (an obviously provocative proposal), Havel thought for a while, then answered: "It is first necessary to examine in which sense we are to look at this question." Then, without answering, he thought for a while, and out of the blue came, "Am I a Marxist or not?" Reflecting for a while again, he answered this question in a halting, self-taught English. "I am not interested in what I am, but in what I do." This did not satisfy him, either, and he rambled on, explaining that his basic troubles started because he came from a bourgeois family, and his father used to be a movie mogul. This was held against him by the Party, and, like many other sons of the former bourgeoisie and the nobility,* he was denied access to higher levels of education. The result was that he became even more rebellious and antiregime. The government, in turn, retaliated in a multitude of petty ways, such as denying him a passport. (He was invited to the P.E.N. Congress in New York, but the Czechs would not permit him—nor Grossman, for that matter—to attend.)

After the 1968 revolution, Havel was permitted to travel abroad and to attend Joseph Papp's production of *The Memorandum* in New York. However, Havel continued to be primarily concerned with the possibilities of a political opposition in Prague. Writing in *Literarni Listy* in the spring of 1968, Havel admitted that although

---

* It is fascinating to follow the fate of some of the former Czech nobility. In 1967, for example, the Earl of Czernin was an assistant to a truck driver in a forestry administration; the Earl of Sternberg was a stagehand in the Karlin Theater; the Knight Stransky was a gas station attendant; the Duke of Kinsky worked in the state co-operative services; Baron Daczicky of Heslov was a storekeeper; and the Earl of Mitrowitz was a truck driver. I was told by one count that there are more titled truck drivers in Czechoslovakia than there are comrade truck drivers, *i.e.*, Party members. But then, in 1968, after Novotny's fall, the Minister of the Interior became a sweeper in an automobile factory.

it would amuse him as a fiction writer "to invent a so-called 'positive' program for a nonexistent opposition party," he was too sensible to "plan strategy without an army." Havel wrote that "political programs do not spring from the desks of writers," but only from the daily activity of those who implement political programs. Havel felt that without a recognition of noncommunist forces, it would be impossible for Dubcek to stem the general alienation of the intelligentsia. Basically, Havel remained a pessimist. After twenty years in the political wilderness, he wrote, "It is difficult to enter the arena of political life when one feels like an outsider who does not enjoy full rights."

During the mid-sixties Czech theater was accused by the Party of being pessimistic, overly serious, and too preoccupied with the challenge of the times. To counteract these charges, the theatrical community in Prague was anxious to persuade "official circles" that seriousness of themes did not necessarily amount to a propaganda of pessimism. Professor Kopecky, who staged a highly successful revival of a classic passion play (*The Crucifixion and Glorious Resurrection of Our Lord and Redeemer Jesus Christ*), asked, "Is there any reason why a drama should be denied the right to depict man in his most tragic and absurd moments?" Answering this rhetorical question in the negative, Kopecky declared, "Such moments, situations, and feelings are a part of dramatic art, just as their opposites are." He then went a step further, maintaining that even without offering any solution or hints at solutions on stage, a theatrical piece need not be regarded as propaganda of despair and impassivity vis-à-vis man's destiny. Nevertheless, the importance of being earnest almost overwhelmed the themes of the relationship between man and society, between one man and a group, between man and woman. Sex, for example, was scarce on the Czech stage. Josef Topol's *Cat on the Rails* was probably as sexy a Czech play as the directors cared to present. A long one-acter revolving around three variations on the same theme, *Cat on the Rails* portrays a couple, approaching thirty, who have been enjoying sexual intimacy for several years and suddenly find themselves at the end of the tether. Eva wants children and a home. Vena, a furniture packer, fails to understand why they should lapse into boring con-

ventionality by getting married. "I want to know what I'm doing
. . . in the daylight. And face to face," he says. He hesitates before
the responsibility of such permanence and cannot make a commitment. There is no resolution, but the audience is given to understand that the couple remain sitting on the parallel rails as a train
is heard approaching. Blackout. The theatergoer is left to decide
their fate for himself.

Topol (b. 1935) is a more profound dramatist than Havel. His
plays border on the poetic. Action consists primarily in subtle shifts
of atmosphere and inflection. A graduate of the Prague Academy of
Drama, Topol was only twenty when his first tragedy, *Midnight
Wind,* was performed. In 1962 he wrote *The End of the Carnival,*
which was produced two years later with an introductory notice by
director Otomar Krejeca: "The hope offered to us by Topol in this
drama is the perspective of freedom, freedom which has to be re-
deemed by conquering fear, freedom on the border of death, yet
freedom that is nevertheless within reach of every man." Topol's
latest one-acter, *Slavik to Supper,* which had its première in March
1967 at the Theater Behind the Gates, is also typical of the new
philodrama, which questions the meaning of life and rejects the
melioristic philosophy of the state. Slavik, which is a common Czech
name as well as the word for "nightingale," is a young man hos-
pitably invited to dinner by a strange family. It soon becomes obvious that not only is he going to be fed supper but that the hos-
pitable family is also going to feed on him. As he realizes his fate,
Slavik begins to show resistance. Inevitably, irresistibly, this melts
into indifferent Czech compliance. The message to the public is
clear.

"I am not looking for complete and definite answers, but for the
logical conclusions of uninterrupted thinking," says dramatist Dali-
bor Plichta. Close to being an unperson in his own land until 1968
(he had only one of his many plays staged, and this was closed down
after a few performances, for "medical" reasons), Plichta has led a
life that reads like a tale out of Kafka. Once a prominent lawyer, he
represented Czechoslovakia at the Paris Peace Conference in 1947.
As the "cult of the personality" descended on Czechoslovakia, he
was no longer permitted to practice law, and for a number of years

241

he was, in fact, jobless. The persecution he suffered caused him to turn inward in his search for a solution. "I am just attempting to express myself through the medium of the theater and to make use of its possibilities—not necessarily all of them—in order to formulate what troubles me and what occupies my mind," he explains. Plichta's plays, which he structures around abstract geometric forms, are written without a preliminary thesis, without an anecdotic core, without any preconceived plot. Although he does not consciously strive for avant-gardism, his outlook is extremely "far out" for the Czech theater.

Like Beckett, whom he greatly admires, Plichta tries to reduce all situations to their simplest form. Readers of his plays, he says, often feel that he produces skeletal figures deprived of all flesh. Czech directors are distressed by the jugular directness with which he asks basic questions and forces fundamental conflict. For example, in his one-acter *Finale* (1964), whose entire cast consists of a drummer, a hairdresser, and two "persons," the dialogue relentlessly probes the meaning of meaning.

PERSON: And what then?

DRUMMER *(much astonished)* : What then?

PERSON: Then! What then?

DRUMMER *(restless)* : I think I don't quite get you.

PERSON: What then? *(Overemphasizing)* *What then?*

DRUMMER *(brusquely)* : There is no "then"! There is nothing but that which existed before! And there will never be more and there will never be anything else except that which existed before! That which existed before and which exists now. Everything there will be is that which existed before and is here now.

PERSON *(persisting)* : And then?

DRUMMER: That which exists now! There has never been a "then"! There never will be a "then"! How could there ever be a "then"? Where do you get this idea? How can you talk like that? You . . . !

PERSON: I am only asking, what then?

DRUMMER: Nothing! Nothing! Nothing!

PERSON: And that would be all?

(DRUMMER *remains silent, at a loss for words*)

242

Finale is a satire on a *perpetuum mobile* of four people spouting phrases. Despite such dialogue—and this is a characteristic sample of his heretical probing—Plichta does not consider that his plays fit into the category of the theater of the absurd. Plichta feels attracted and repelled by the objective world and would like to look at it, if not entirely objectively, then at least more so than the dramatists of the theater of the absurd. To Plichta, "the absurd theater represents decay, and merely states the triumph of the senselessness of the world, often in a provocative manner." Under socialism, man is oppressed by forces more immediate, more concrete than the absurdity of the individual in existentialist space as represented, for example, in Ionesco's *The Chairs.* "What is felt here in Prague is not fateful, but caused and effected by man," says Plichta. Calmly, the graying, spent Plichta explains that no dramatist in the West works under the artificial atmosphere of officially canonized aesthetic norms that exist under the dictatorship of the proletariat. One can, perhaps, fight the unity of thought demanded by the Party by means of satire bordering on the absurd, but this, in itself, is far removed from the theater of the absurd.

Plichta says, "Drama must be exposed as a world *per se,* which has no continuation and in which there is no outside interference from the empirical world." His other plays, such as *Improvisation,* which is actually a spoof on conformism, and *Intermezzo,* which ridicules the notion of eternal life, are in a dramatic category of their own. "I felt compelled to go as far as possible in the negation of the devices of rigid academism in the theater," says Plichta, who is constantly striving for a higher degree of stylization, for greater compactness, synchronized organization, and finality of form. He feels that he has sought to express the sequence of events in ascetic and geometric fashion. In *Intermezzo* he arrives at the figure of a square in his search for a perfectly lucid intellectual solution to the problem of life. The corners of his square possess the following "coordinates": A. can but does not want to (be on top, let us assume) ; B. cannot and does not want to; C. cannot but wants to; D. can and wants to; E. is like A. again—he can but does not want to. "This had led me to a high degree of abstraction," says Plichta, "and to an approach comparable to the principles used in musical composition —to permutations, variations, counterpoints, fugues." Plichta says his *Intermezzo* is propelled forward by the human impossibility of co-ordinating these four geometric points and by the intrinsic conflict in the various postures of human existence. Plichta recognizes this inner structure cannot be followed readily by the audience, but "for me," he says, "this form serves as a check on my postulates and proves to myself that I have thought out the problem to the end." The combination of Plichta's introverted vision, his intellectualizations, his own political background, and the radical philosophy of his plays makes it unlikely that his dramas will be performed in Prague for some time to come. As he admits, "My plays are political to the core because they methodically attack the very foundations of the modern state." It is to be hoped Plichta's dramas will soon be performed in the West.

The Kafka cult is now almost as strong in the Prague theater as it is in Czech life. Edward Albee's *Who's Afraid of Virginia Woolf?* was symbolically retitled *Who's Afraid of Franz Kafka?* Since that time even the Czech Communist Party has ceased worrying about this prewar archprophet of alienation. Director Jan Grossman, who lived through the Kafkaesque era of the cult of personality, has been the leading figure in rehabilitating Kafka on stage. Certainly one of the most exciting theatrical productions in the socialist world today is Grossman's rendition of *The Trial*. Kafka's nightmarish fable has been faithfully but unconventionally interpreted—as only a Czech who understands the ways and means of bureaucratic death could: Grossman's version is introduced to theatergoers as "the story of a man who died like a dog."

Grossman calls André Gide's version of *The Trial*, in which the hero searches for a solution to his sufferings, "too heroic." Grossman's Josef K. is not involved in Orson Wellesian melodrama; he seeks to discover the meaning of his strange fate. He is not concerned with seeking a way out or with rebellion; instead, he accepts the logic of the system. And that is because he is a well-dressed bureaucrat himself, in a land where bureaucrats are accustomed to acquiesce. The playgoers feel no rebellion against the system is feasible, and this is important, because Grossman implies by this acquiescence that Josef K. is almost as guilty as his persecutors. The conclusion is that—although, at the end, K.'s tormented figure is jumped upon by his executioners, and he falls back, half-naked, a modern Christ figure—there is little pity for him because he accepted his fate from the beginning.

Grossman is not a man to accept fate passively. He was exiled to central Czechoslovakia during the Stalinist terror of the fifties because he had dared to criticize the National Theater. This institution had become sacrosanct, but Grossman refused to agree that a plan could be worked out for a theater, just as for any other industry, and that it could be ordered to fill its quota of so many plays per year. "The didactic drama of the fifties saw man only as a functional, mechanical component, a cog in the social machinery," says Grossman. Such drama presented the viewer with a finished world in which his role had been determined once and for all. "But the theatergoer," Grossman insists, "needs a world in whose shaping he can participate, if he wants to satisfy his desire for self-realization." It was with this in mind that he established the Theater on the Balustrade in the early sixties. This small, charming theater, which seats fewer than one hundred and fifty persons, was originally used by the Knights Templar and converted into a nunnery for the Sisters of St. Anna in 1330. The immense problems the small, cramped medieval quarters originally posed for Grossman were turned into a challenge and, ultimately, into an advantage. The stage is only fourteen feet wide and twenty feet deep and formerly had no side entrance or exits and no storage space for scenery. These limitations forced Grossman and set designer Josef Svoboda to come up with such original, imaginative solutions that the Balustrade is recognized today as one of the best dramatic workshops in the world.

"In our presentations of *The Trial* and *Ubu Roi*, I had an opportunity to rewrite scenes during rehearsals. It was possible for everyone in our fourteen-man ensemble to present his views and criticisms, as we went through the different versions and interpretations of the same scene," Grossman explained. Svoboda, meanwhile, thought out the sets during the four months they prepared each play. The result is that the company is so thoroughly integrated and the plays are so fantastically tooled that each performance becomes trapezelike in its rhythm. The gusto with which Grossman orchestrates movement arouses awe. In *Ubu Roi,* for example, the actors throw heavy packing crates around the stage with Harlem Globetrotter precision. Moreover, their every movement is co-ordinated to the stereophonic sounds and music specified by Svoboda. Such clockwork and harmony are inconceivable on Broadway. Aside from the thoroughness and discipline of the rehearsals, Grossman's repertory system does not permit understudies and assumes that there will be no turnover in actors or personnel. In Czechoslovakia, as in most socialist countries, actors and technicians are engaged by the state for life after they have finished their schooling and spent a single probationary year with a company. Consequently, there is no incentive for them to look elsewhere for a better job or to flit from one theater to another.*

Josef Svoboda (b. 1920), the designer for the National Theater as well as for numerous smaller theaters in Prague, is now recognized as Europe's leading scenic creator. Although one might be tempted into thinking that he liked to tinker with ingenious mechanisms, Svoboda aims for integrated, highly abstract sets that express the mood of the play. He feels that the theater "is entitled to new techniques just as modern houses are entitled to elevators, automatic laundries, and convenient garbage disposal units." Accordingly, he incorporates multiple-slide projection systems, rotat-

---

* Jerzy Grotowski's Teatr Laboratorium near Wroclaw, Poland, is also an example of a theatrical group whose devotion has no equal in the United States. The thirteen members of this ensemble attend work sessions eight hours a day, six days a week, eleven months a year—almost as an exercise in Hatha Yoga. To them, the theater is, first of all, an attitude toward life, while their work is a way of life. The result is success. Grotowski has transformed his small theater into a tribal ritual room: The audience participates in the ceremony and is brought into the play. There is no stage, and the actors, on occasion, serve as chorus leaders for the audience. The word becomes more than a means of intellectual communication; its sound is used to arouse the instincts, much like incantations.

No technique is sacred to Grotowski, whose thesis is that "everything that is art is artificial." The deficiencies of the actor are exploited, not hidden. Make-up is considered unnecessary, since perspiration, lighting, and breathing, as well as carefully controlled muscular movements, transform the skin into a mask.

Grotowski believes the cinema and television have taken over the social functions of the theater, so the only way for the theater to survive is for it to exploit the direct contact, the interplay between actor and public.

ing platforms, mobile reflectors, and other special effects into the sets. An architect by profession (as well as a designer and a carpenter), Svoboda is capable of creating complex forms by setting simple structures in motion. In *The Trial* he built a hand-operated revolving set on which he joined a group of scaffolding poles in the form of monkey bars. As the set was turned, abstract spaces and forms created the illusion of an apartment, an office, a courtroom, and a church. Moreover, the dramatic action continued during each revolution of the platform and the scene changes seemed entirely natural. Similar illusions of space and form were provided in *Ubu Roi,* where two iron beds were transposed by the actors themselves into a tribunal, a prison, a church, an altar, and a battlefield. For the new production of *The Insect Play* by the brothers Capek (who were taboo only a few years ago), Svoboda built two flats made of hexagonal metal reflectors tilted toward the audience in such a way as to give a view of the stage from directly overhead. This has enabled Svoboda to pick up designs and forms on the stage floor so as to create kaleidoscopic images of great originality—evoking a microscopic view of a fly's eye, or the honeycomb reflector of a science-fiction heating unit. And Svoboda's genius is winning acclaim not only in Prague. His new cinema techniques were hailed at the Montreal Expo. Diapolyecran, with its 224 slide projectors placed inside 112 blocks that moved back and forth in concert, formed patterns out of flowers, faces, and even industrial circuitry.

Czechoslovakia's ideological boss until January 1968, Jiri Hendrych, on occasion denounced the "so-called 'voguish experiments' . . . that distort reality and even negate it." When such experiments as Diapolyecran won international attention for Czechoslovakia at a world's fair, that was fine, but when King Ubu wound up as king of a group of slaves who realize that prison is the only place they can find freedom from responsibility, that was another matter. Party officials apparently were upset by this concluding scene, which portrayed a couple of gawking, American-style tourists, with cameras swinging around their necks, coming to take pictures of the king of slaves behind bars. The Falstaff-like Ubu, whom Grossman portrays as a fat, stupid, cruel, greedy, sadistic, but nevertheless endearing figure, is most obliging; he even lets the tourists (one of

247

whom was sometimes played by Havel) come into the prison and view life for a few minutes from the other side of the Curtain.

In Prague, as in Budapest and Warsaw, the Party tried with all the guile at its disposal to undermine the status of theater of protest.* Rather than pass down closure orders from above, the Central Committee has been known to instruct local Party units to write damning editorials demanding that such and such a play be closed. Hendrych justified such Party interference on the ground that "art for the elite," which is incomprehensible to the wide masses, usually exists only as a cover-up for its own weaknesses. To authors such as Havel, Karvas, Topol, and Klima, the attitude of the Party presented an inviting challenge, and the make-believe propagandistic image the Party sought to disseminate offered a convenient target. For example, Pavel Kohut (b. 1928) opened his latest play, *Augustus,* with the following line: "I love the circus because we live in it." Ivan Klima, in his play *The Castle,* portrayed a group of artists and scientists who live a useless, parasitic existence in an undefined castle (actually patterned on a very real castle not far from Prague).

* In Moscow, where drama flourished more than thirty years ago, the theater of protest is still in its infancy. The Soviet stage is, in fact, now about a decade behind Prague. The best indication of this regrettable state of affairs is that a banal play, *The Warsaw Melody,* was one of the hits of the 1967 season in Moscow. The play, which revolves around a 1947 law prohibiting Russians from marrying foreigners, opens as a young Polish conservatory student meets her Russian botanist at a concert. He has never heard of Chopin, but that doesn't prevent them from falling in love. Stalin's new law separates them, and he goes off to grow wine in the Caucasus. In Act Two, which takes place ten years later, he is the successful director of a vineyard on a business trip to Warsaw, while she is married to a music critic and has become a respected singer. In Act Three, he has made it to the top of the wine industry, and she is a Polish celebrity singing in Moscow—but twenty years have passed, and there is no love between them any more. Like the Moscow public, the two sacrificed their personal happiness to create a new middle-class society. It is no more than well-acted but mawkish Soviet retrospection. It would seem that overexplicitness remains the bane of the Russian theater.

Performances in Moscow seem arithmetical and, somehow, perversely overregulated. Soviet theater censors ban every play that offers "a serious answer to the serious problems of life," said two Soviet critics, Fedor Burlatsky and Lev Karpinsky. They condemned the incompetent meddling of theater censors who were afraid of "a fresh and sharp idea or an unexpected treatment of a subject."

Having retired with full honors amassed during the Stalin era, this distinguished collective is naturally fearful of anything that might upset their privileged *status quo*. A young man, symbolic of the new Czech generation, is murdered by them when he threatens to expose their unwarranted status. Symbolically, as the curtain goes down this young man is replaced by another visitor who will eventually succeed in upsetting their gravy train. Klima's *Castle* suggests that the "apparatchiks," dogmatists, and those whom Radio Free Europe still refers to as "die-hards," stand ready to re-enact their dark deeds even now. Playwright Peter Karvas (b. 1921), in another vicious Slovak satire, *The Big Wig*, portrays the persecution of the minority by the majority. The action takes place in a distant country where a general, a dictator acting on behalf of a foreign power, is looking for a scapegoat. The supply of Jews ran out with Hitler, the gypsies were deported, yet someone must be made responsible for the economic mess in which the country finds itself. The general decides to lay the blame for mismanagement on the international conspiracy of the bald. The antibald pogrom commences as the Antibald League roams the streets in search of glistening heads. The only dissenter to this pogrom is a barber-chemist who has just placed a new miracle tonic on the market. This tonic makes people's hair sprout like weeds. The barber is arrested and ordered to face a show trial. However, it suddenly develops the tonic has an aftereffect that makes all the hair fall out. The upshot of this nonsense is that the bald-headed gain the majority and stage a coup—with the general at their head. And the barber, who for professional reasons refuses to become the hero of the bald-headed, is executed as the curtain falls. In thematic structure, this satire basically differs little from Havel's *Memorandum* or Grossman's *Ubu Roi;* its barbs are equally pointed and obvious.

These snarling, provocative satires distressed Party ideologists prior to the 1968 revolution, with good reason; it is the Czech state that hands out huge annual subsidies to keep these theaters alive and to make *"kultura"* available to the masses at low cost. All but two of Czechoslovakia's theaters are state-subsidized. Tickets are artificially priced between fifty cents and a dollar and twenty-five— which means that the average theater gets an annual subsidy of close to sixty thousand dollars. This may not seem much by American standards, but it means the difference between red and black for nearly all the repertory groups. For its fifteen million dollars in yearly subsidies, the Party wanted at least to see some of its own favorite color, Red.

Despite official denials, censorship of plays was prevalent in Czechoslovakia until 1968. The praesidium of the theatrical union in Prague was informed in the mid-sixties that a commission would be set up in the Ministry of Culture "to clarify opinions on those original plays that even before rehearsals are regarded as controversial." The theatrical community reluctantly yielded to the establishment of this body and issued a statement to the effect that this new "commission should in no case curtail the powers and responsibilities of leading theatrical workers." Grossman explained that the Ministry got the text of every new play about to be produced, and, while in principle it was supposed to give yes or no responses, in practice many hours were lost debating particular scenes and even individual lines. Most of the directors I talked to admitted, after some probing, that they faced bureaucratic interference with each topical play they produced or attempted to produce. Speaking to the members of the Theater Congress, Professor Kopecky regretted there were certain people "whom we unfortunately do not see in our theaters, but who nevertheless pass decisions on our work and our destinies." Kopecky thought the anticensorship statements of the theatrical workers would have to be reiterated for a long time until, "by the force of our argument, we finally get the message across to them." However, by the spring of 1968, they had felicitously succeeded, and for the first time since 1948 there was no censorship on the Czech stage. It was not to last for long.

"The tragic history of the Czech theater is that it always has been a theater of opposition," says Jan Grossman. "You cannot create much if you spend your whole life fighting against something," explained the director. Paraphrasing Eugene O'Neill to the effect that "if you fight too long against small things you become small yourself," Grossman expressed his doubts about the wisdom of the Czech theater's direct challenge of the political realities. Instead, he felt drama would be much more effective if there were less satire on the Prague stage. Grossman thinks the vogue for satiric protest grew out of opposition to the artistic horrors of socialist realism. "Satiric theater stays on one level; it cannot grow beyond what it attacks," he maintains. For example, dramatists used to write, "The Minister is a fool," and the audience would laugh and clap nervously. Such simple reactions quickly killed the dramatic possibilities of satire. Moreover, satiric theater is a didactic theater, and Grossman does not think it can provoke the fantasy of the audience. The role of the theater is not to show everything that is wrong, maintains Grossman. "I believe its aim is to have people arrive at their own vision of reality." In his splendid renditions of *The Trial* and *Ubu Roi* Grossman illustrated that in Prague this reality still borders on the nightmarish, but once audiences have an understanding of their nightmares they can at least try to live more rational and perceptive existences by day. Up to 1968 the Czech theater had something to say, it said it well, and its presentations were most relevant to the life spirit of the nation. This is more than can currently be said for theater in the West.

Epilogue

Upon my return to the Uneasy States of America, I was greeted by a bombardment of impossible questions:

● "I find all these Czech films a dreadful bore," noted one of our most distinguished career ambassadors. "Between you and me," he asked, "is their literature equally dull?"

● A prominent art critic, who had never seen a comprehensive exhibit of Eastern European painting, said, "The Poles just seem to be imitating us. Why are you bothering to write on such an insignificant field?"

● "Why are you American journalists so taken in by all those poseurs, those make-believe intellectuals? Don't you understand they are only front-men?" demanded a recently naturalized emigré writer.

These questions, and many more like them, seem a sullen commentary on the low spiritual state of the times. Clifford C. Nelson, President of Columbia University's American Assembly, has pointed out that "the general ignorance concerning Eastern Europe is colossal." Until Soviet tanks rolled into Prague, many Americans were convinced that the evolutionary process in Eastern Europe would continue until Communist orthodoxy was so eroded only the old facade of Marxism would be left. They refused to hear any arguments which suggested that liberalization might not be following a steady upward curve. I can only counter that I have described what I have seen and what I have read—with a minimum of a priori notions or designs. Let me then summarize some afterthoughts:

Things have changed in Eastern Europe, and somewhat for the better. Darkness no longer falls at noon, but at three or four in the afternoon, from Warsaw to Bucharest. While the communist leaders find artistic polycentrism as difficult to accept as political polycentrism, they are aware that only two alternatives are open to them: a rear-guard action or a return to ruthless suppression. In culture, the unbearably false optimism of the previous generation is gone; so is the boredom and exasperation which accompanied theatergoers and moviegoers of the early fifties. *Partinost* (party-mindedness), the notion that the party must use literature according to given dictates and that the writer must accept party guidance without asking questions, is no longer the predominant force in Eastern European literature. While criticism of socialism is still interpreted as interference with the building of an idealized communist society, the sugary skies of socialist realism have a much more natural coloration now.

Yet the seesaw tips both ways. Jerzy Putrament (b. 1910), author of Poland's recent best seller *Malowierni* (*Men of Small Faith*), described the mores of Party officials and hangers-on during the Stalin era. Evasive, kowtowing Party hacks objected that Putrament concentrated on bureaucrats, black marketeers, and professional careerists, while, they said, in reality, most of the workers and peasants led correct, proletarian lives. Putrament, in a rage, countered, "You will never live to see political literature, as distinct from hagiography, if you base your appraisal of this literature not on what it is, but on what it lacks." Even so, such a novel still had a long way to go before it could be categorized as "honest." Another Polish critic wrote in the daily press: "Personally, I did not like *Malowierni* because of the embarrassment that accompanied my reading. . . . My embarrassment was born of the thought that I, and thousands of other readers, know more than the book tells us, and that we know it in more dramatic form. We know that the course of the swing on which we rose and fell was more ample, more breathtaking."

A desolate chapter was added to this history when, in the spring of 1968, Putrament (under strong pressure from the Party) argued that unless his colleagues in the Warsaw Union purged some of the dissident writers, "the Union would be forced to undergo changes of one kind or another." As the anti-Zionist campaign was stepped up by the regime, Putrament menacingly declared that "the Writers' Union will no longer tolerate the activities of enemies of the system, particularly within the Union itself." Despite his anti-Stalinist novel, it would seem that Putrament, like millions of others in Eastern Europe, was not entirely successful in shaking off the past.

The communists are still convinced their system is right. Czech playwright Vaclav Havel says, "The communists believe their mistakes are lesser than the mistakes of others." But it is much more than that: Marxism pretends that the old ideologies must be cleared away so that the socialists can freely create new and more rationalist values. Their reasoning closely parallels the analogy of Bertolt Brecht, for whom the mass of men are like a crowd that screams that the theater is on fire and, in its panic, clogs the exits and perishes. Watching from the balcony, the communist realizes everyone could be saved if the crowd would only go out in an orderly manner. To Brecht, the fact of the matter was that, while stupidly asserting himself, man cuts off his own path; he is too greedy, selfish, assertive. In his efforts to push his neighbor out of the way, man only limits his own mobility. So the communists have felt it imperative to establish a system that limits each individual, but that will permit the crowd to get out of the fire exit. What is beginning to appear intolerable, even to the communists, is that while waiting for this hypothetical fire everybody must stand at perpetual attention—facing the exits.

The differences between the Soviet Union and Eastern Europe remain enormous. It's not only that Eastern Europe has no Siberia, it's that when intellectual dissidents are called to task or jailed in Budapest or Warsaw, they do not become unpersons. To me, the spiritual distance between Budapest and Moscow is greater than the distance between Budapest and Paris. Moscow is suspicious, repressed, Asiatic in its lack of openness. Budapest is melancholy, cynical, sophisticated. The difference can most graphically be illustrated in the literature of protest. In Czechoslovakia, for example, the novels and plays of the mid-sixties express the doubts and uncertainties of the authors. In the Soviet Union, on the other hand, both the reformers (like Dudintsev or Sinyavsky) and the Stalinists (like Vsevolod Kochetov, editor of the literary monthly *Oktyabr*) are equally clear and certain that they are right, that they have the answers. Neither Russian conservatives nor liberals betray the slightest hesitation; both are equally single-minded, both are equally free of that human characteristic known as doubt.

Police terrorism has largely disappeared, but fear lingers. The vicissitudes of Central Europe are such that the intellectuals wonder whether the hundred flowers bloom only to be razed by a state lawnmower. "What would happen to us if the Vietnam war were expanded?" was a question I heard frequently. The cultural community is not anxious for any Pyrrhic victories. To be sure, some writers and academics now exaggerate their own fears and uncertainties. The communists exploit these fears by the clever use of allusion and innuendo. They know that the intellectuals have, to a certain extent, been conditioned by Pavlovian punishment: For a decade, if a writer overstepped the prescribed limits of freedom, it marked the end of his career or even his life. Now all the party has to do is to ring the bell. However, for the younger generation, no such reflex exists. For them, there is only cynical doubt and ideological confusion. These uncertainties were well illustrated in the following Dresden (East Germany) cabaret song of the mid-sixties:

> In the old days, when they showed you a picture,
> If it showed fellows working, it was art.
> If it showed a slogan in the background,
> That was realism to boot.
> In the old days, comrades, you knew where you stood.
> The old days were easy—but now?
>
> In the old days a central soup was brewed at the top.
> That was it, and you only had to pass it down.
> If you were wrong in those days you quickly knew.
> In the old days, well, that was just the end of you.
> But in the old days at least you knew where you stood.
> In the old days, yes, but comrades—now?*

* Translated by Uwe Kitzinger.

The communist attitude toward aesthetics is evolving. Art, which was reduced to a subsidiary mode of describing reality during the Stalin era, has become less pedagogical and slightly less burdened by self-righteous and moralistic overtones. To be certain, communist aesthetics have been spotty ever since Hegel declared that "Thought and reflection have superseded fine art." Neither Marx nor Lenin devoted much attention to the problems of culture. To them, culture was a luxury. Only the gross distortions and intentional misinterpretations of aesthetics by Plekhanov in the twenties and Zhdanov in the forties passed for theory while Stalin lived. However, as I have tried to show, imagination and creativity simply cannot be kept refrigerated forever in Siberia or pigeonholed by bureaucrats trying to apply the principles of a "socialist realism" that hardly anybody understands. Reluctantly, the Soviet writers admitted for the first time in 1967 that a work could be ideologically "decadent" and still be a work of art. This was a timid step forward.

"Art is revolution," wrote Herbert Read, and the truth of this provocative statement extends beyond the confines of ideology. In Eastern Europe, merely the description of reality by a writer who honestly accounts for his own life has revolutionary implications. However, the necessity for confession, the impulse to share experience transcend ideology. The gradual realization of the structuralist relationship between art and the human personality is slowly leading toward broader definitions of the role of aesthetics. Georgy Lukacs said at the end of 1967 that "the real mission of literature and the arts is to make people understand the great human problems of an era"—a catchall that could easily encompass Bob Dylan or Robert Rauschenberg. Perhaps this approach only reflects the softening of age, but such a statement is illustrative of the change that is taking place in the communist rethinking of aesthetics.

The intellectuals are achieving concrete and positive results. Surrounded by a vast majority who are content to live as best they can and who talk about political developments much as we do about the weather, the intellectual activists maintain persistent pressure for liberalization on the communist hierarchy. Novotny's failure to quiet the dramatic protests of the Czech Writers' Congress in 1967 led to his ouster from office and to the temporary establishment of a liberal regime. But freedom is also painfully frustrating if it cannot be used to promote social and political change. This is especially true in Poland, where the intellectuals resent their impotence. "We're exactly as free as we dare to be," said one Polish abstract painter. "I can say, 'Gomulka's communism is crap' all day long, and no one will arrest me as long as I don't cause a public commotion." Freedom of speech? Yes. But should he try to type out a pamphlet to that effect, he would quickly land in jail. In most of the communist world there is still no recognition of the survival of the fittest in the realm of ideas; bureaucrats refuse to conceive of truth as multidimensional.

At the first conference of the Association of Czechoslovak Film and Television Artists in the spring of 1968, the philosopher Ivan Svitak delivered an address that indicated how rapidly freedom of speech flowered in Czechoslovakia after Novotny's overthrow.

When the nation is silent it is the artist, the scientist, the intellectual who must speak. When the nation talks, what is the artist, the scientist, the intellectual to do? He must think, because whatever the circumstances, his main cultural role is to think. Every culture is the result of intellectual effort, of the power of reason. . . .

The central question always of every culture is not art but the measure of civil rights, their existence or nonexistence. Every culture that in the name of power-political considerations permits curtailment of the freedom of thought and of human rights is qualitatively poorer than a culture in which the citizen acts and works as an equal, free citizen, as the creator and recipient of cultural values.

Therefore, of decisive importance to us is not the enthroning of the president but rather the enthroning of civil rights, the enthroning of civil freedom. The accidental play on words may be symbolic and a favorable sign that freedom and not an emperor will be given to us. ["*Svoboda*" means "freedom"; it is also the name of the new President of Czechoslovakia.]

Connected with the central question of human rights is the process of the democratization of culture. The decisive factors in the cultural policy of the present state have been responsible for the establishment of bureaucratic control, which has not only been guilty of erroneous and incompetent decisions, but which should not have possessed any cultural authority

257

whatsoever. The notion that values, culture, art, social relations are to be guaranteed by institutions or governments is nothing else but another form of totalitarian thinking. The conflict between culture and the ideologies of the governing bodies was inevitable, because every free culture, and especially a humanistic culture, is bound to find itself at variance with the contemporary state. Without overcoming the totalitarian attitude to culture a democratization process is impossible.

An artist, a film artist, an intellectual, or a scientist should not have to render an account to any official or to any organization, regardless of whether it is a democratic, democratized, or totalitarian organization. The discipline of truth is the hardest of all, but every artist and every scientist must accept it. The discipline of truth is superior to the discipline of institutions. This great idea, one of whose propagators was Karl Marx, may today not only be expressed but also defended. We cannot sacrifice critical thinking to anything or to anybody—to individuals or to institutions, to Party or to democracy. The freedom of the artist is an axiom of culture not because the artist is different from the others but because the same civil rights apply to him that apply to everybody else.

Intellectuals, artists, and scientists on the one hand, and the working people on the other, had in the past and have now a common enemy—bureaucratic dictatorship—of which they want to be rid. The apparatus nourished the conflicts of social groups in order to prove its seeming usefulness; it is up to us artists, scientists, and intellectuals to tell the working people and the workers' class that we do not defend only our special interests but also the interests of the overwhelming majority of people living in this country. We are now returning through a dramatic and momentous evolution of history to the same curve of the spiral that we left twenty years ago. Today we can define our aim by the slogan: "Long live the unity of working hands and working heads."

Eastern Europe has something of value to offer civilization. As representatives of Western culture, we must care what Poles or Czechs think. The intellectuals I have portrayed in this book have suffered for two decades under one of the most onerous social experiments in human history. Their experience warns us not to let extremes or absolutes, under any guise, enter our political existence. They have also shown us that, despite the insurmountable obstacles of the most restrictive political ideology of our time, talent must out. Throughout the chapters of this book the interplay between culture and politics has been spotlighted. I believe that, in the course of the resulting seesaw movement, culture has become a powerful tool of political expression, and that the force of the message in painting, theater, poetry, films, novels, sculpture, and architecture is getting stronger all the time, that all of these media are moving toward a liberation of form. If one looks at the developments in Eastern Europe since the death of Stalin, the inevitable conclusion must be that the arts have, by sheer persistence, corroded orthodox communist ideology.

I do not pretend the cultural achievements of Eastern Europe are immutable. Polish novelist Leopold Tyrmand contends from the comfort of his American exile that "so far, postwar Eastern Europe has produced nothing of lasting value, the half-dozen good films produced by Poland and Czechoslovakia notwithstanding." Although I can hardly assume to be the judge of what will be of lasting value, I disagree. Tyrmand's position is that the movies, literary creations, and paintings were all produced by political hypocrites and sellouts. My own contention is that the political criterion under which a work of art is created should not color one's opinion. During the worst period of Czechoslovakia's Stalinist repression, Jiri Trnka created some of the best animated films ever produced. Of course, the context in which I saw paintings in Warsaw and Prague did endow them with a romantic message that is absent when I look at them on the walls of my New York apartment. In Warsaw, the canvases appeared daring and symbolic of the aesthetic liberation the Poles wished to attain. In New York, the same paintings look somewhat somber. They are brushed off as "passé" without so much as a second glance by some American painters, who argue that these works "could not have been produced without the American experience, that they lack originality."

On the other hand, the vacuity of some U.S. art forms, ranging from Claes Oldenburg's Central Park "sculptural grave" to the dry-ice monuments built in Southern California, illustrate the absurdity to which the American artists can descend. Those painters and sculptors, who have nothing left to fight but their own lack of talent and the public's indifference, are the ones who shout loudest that their counterparts in Eastern Europe are masters of the *"déjà vu."* Critic Harold Rosenberg maintains that form in Western art is "no longer capable of arousing deep feelings or affecting major experiences." American vanguardists are apparently convinced of the collapse of the traditional forms of artistic expression. Rosenberg wrote in 1968 that Hans Hofmann, Jackson Pollock, and Willem de Kooning "share a concept of creation based on the intuition that there is nothing worth painting. No object, but also no idea." This intuition is not shared in Eastern Europe and the Soviet Union. Art still stirs strong feelings and affects the daily life of the intellectual community. To a Hungarian painter, the very idea of representing poverty or portraying misery seems like a worth-while act of rebellion. The tensions produced on canvas are intended to arouse the intelligentsia to action, toward protest. The vision of the collapse and disintegration of forms now so prevalent in American culture remains foreign to Eastern Europe. Painting, poetry, drama, and music represent both social action and individual sanctuary.

I believe art does proffer values that are universal, but for fear of being presumptuous, I shall restrict myself to concluding that culture in Eastern Europe holds a greater promise for the people of this area than most Americans can begin to understand. Art behind the Iron Curtain is a liberalizing notion, a challenge to authority, an instrument for social change. Ultimately, I believe, the outcome of the seesaw motion between art's promise and the realization of its potential will determine the fate of all men.

Acknowledgments

This volume owes much to many: The late Philip Graham of the Washington Post Company paved the way for this book's realization through his faith and intuition; Mrs. Katharine Graham and the editors of *Newsweek* gave me the opportunity to open up *Newsweek*'s first East European bureau; my fellow journalists, and in particular Eric Bourne of the *Christian Science Monitor*, taught me much that I could not otherwise have learned; and Professor Richard Pipes, of Harvard's Russian Research Center, sparked my youthful interest in the quandaries of the intellectual under communism.

Special thanks must go to the editors of Radio Free Europe, without whose voluminous situation reports, press surveys, and other documents, I could never have checked the material that went into writing these chapters. And, on the other side of the "fence," I wish to thank the editors of the *New Hungarian Quarterly*, and in particular Ivan Boldizsar, for their assistance and co-operation.

Georg Eisler and Stephen Dummer were most helpful in collating material on the East German opera, while Philip Arnold and Dr. Rudolf Sobotka, both of the United States Information Service, provided me with contacts, insight, and material on People's Poland. Miodrag Maximovich, of *Politika*, was extremely kind in providing me with numerous contacts in Yugoslavia, and editor Georg Ivascu, of Bucharest, spent many hours explaining the ins and the outs of the situation in Rumania.

I also wish to thank Barbara Frischmuth and Hilde Bennett for their assistance on the translations; Lorna Morley for her invaluable proofreading; Ted Slate, of the *Newsweek* Library, who endured my many requests; and Heidi Kieslinger, my Vienna secretary, who participated in so many stages of these travails.

Even more crucial to this book were the hundreds of East Europeans to whom I talked over the past years. To them I have dedicated this volume. All of them helped to form my ideas, but for the judgments, prejudgments, and mistakes I assume the full responsibility.

To Signora Inge Feltrinelli—a special acknowledgment for her diplomatic contacts.

Finally, I wish to thank my wife, Helaine, who had to suffer the disappointment of so many weekends at home and had to put up with my fits of distemper while I was writing this book. Without her encouragement and suggestions this volume would not have been.

April 11, 1968

Index